WHEN I'M OLD
and other stories
Gabrielle Bell

for Tony

When I'm Old is published by Alternative Comics, 503 NW 37th Ave., Gainesville, FL 32609-2204; 352.373.6336; jmason@indyworld.com; www.indyworld.com/altcomics. All contents copyright © 1998, 1999, 2000, 2001, 2002 Gabrielle Bell. All rights reserved. Characters and likenesses are properties of the cartoonists. Graphic Design: Charles Orr. Publisher: Jeff Mason. No portion of this book may be reprinted or reproduced without permission except for journalistic or educational purposes. First Printing, March 2003. Printed in Canada.

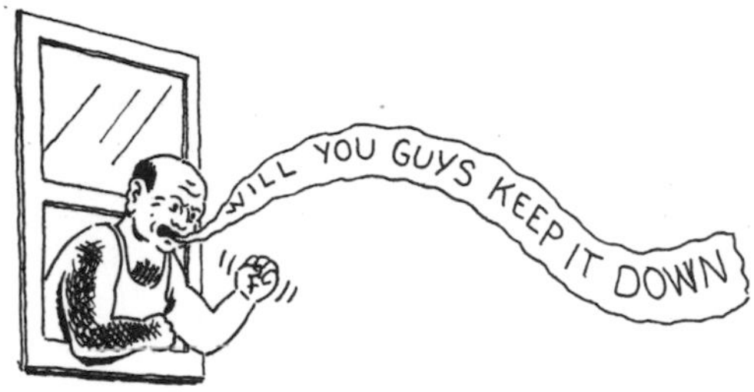
WILL YOU GUYS KEEP IT DOWN

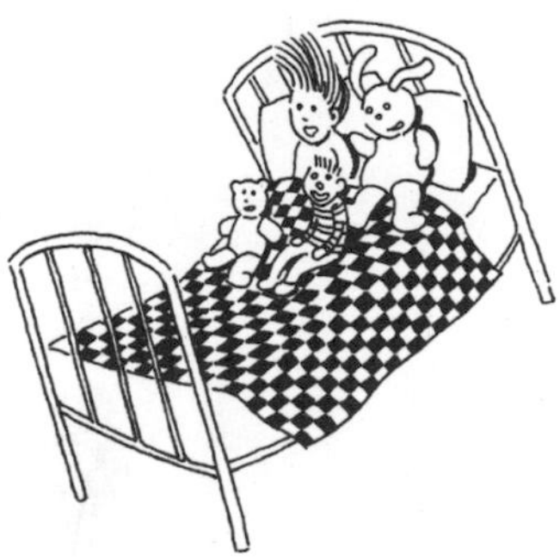

AMY WAS A

BABYSITTER

 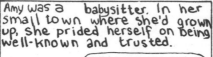

AMY WAS THE BEST A BABY SITTER

Amy was a babysitter. In her small town where she'd grown up, she prided herself on being well-known and trusted.

KIDS, I'M GOING OUT TO-NIGHT SO AMY'S COM-ING OVER TO KEEP AN EYE ON YOU.

YAY!!!

NOW, DON'T BE BUG-GING HER ALL THE TIME AND DO AS SHE SAYS.

Both responsible and popular with the children, she was welcome in any home.

AMY! CAN WE MAKE A FORT CITY IN THE LIVING ROOM?

NO!...WELL, OKAY. BUT BRUSH YOUR TEETH, ALL RIGHT?

But there was something wrong in Amy's life.

AMY?

She was dissatisfied. At nineteen, she was both cynical and full of irrational dreams.

HUH?

DO YOU KNOW ANY THING ABOUT LONG DIV-ISION?

JUST THAT IT ROTS YOUR BRAIN AND HAS NO RELEVANCE TO REAL LIFE.

DON'T TELL YOUR MOM I SAID THAT, OKAY?

She was discontented, but she devoted everything to the children, and never so much as grew impatient with them.

WHERE Y'ALL GOING?

WE'RE RUN-NING AWAY FROM HOME.

WELL, BE HOME BY DINNERTIME.

The one thing that distinguished her most as a great babysitter was her ability to captivate anyone around with her imaginative stories.

JUST LIKE THIS ONE WERE SITTING UNDER NOW; ONLY THIS TREE WAS HUGE; AS BIG AS A SUPERMARKET; AND IT HOUSED MANY ANIMALS, AND SOME CHILDREN LIVED THERE TOO; CHILDREN THAT'D BEEN ABANDONED OR BEATEN OR KIDS THAT JUST DIDN'T FIT IN AT SCHOOL...

Secretly, she saved up her money, and planned a trip to the city.

But she was relied on by both parents and children, and life without her could not be imagined.

...AND IN THIS TOWN THERE WERE NO DOORBELLS SO YOU HAD TO SHOUT UP AT THE WINDOWS OR THROW LITTLE STONES, AND IT WAS CUSTOMARY, UPON ENTERING SOMEONE'S HOUSE, TO TELL YOUR HOST A SECRET YOU'VE NEVER TOLD BEFORE...

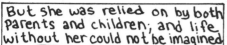

It seemed to her that there was a conspiracy to keep her home forever.

AMY! WHAT ARE YOU DOING?

I'M LEAVING TOWN. I CAN'T STAND ANOTHER SECOND HERE

CAN I JUST GET YOU TO STAY WITH JAMIE FOR A COUPLE HOURS, AND THEN WE CAN ALL GO OUT FOR PIZZA...?

PIZZA?

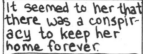

SAY YES SAY YES SAY YES SAY YES SAY YES

She was a very melodramatic girl.

AND THEN, ONE DAY, AFTER YEARS OF PRACTICE, SHE FINALLY TAUGHT HERSELF TO FLY. IT CAME AS NATURALLY TO HER AS BREATHING, AND AS SHE DARTED UP TO THE CLOUDS, SHE FOUND THAT ALL OF HER WORRIES WERE TOO HEAVY TO COME WITH HER, SO THEY DROPPED DOWN TO THE EARTH WITH A THUD...

So, on one sad day she got up the courage to leave, and all the children cried.

NOW, REMEMBER WHAT I TOLD YOU ABOUT LONG DIVISION...

GATE 3

On the bus she experienced the lonliest time of her life.

She found herself a cheap, cozy little studio. She would have been excited but she was too miserable and scared.

She tried to get a job but she didn't know how to act at the interviews.

SO, AMY, TELL ME, HOW CAN WE APPLY YOUR SKILLS AS A BABYSITTER TO OUR COMPANY?

She spent a lot of time at the bookstore.

EXCUSE ME BUT IF YOU'RE GOING TO READ THAT WHOLE THING YOU'LL HAVE TO BUY IT.

Because of her excellent references, she managed to find a babysitting job, but the city kids found her weird.

NO I DON'T WANT TO HEAR NO STORY.

AND IF YOU TRY AN' MAKE ME GO TO BED, BITCH, I'LL TELL MY PARENTS YOU DID DIRTY THINGS TO ME.

She read constanty, often a book a day.

The city frightened her. Soon she was only leaving her house to go to the market or the bookstore.

When she was down to her last hundred dollars, she bought herself a bus ticket home, and took herself out to dinner.

AND A CARAFE OF HOUSE RED!

ALL RIGHT... CAN I SEE YOUR I.D. PLEASE?

MY I.D? HA HA! OH YOU FLATTER ME!

She would be needing a job as soon as she got home.

AMY!!!

She dreaded the time she would be asked;

SO; HOW WAS YOUR TRIP?

THE EMPIRE STRIKES

So she made something up.

WELL, I MET THESE GIRLS ON THE BUS AND WE GOT KICKED OFF IN SOME NO-WHERE TOWN SO WE ENDED UP HITCHHIKING DOWN TO TEXAS WHERE WE STARTED A BAND, WHICH WAS COOL UNTIL ONE OF THE GIRLS GOT PREGNANT...

And they wanted to hear more; so she kept making things up, until she began to believe them herself.

IN ISTANBUL I MET THIS FORTUNE TELLER WHO WAS TRYING TO KILL ME BECAUSE SHE KNEW HER HUSBAND WAS DESTINED TO FALL IN LOVE WITH ME...

She spoke so much of her imagined adventures that she soon thought of herself as a world traveller.

NEVER, IN ALL MY TRAVELS HAVE I EVER TASTED A COOKIE THIS DELECTABLE!

She was a strange girl, but with children she could always be trusted.

IN CHINA THERE'S A TOWN WHERE THEY'VE PROGRAMMED ROBOTS TO DO ALL THE CHORES LIKE THE FARMING AND COOKING AND CLEANING SO THE PEOPLE DEVOTE THEIR TIME TO MAK-ING WIND CHIMES AND BELLS AND DRUMS AND YOU CAN HEAR IT FOR MILES AROUND

And through the years her fame spread, and wealthy parents brought their kids from miles around, and she charged ridiculously large sums of money.

AMY'S BABYSITTING SERVICE NEXT EX

MAIN STR NEXT ST

Except, of course, for all her friends in town, for whom she always had time.

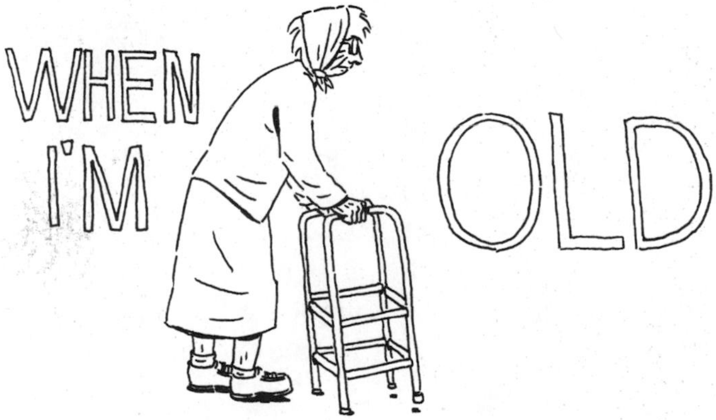
WHEN I'M OLD

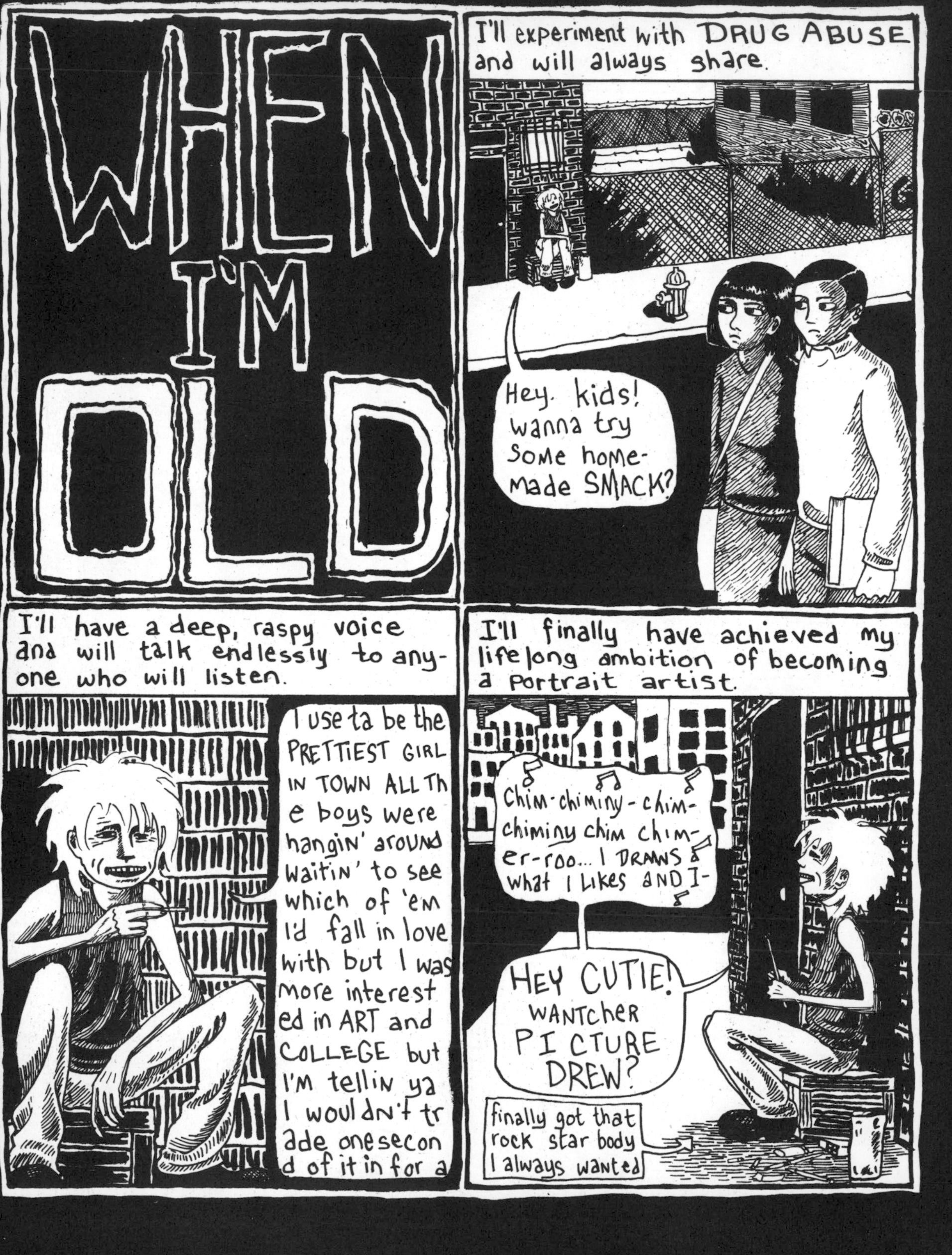
WHEN I'M OLD
I'll experiment with DRUG ABUSE and will always share.
Hey. kids! wanna try some home-made SMACK?
I'll have a deep, raspy voice and will talk endlessly to any-one who will listen.
I use ta be the PRETTIEST GIRL IN TOWN ALL Th e boys were hangin' around waitin' to see which of 'em I'd fall in love with but I was more interest ed in ART and COLLEGE but I'M tellin ya I wouldn't tr ade one secon d of it in for a
I'll finally have achieved my lifelong ambition of becoming a portrait artist.
Chim-chiminy-chim-chiminy chim chim-er-roo... I DRAWS what I LIKES AND I-
HEY CUTIE! WANTcher PICTURE DREW?
finally got that rock star body I always wanted

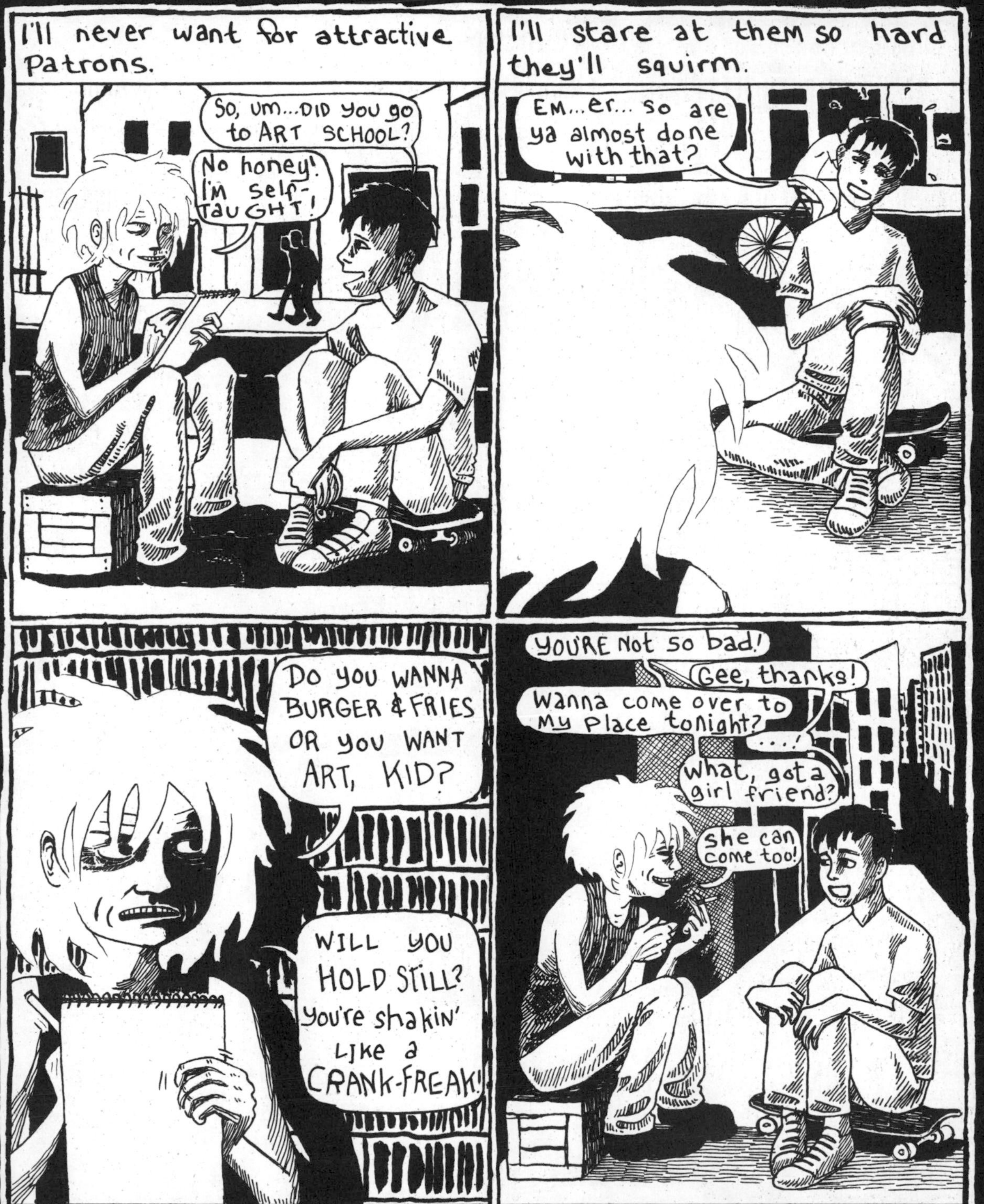
I'll never want for attractive Patrons.
So, um...DID you go to ART SCHOOL?
No honey! I'm self-TAUGHT!
I'll stare at them so hard they'll squirm.
EM...er... so are ya almost done with that?
Do you WANNA BURGER & FRIES OR you WANT ART, KID?
WILL you HOLD STILL? You're shakin' like a CRANK-FREAK!
I'll be a tad eccentric.
YOU'RE Not so bad!
Gee, thanks!
Wanna come over to My Place tonight?
...!
What, got a girl friend?
She can come too!
I'll still have my MOJO WORKIN'!

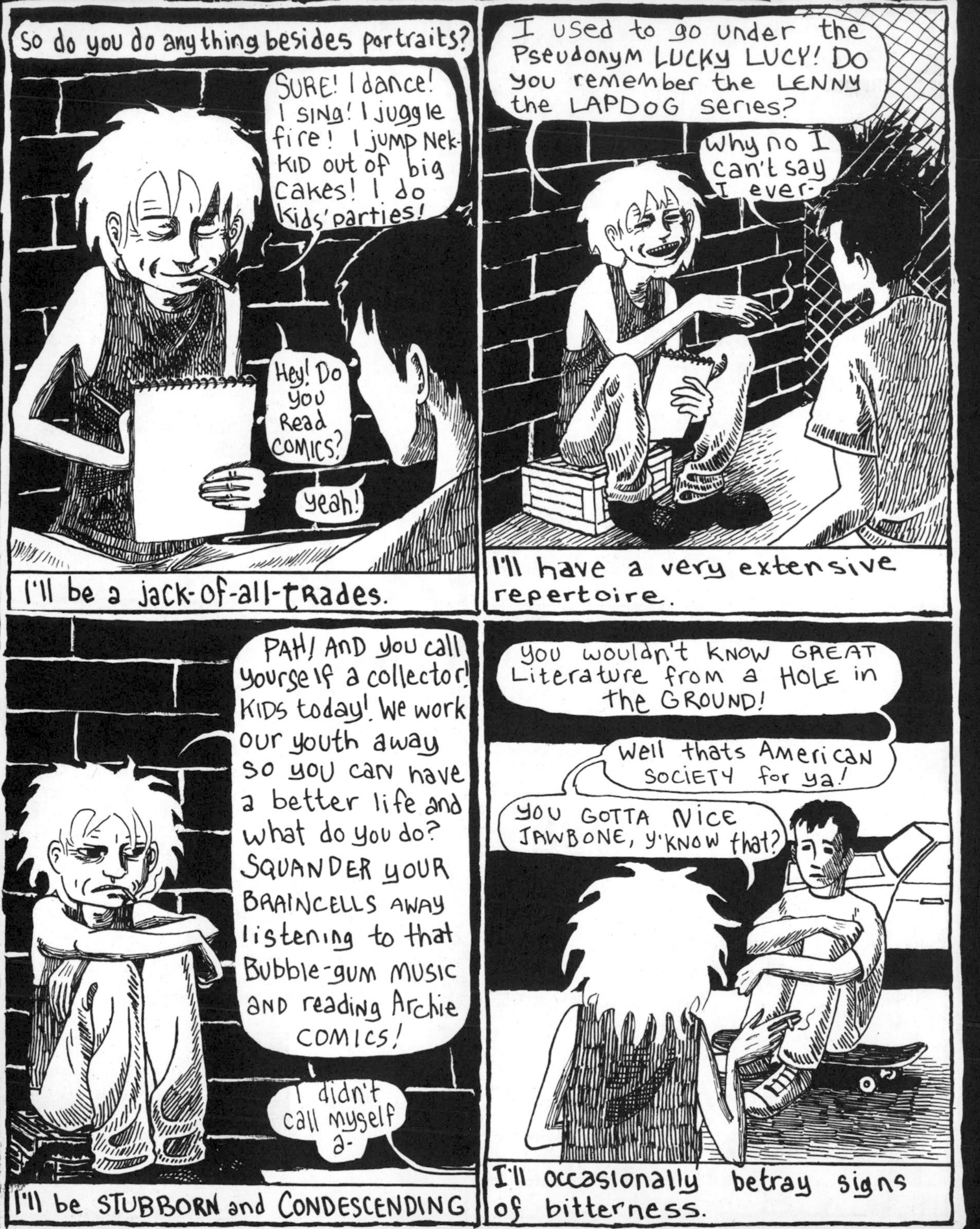

So do you do anything besides portraits?
SURE! I dance! I SING! I juggle fire! I jump NEK-KID out of big cakes! I do Kids' parties!
Hey! Do you Read COMICS?
yeah!
I'll be a jack-of-all-trades.
I used to go under the Pseudonym LUCKY LUCY! Do you remember the LENNY the LAPDOG series?
Why no I can't say I ever-
I'll have a very extensive repertoire.
PAH! AND you call yourself a collector! KIDS today! We work our youth away so you can have a better life and what do you do? SQUANDER YOUR BRAINCELLS AWAY listening to that Bubble-gum MUSIC AND reading Archie COMICS!
I didn't call myself a-
I'll be STUBBORN and CONDESCENDING
YOU wouldn't KNOW GREAT Literature from a HOLE in the GROUND!
Well thats American SOCIETY for ya!
YOU GOTTA NICE JAWBONE, Y'KNOW that?
I'll occasionally betray signs of bitterness.

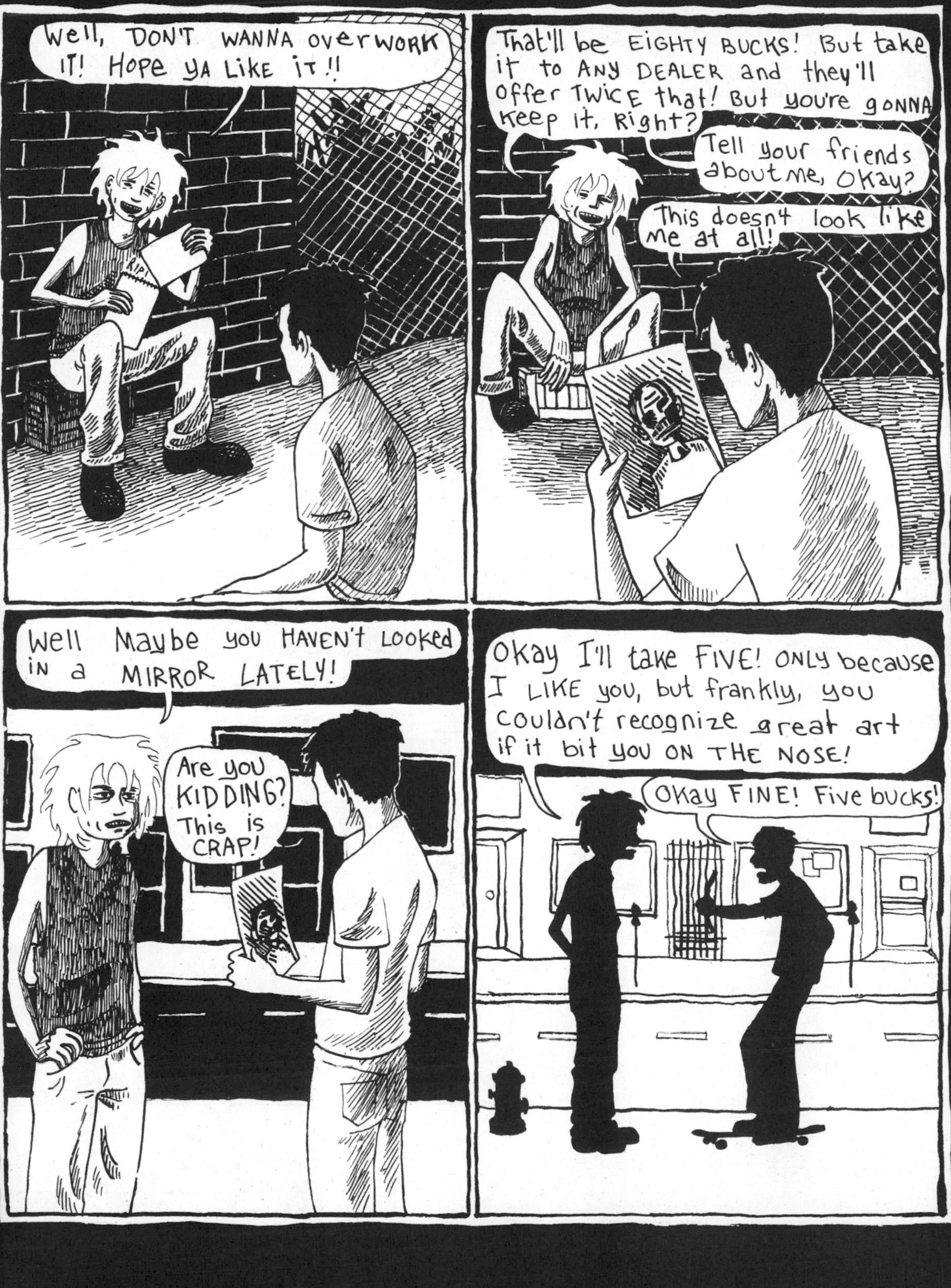
Well, DON'T WANNA overWORK IT! HOPE YA LIKE IT!!
RIP!
That'll be EIGHTY BUCKS! But take it to ANY DEALER and they'll offer TWICE that! But you're gONNA Keep it, Right?
Tell your friends about me, Okay?
This doesn't look like me at all!
Well Maybe you HAVEN'T LOOKED in a MIRROR LATELY!
Are you KIDDING? This is CRAP!
Okay I'll take FIVE! ONLY because I LIKE you, but frankly, you couldn't recognize great art if it bit you ON THE NOSE!
OKay FINE! Five bucks!

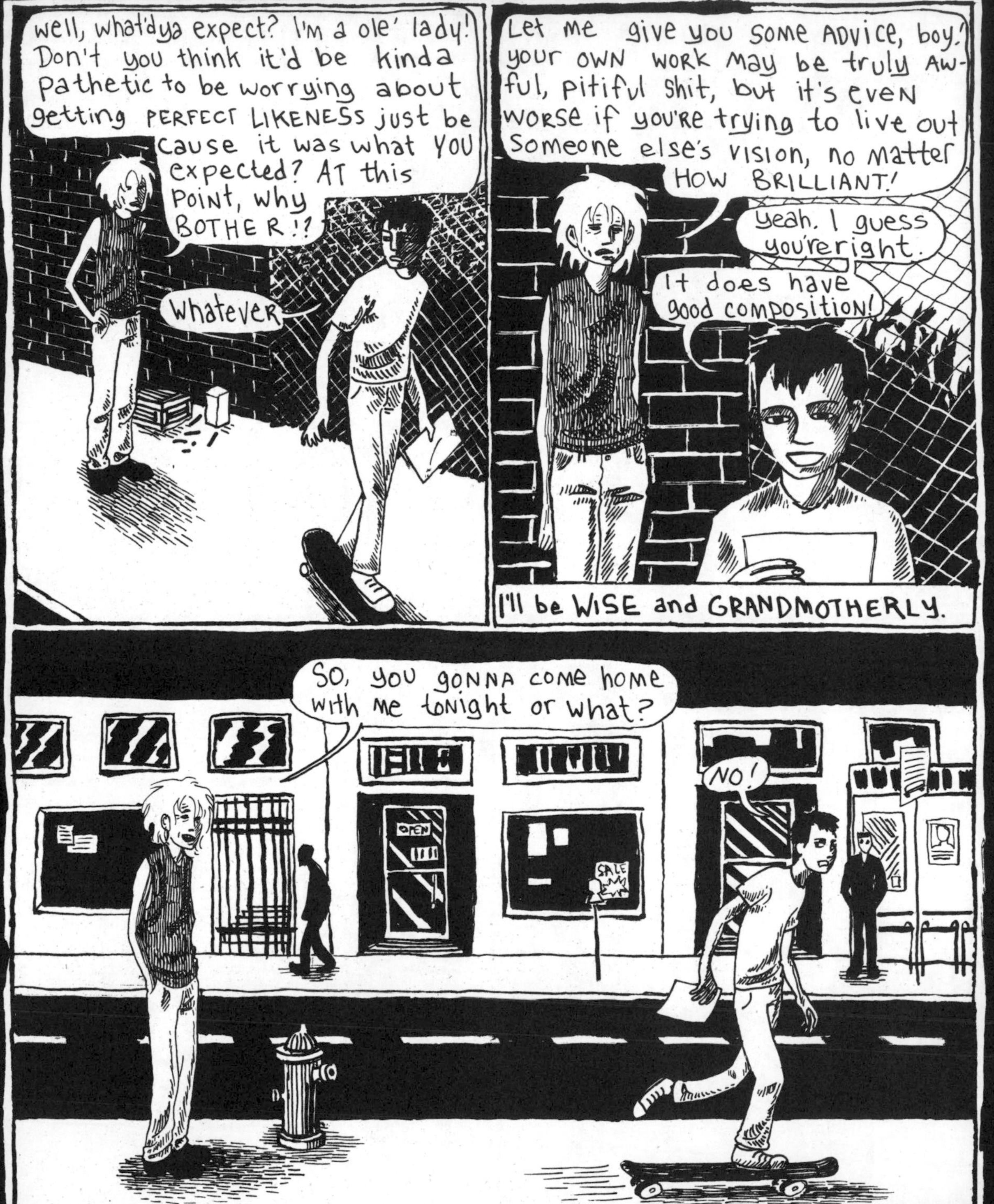
well, what'dya expect? I'm a ole' lady! Don't you think it'd be kinda pathetic to be worrying about getting PERFECT LIKENESS just be cause it was what YOU expected? AT this Point, why BOTHER!?
Whatever
Let me give you some ADVICE, boy! your OWN WORK may be truly awful, pitiful shit, but it's even worse if you're trying to live out someone else's vision, no matter HOW BRILLIANT!
Yeah. I guess you're right.
It does have good composition!
I'll be WISE and GRANDMOTHERLY.
So, you gonna come home with me tonight or what?
NO!
OPEN
SALE
I'll never give up.

JUST ONE REASON

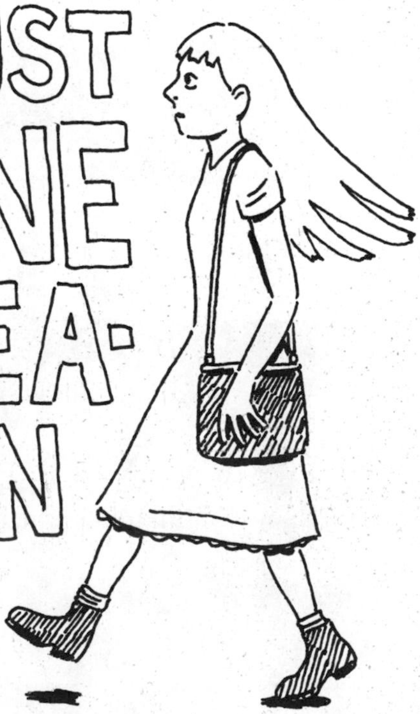

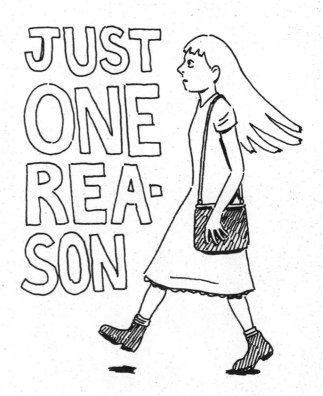

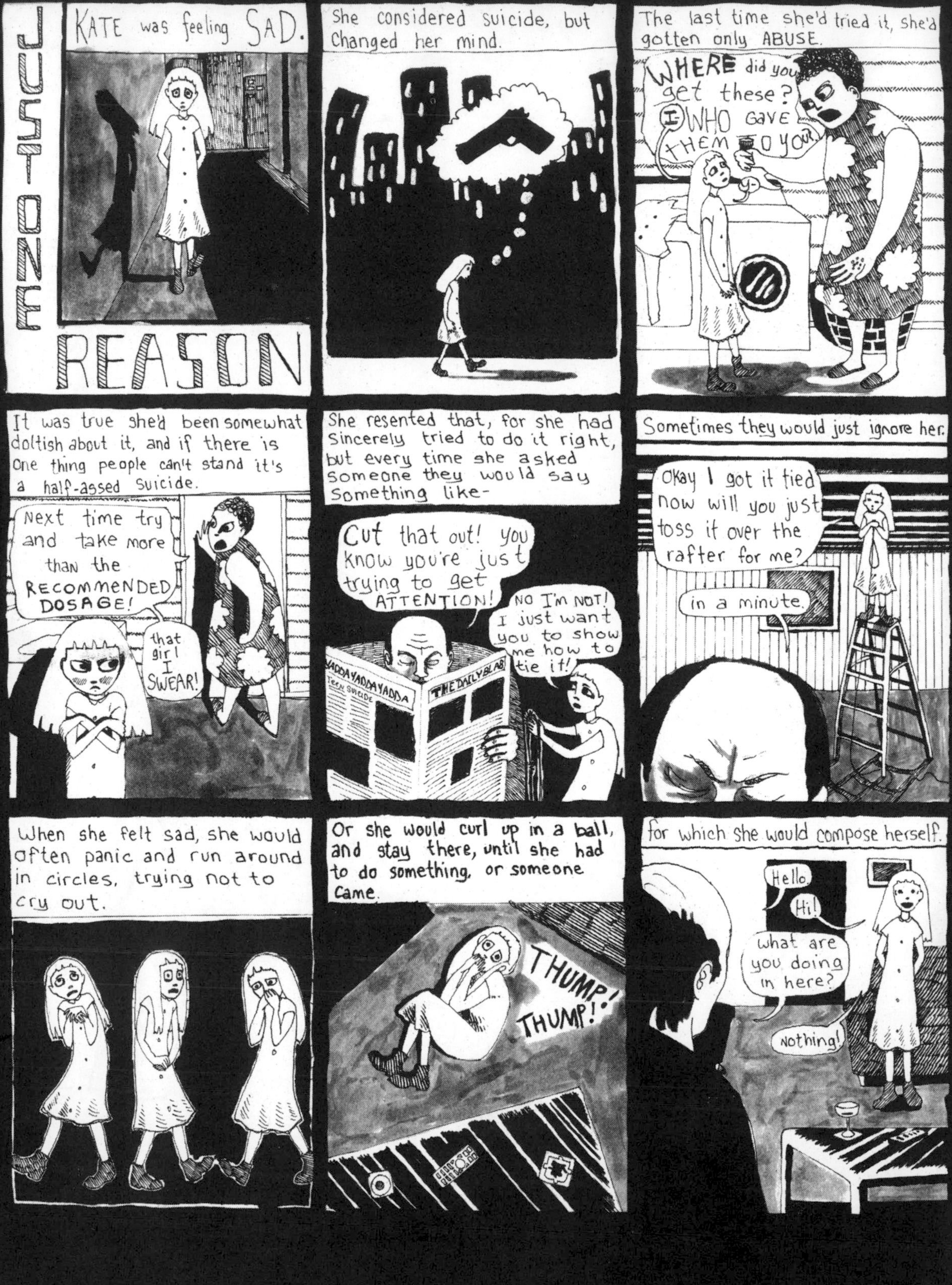
JUST ONE REASON
KATE was feeling SAD.
She considered suicide, but changed her mind.
The last time she'd tried it, she'd gotten only ABUSE.
WHERE did you get these? WHO GAVE THEM TO YOU?
I
It was true she'd been somewhat doltish about it, and if there is one thing people can't stand it's a half-assed suicide.
Next time try and take more than the RECOMMENDED DOSAGE!
that girl! I SWEAR!
She resented that, for she had sincerely tried to do it right, but every time she asked someone they would say something like-
Cut that out! you know you're just trying to get ATTENTION!
NO I'M NOT! I just want you to show me how to tie it!
YADDA YADDA YADDA
TEEN SUICIDE
THE DAILY BLAB
Sometimes they would just ignore her.
Okay I got it tied now will you just toss it over the rafter for me?
in a minute.
When she felt sad, she would often panic and run around in circles, trying not to cry out.
Or she would curl up in a ball, and stay there, until she had to do something, or someone came.
THUMP! THUMP!
for which she would compose herself.
Hello.
Hi!
what are you doing in here?
Nothing!

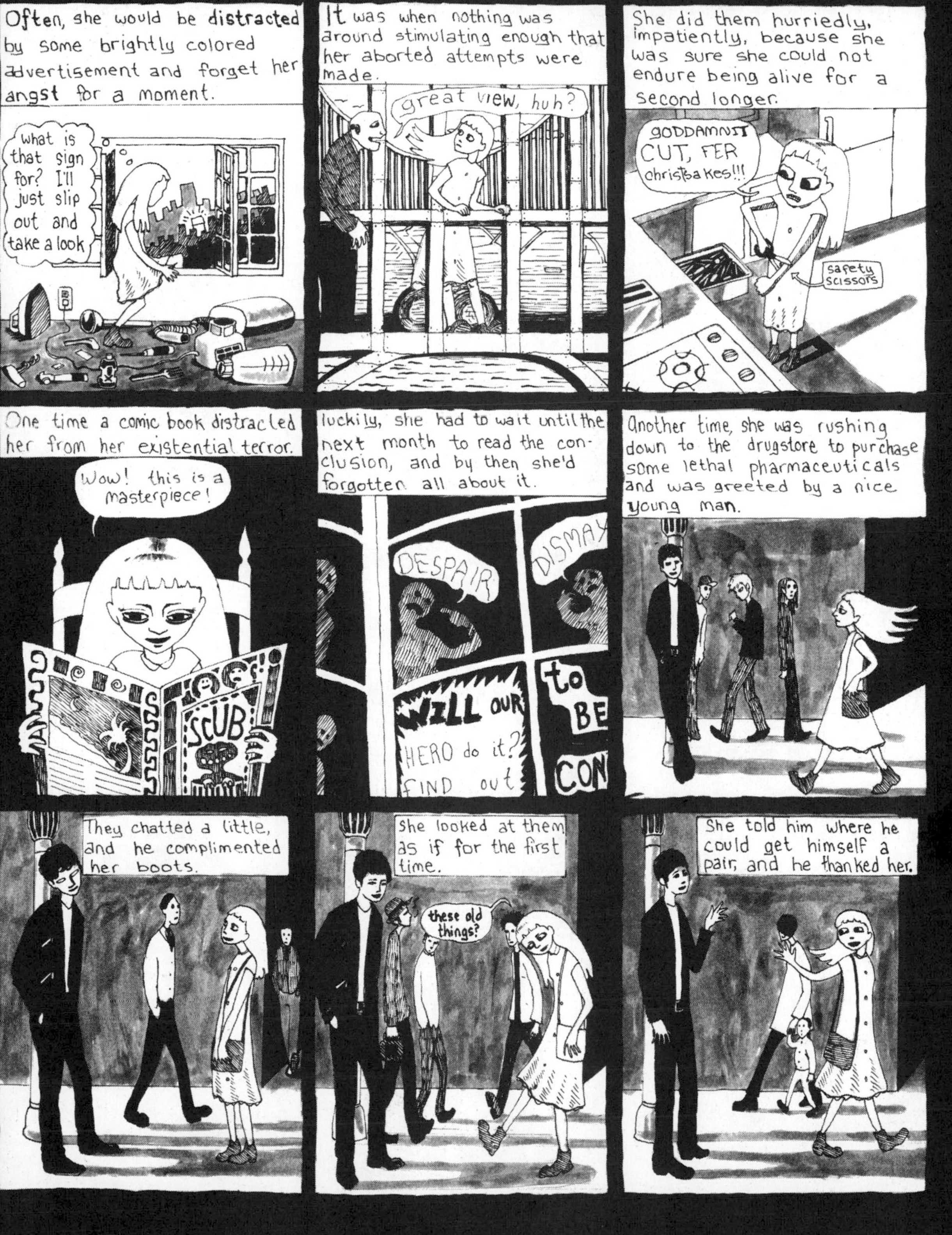
Often, she would be distracted by some brightly colored advertisement and forget her angst for a moment.
what is that sign for? I'll just slip out and take a look
It was when nothing was around stimulating enough that her aborted attempts were made.
great view, huh?
She did them hurriedly, impatiently, because she was sure she could not endure being alive for a second longer.
GODDAMNIT CUT, FER christsakes!!!
safety scissors
One time a comic book distracted her from her existential terror.
Wow! this is a masterpiece!
SCUB
luckily, she had to wait until the next month to read the conclusion, and by then she'd forgotten all about it.
DESPAIR
DISMAY
WILL OUR HERO do it? FIND out
to BE CON
Another time, she was rushing down to the drugstore to purchase some lethal pharmaceuticals and was greeted by a nice young man.
They chatted a little, and he complimented her boots.
She looked at them as if for the first time.
these old things?
She told him where he could get himself a pair, and he thanked her.

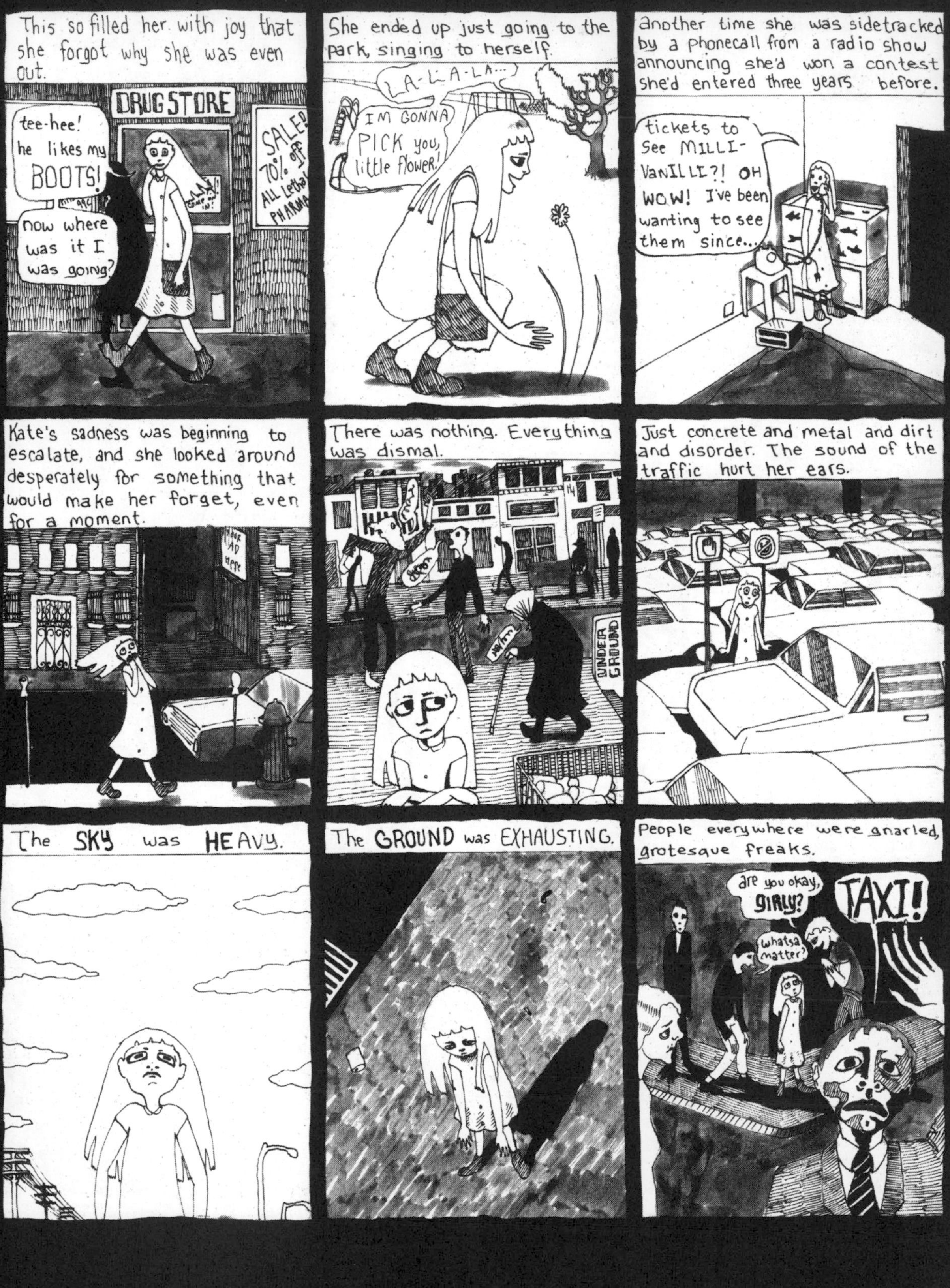

This so filled her with joy that she forgot why she was even out.
DRUG STORE
SALE! 70% off ALL Lethal PHARMA
tee-hee! he likes my BOOTS!
now where was it I was going?
She ended up just going to the park, singing to herself.
LA-LA-LA...
IM GONNA PICK you, little flower!
another time she was sidetracked by a phonecall from a radio show announcing she'd won a contest she'd entered three years before.
tickets to see MILLI-VANILLI?! OH WOW! I've been wanting to see them since...
Kate's sadness was beginning to escalate, and she looked around desperately for something that would make her forget, even for a moment.
There was nothing. Everything was dismal.
UNDER GROUND
Just concrete and metal and dirt and disorder. The sound of the traffic hurt her ears.
The SKY was HEAVY.
The GROUND was EXHAUSTING.
People everywhere were gnarled, grotesque freaks.
are you okay, GIRLY?
whatsa matter?
TAXI!

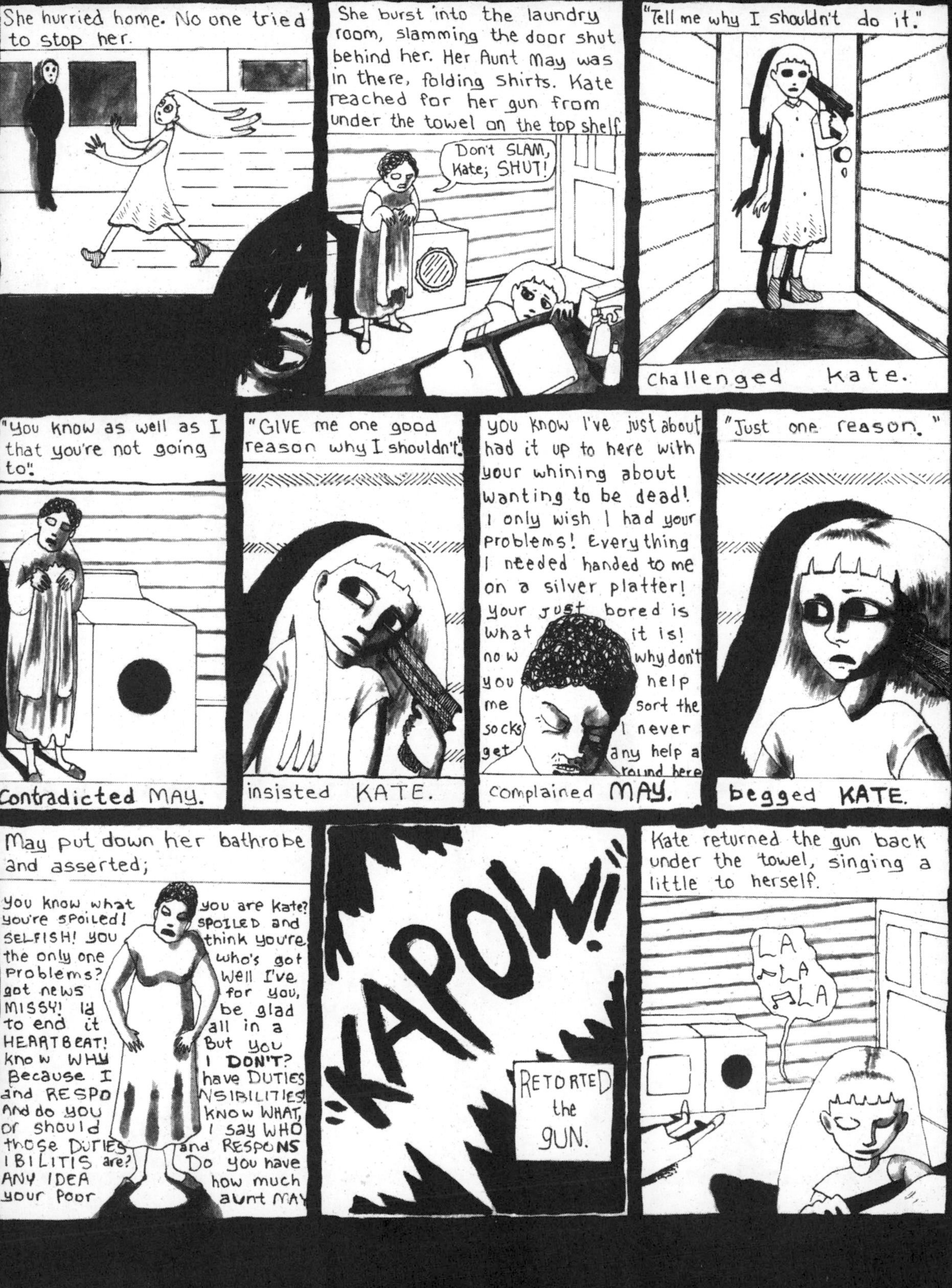

She hurried home. No one tried to stop her.
She burst into the laundry room, slamming the door shut behind her. Her Aunt May was in there, folding shirts. Kate reached for her gun from under the towel on the top shelf.
Don't SLAM, Kate; SHUT!
"Tell me why I shouldn't do it."
Challenged Kate.
"You know as well as I that you're not going to."
Contradicted MAY.
"GIVE me one good reason why I shouldn't."
insisted KATE.
you know I've just about had it up to here with your whining about wanting to be dead! I only wish I had your problems! Everything I needed handed to me on a silver platter! your just bored is what it is! now why don't you help me sort the socks I never get any help around here
complained MAY.
"Just one reason."
begged KATE.
May put down her bathrobe and asserted;
You know what you are kate?
you're spoiled! SPOILED and
SELFISH! YOU think you're
the only one who's got
Problems? Well I've
got news for you,
MISSY! I'd be glad
to end it all in a
HEARTBEAT! But YOU
know WHY I DON'T?
Because I have DUTIES
and RESPO NSIBILITIES!
And do you KNOW WHAT,
or should I say WHO
those DUTIES and RESPONS
IBILITIS are? Do you have
ANY IDEA how much
your poor aunt MAY
KAPOW!
RETORTED the GUN.
Kate returned the gun back under the towel, singing a little to herself.
LA LA LA

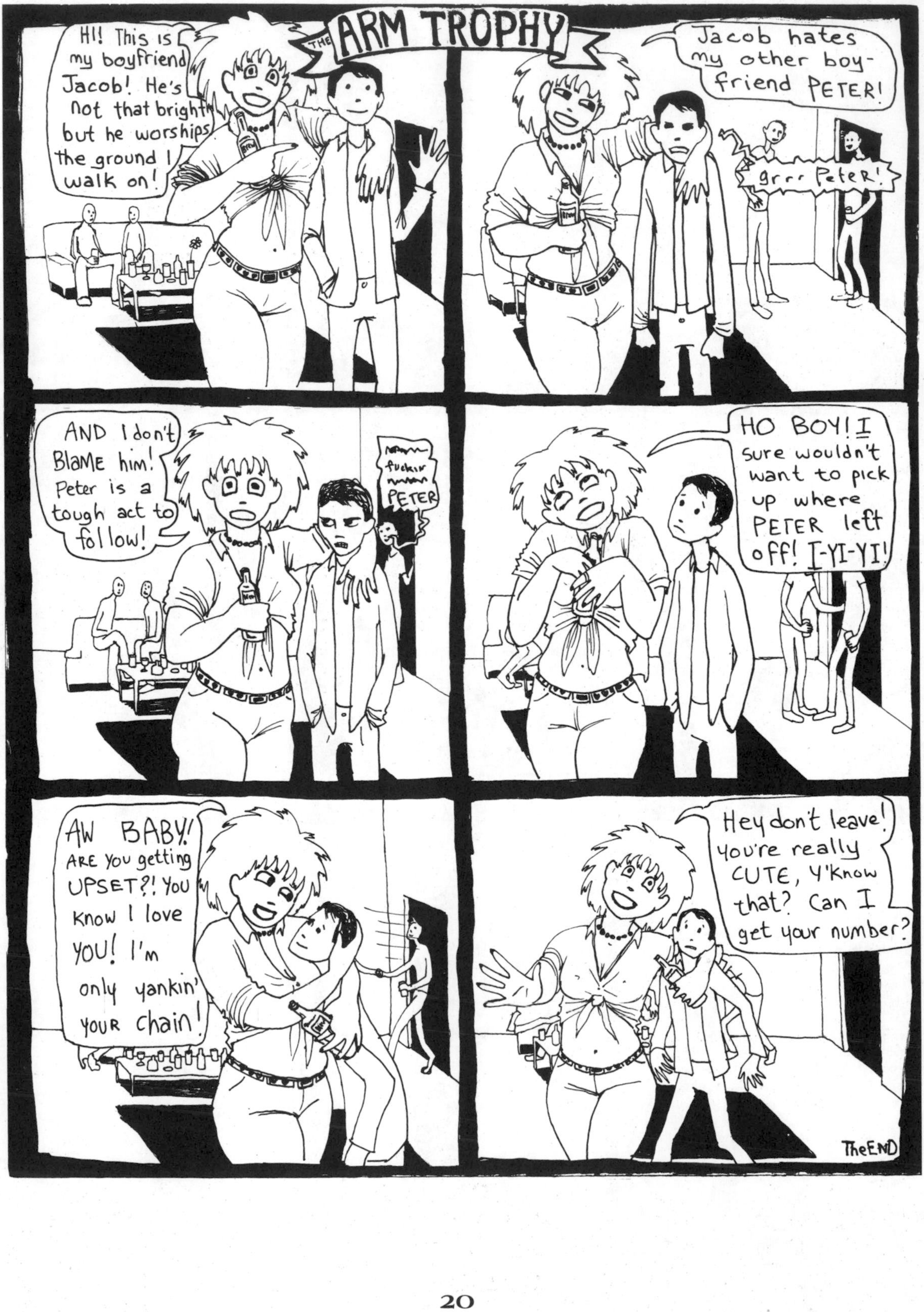
THE ARM TROPHY
HI! This is my boyfriend Jacob! He's not that bright but he worships the ground I walk on!
Jacob hates my other boy-friend PETER!
grrr Peter!
AND I don't Blame him! Peter is a tough act to follow!
fuckin PETER
HO BOY! I sure wouldn't want to pick up where PETER left off! I-YI-YI!
AW BABY! ARE YOU getting UPSET?! YOU Know I love YOU! I'm only yankin' YOUR chain!
Hey don't leave! You're really CUTE, Y'Know that? Can I get your number?
The END

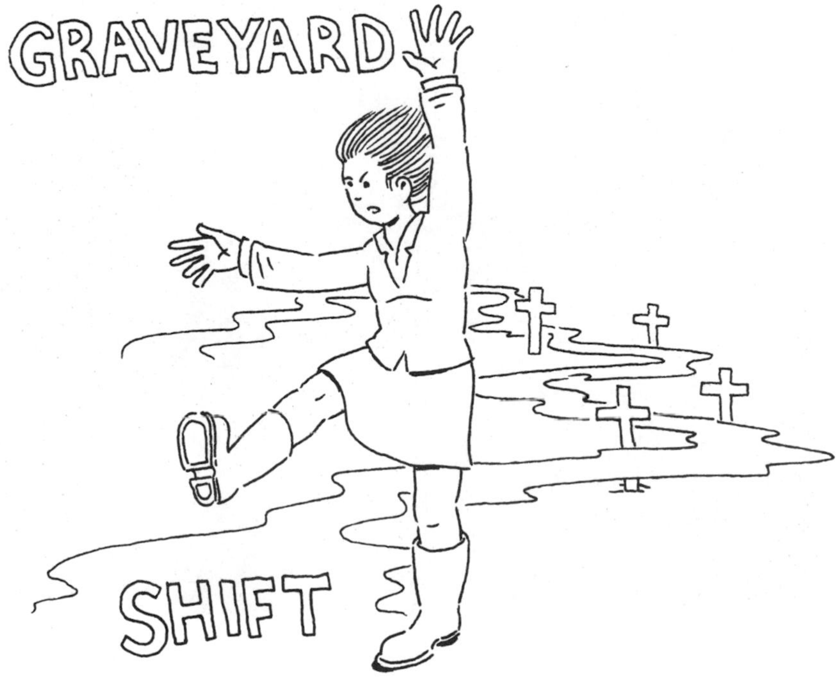
GRAVEYARD
SHIFT

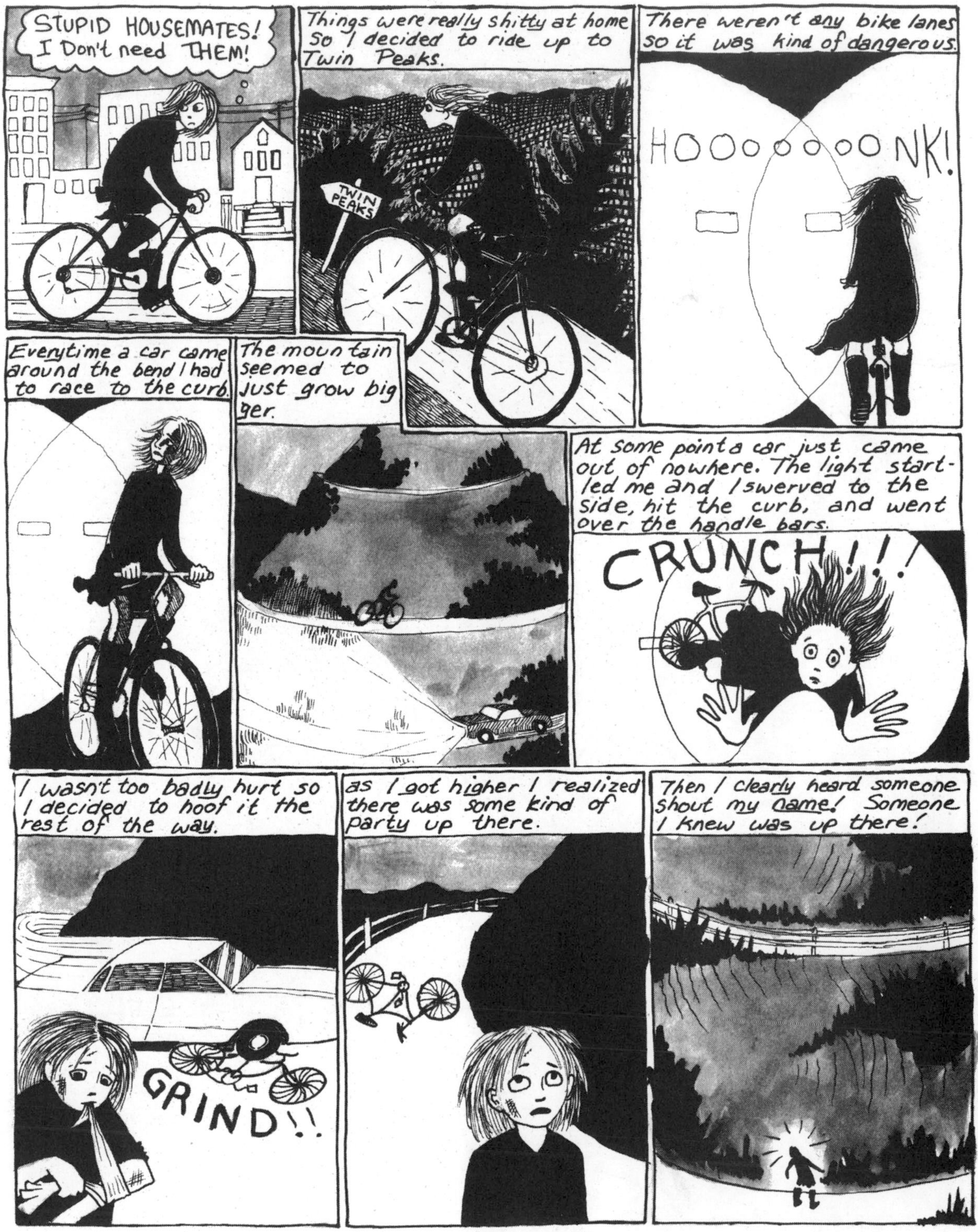
STUPID HOUSEMATES! I Don't need THEM!
Things were really shitty at home so I decided to ride up to Twin Peaks.
TWIN PEAKS
There weren't any bike lanes so it was kind of dangerous.
HOOOOOOOONK!
Everytime a car came around the bend I had to race to the curb.
The mountain seemed to just grow bigger.
At some point a car just came out of nowhere. The light startled me and I swerved to the side, hit the curb, and went over the handle bars.
CRUNCH!!!
I wasn't too badly hurt so I decided to hoof it the rest of the way.
GRIND!!
as I got higher I realized there was some kind of party up there.
Then I clearly heard someone shout my name! Someone I knew was up there!

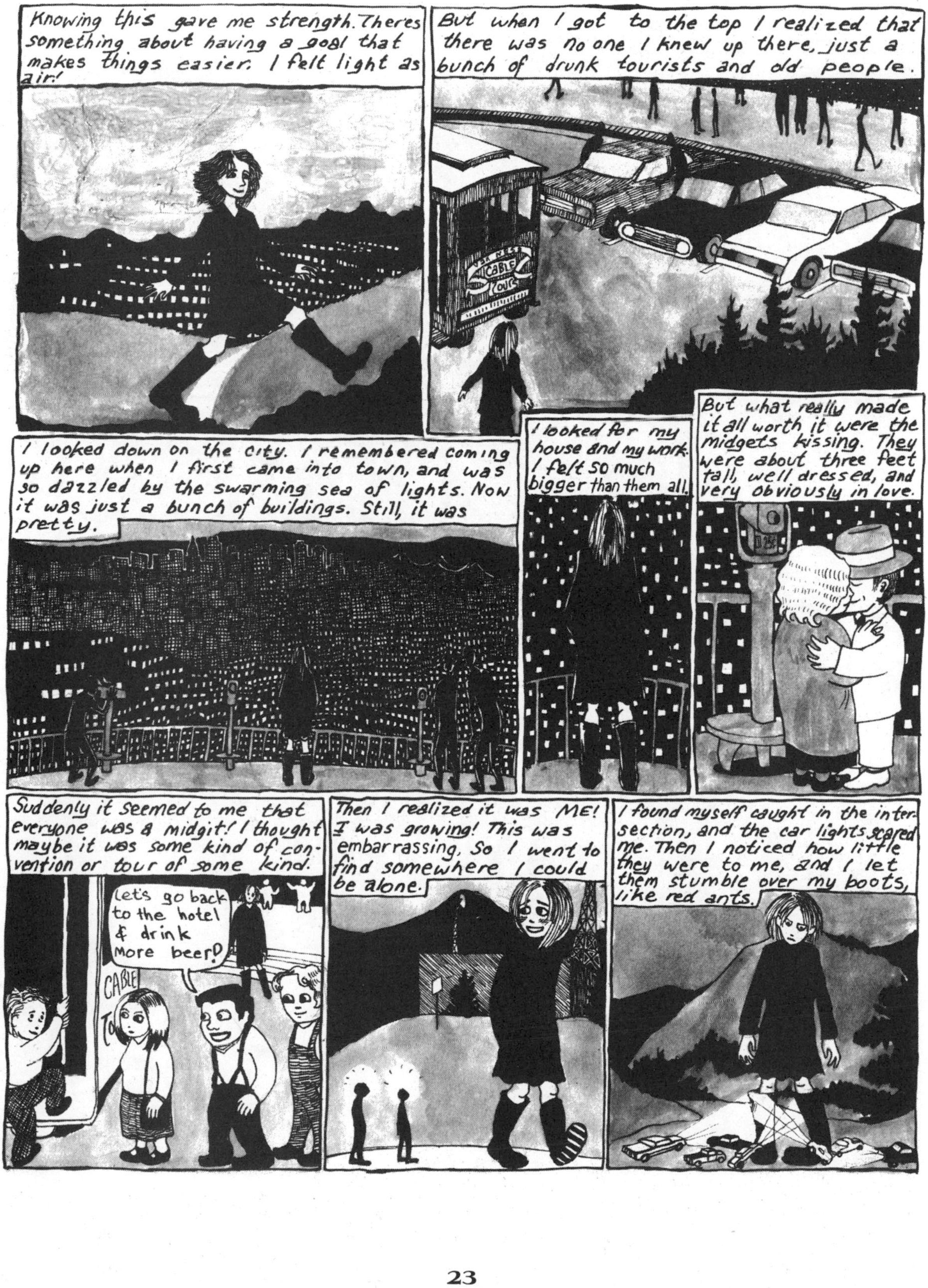
Knowing this gave me strength. Theres something about having a goal that makes things easier. I felt light as air!
But when I got to the top I realized that there was no one I knew up there, just a bunch of drunk tourists and old people.
CABLE
I looked down on the city. I remembered coming up here when I first came into town, and was so dazzled by the swarming sea of lights. Now it was just a bunch of buildings. Still, it was pretty.
I looked for my house and my work. I felt so much bigger than them all.
But what really made it all worth it were the midgets kissing. They were about three feet tall, well dressed, and very obviously in love.
Suddenly it seemed to me that everyone was a midgit! I thought maybe it was some kind of convention or tour of some kind.
Let's go back to the hotel & drink more beer!
CABLE
Then I realized it was ME! I was growing! This was embarrassing. So I went to find somewhere I could be alone.
I found myself caught in the intersection, and the car lights scared me. Then I noticed how little they were to me, and I let them stumble over my boots, like red ants.

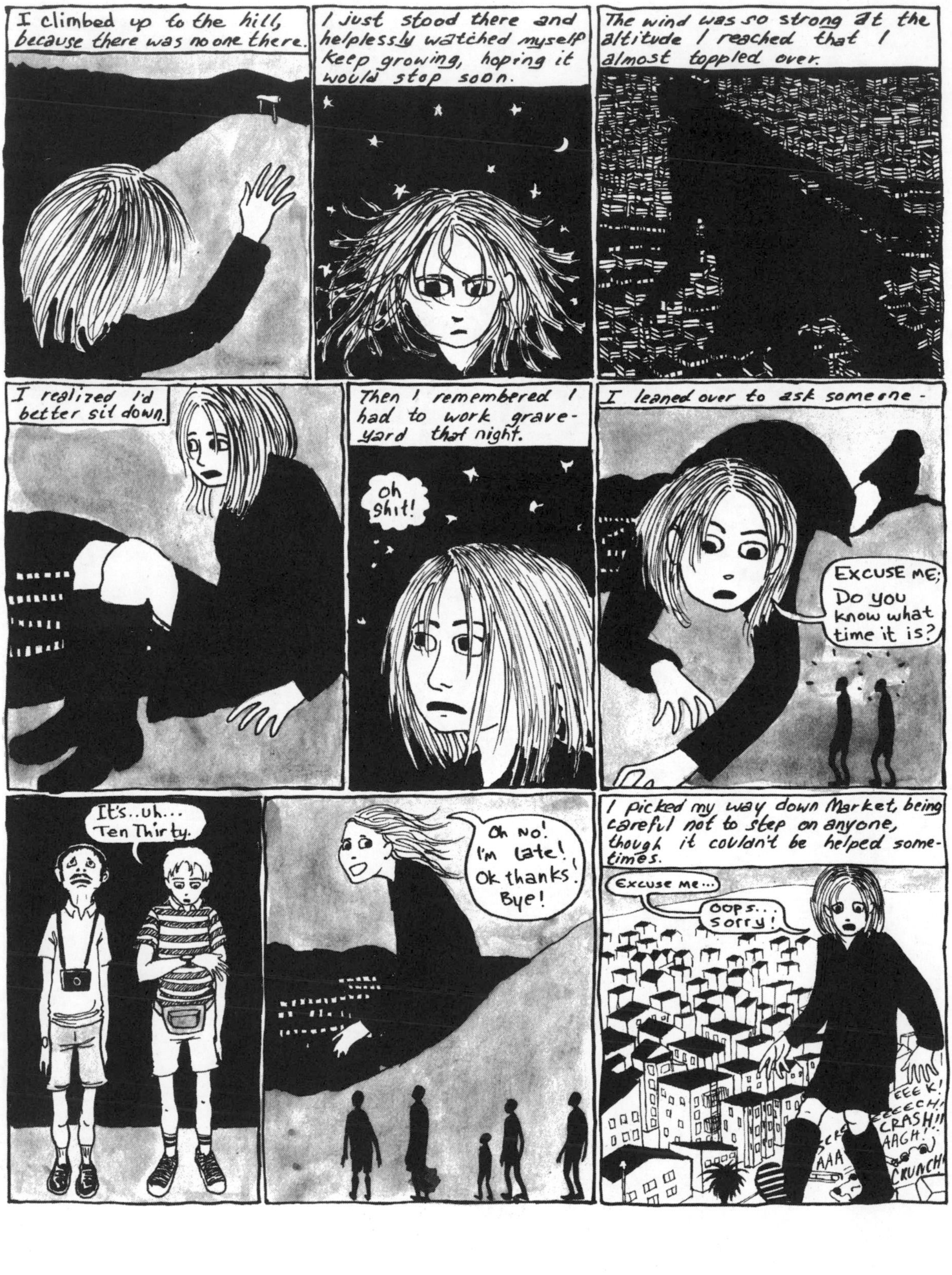
I climbed up to the hill, because there was no one there.
I just stood there and helplessly watched myself keep growing, hoping it would stop soon.
The wind was so strong at the altitude I reached that I almost toppled over.
I realized I'd better sit down.
Then I remembered I had to work graveyard that night.
Oh shit!
I leaned over to ask someone -
EXCUSE ME; Do you know what time it is?
It's..uh... Ten Thirty.
Oh No! I'm Late! Ok thanks! Bye!
I picked my way down Market, being careful not to step on anyone, though it couldn't be helped sometimes.
Excuse me...
Oops... Sorry!
EEEK!
EEEECH!
CRASH!!
AAGH!
AAA
CRUNCH!

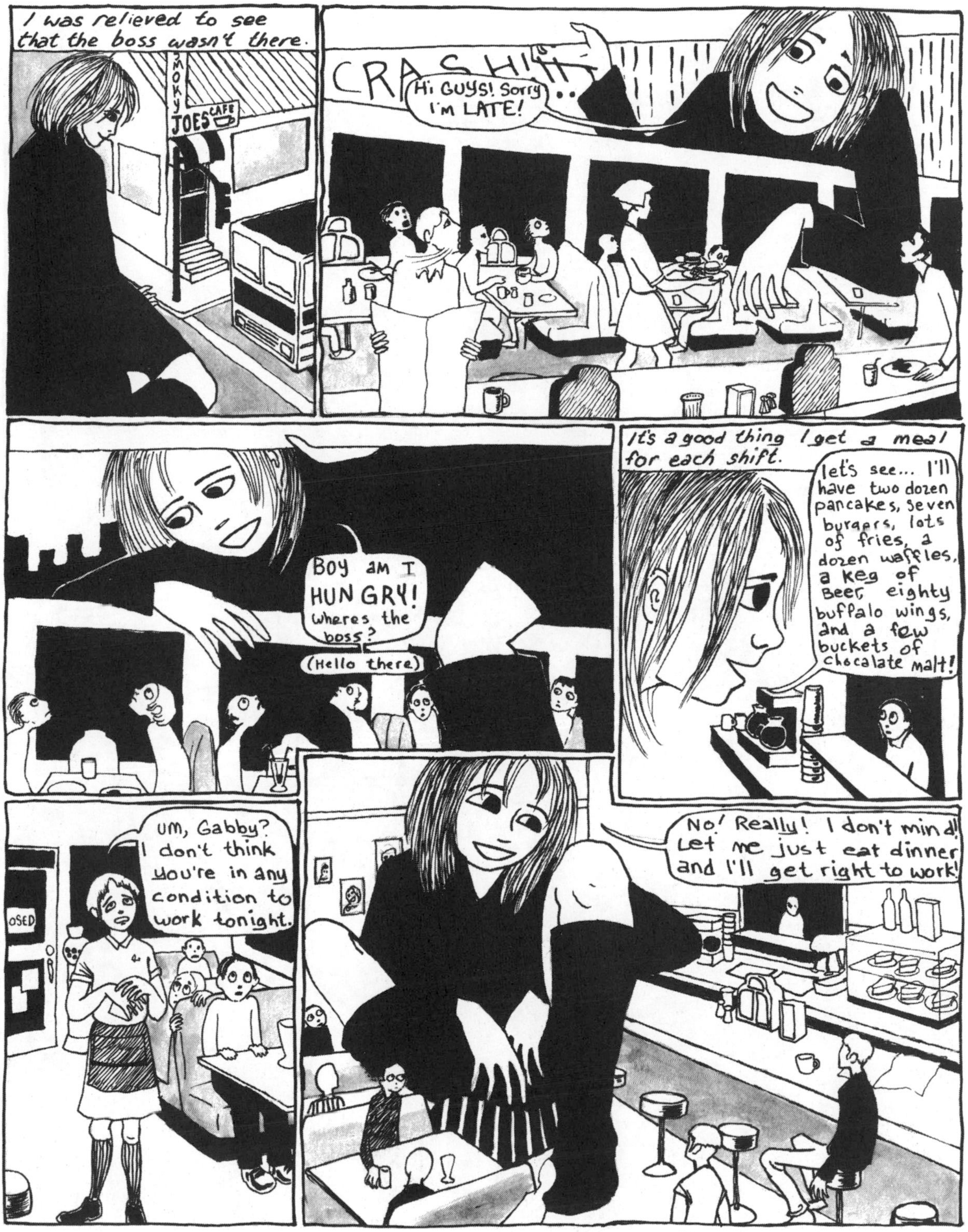

I was relieved to see that the boss wasn't there.
SMOKY JOES CAFE
CRASH!!!
Hi GUYS! Sorry I'M LATE!
Boy am I HUNGRY! wheres the boss?
(Hello there)
It's a good thing I get a meal for each shift.
let's see... I'll have two dozen pancakes, seven burgers, lots of fries, a dozen waffles, a keg of Beer, eighty buffalo wings, and a few buckets of chocalate malt!
UM, Gabby? I don't think you're in any condition to work tonight.
OSED
No! Really! I don't mind! Let me just eat dinner and I'll get right to work!

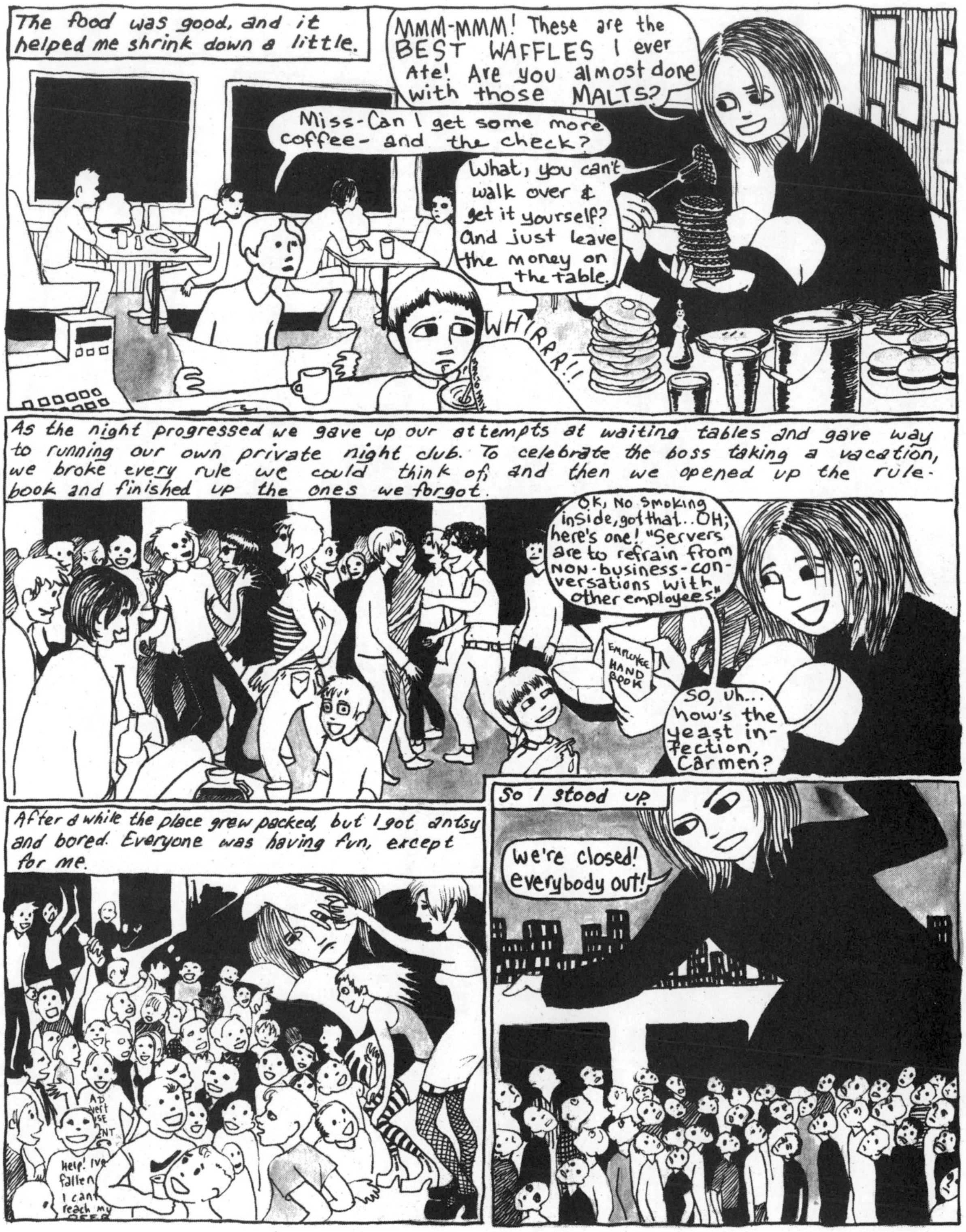
The food was good, and it helped me shrink down a little.
MMM-MMM! These are the BEST WAFFLES I ever Ate! Are you almost done with those MALTS?
Miss-Can I get some more coffee- and the check?
What, you can't walk over & get it yourself? And just leave the money on the table.
WHIRRR!!
As the night progressed we gave up our attempts at waiting tables and gave way to running our own private night club. To celebrate the boss taking a vacation, we broke every rule we could think of, and then we opened up the rule-book and finished up the ones we forgot.
OK, No smoking inside, got that... OH; here's one! "Servers are to refrain from NON-business-conversations with other employees."
EMPLOYEE HAND BOOK
So, uh... how's the yeast infection, Carmen?
After a while the place grew packed, but I got antsy and bored. Everyone was having fun, except for me.
Help! Ive fallen I cant reach my
So I stood up.
We're closed! everybody out!

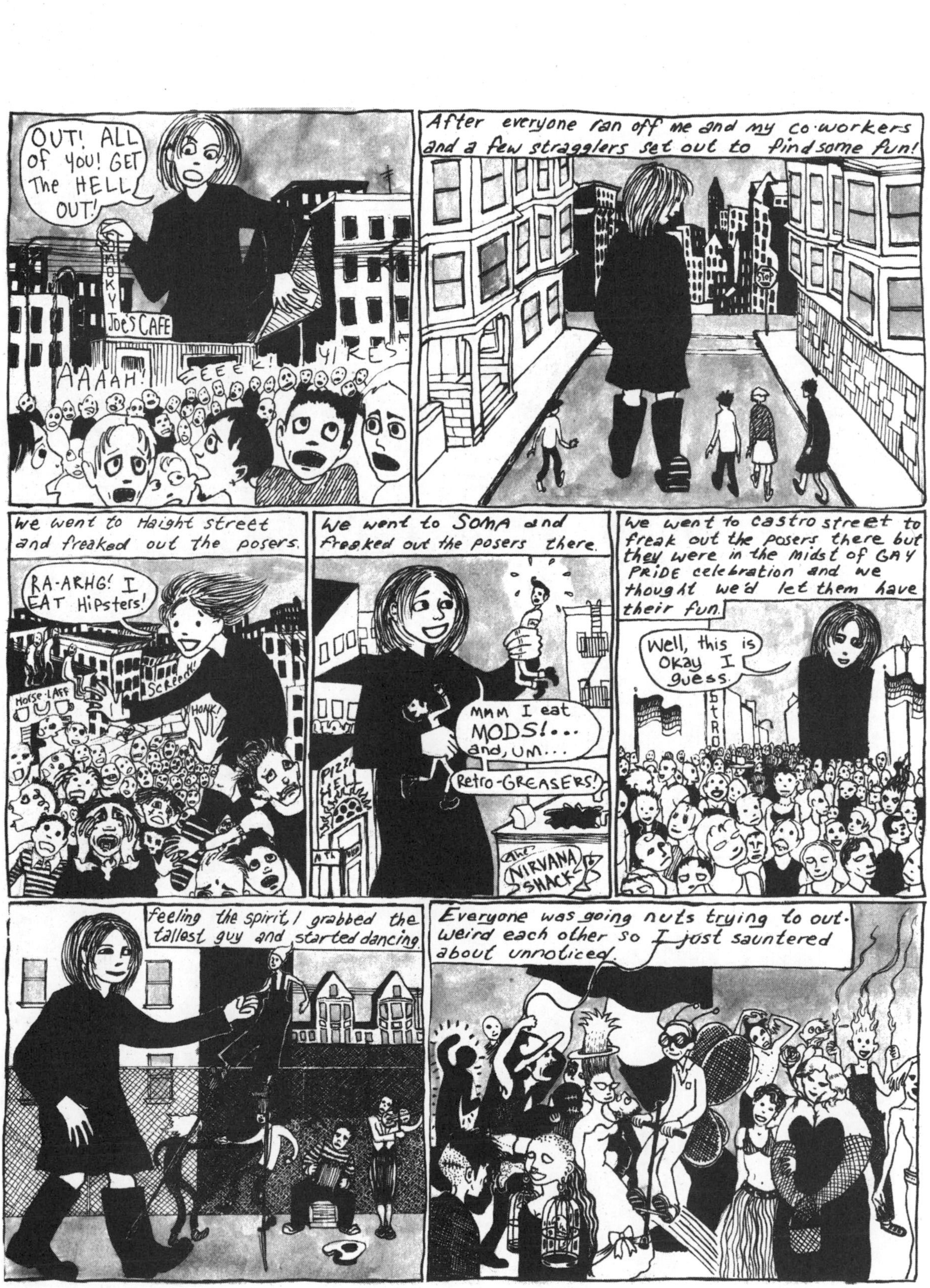
OUT! ALL OF YOU! GET The HELL OUT!
SMOKY Joe's CAFE
AAAAH!
EEEEK!
YIKES!
After everyone ran off me and my co-workers and a few stragglers set out to find some fun!
STOP
We went to Haight street and freaked out the posers.
RA-ARHG! I EAT Hipsters!
SCREECH!
HONK!
We went to SOMA and freaked out the posers there.
MMM I eat MODS!... and, UM...
Retro-GREASERS!
PIZZA HELL
The NIRVANA SHACK
We went to castro street to freak out the posers there but they were in the midst of GAY PRIDE celebration and we thought we'd let them have their fun.
Well, this is Okay I guess.
feeling the spirit, I grabbed the tallest guy and started dancing.
Everyone was going nuts trying to out-weird each other so I just sauntered about unnoticed.

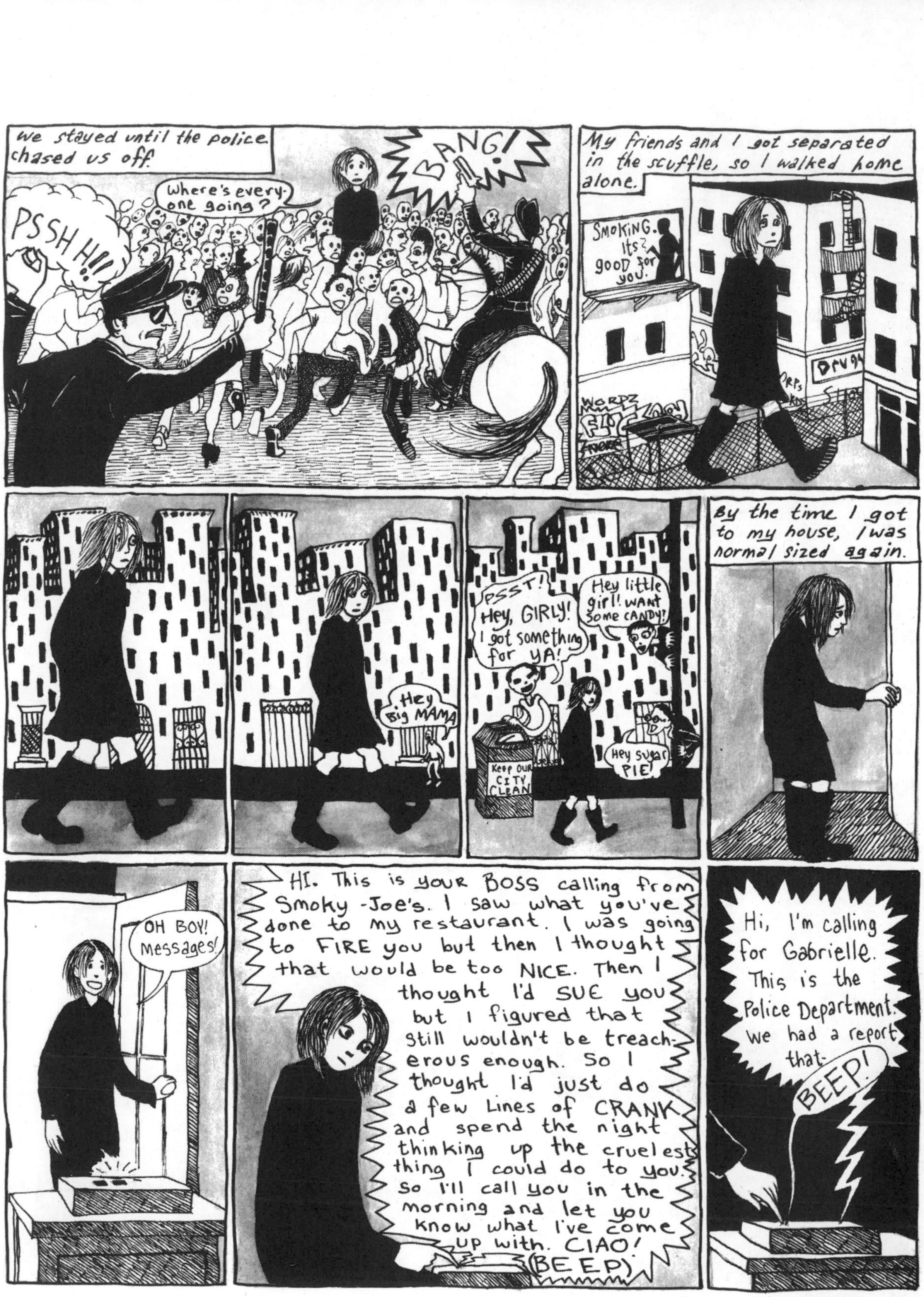
we stayed until the police chased us off.
PSSH H!!
Where's every-one going?
BANG!
My friends and I got separated in the scuffle, so I walked home alone.
SMOKING. Its good for you.
Drugs
Hey Big MAMA
PSST! Hey, GIRLY! I got something for YA!
Hey little girl! WANT SOME CANDY!
Keep OUR CITY CLEAN
Hey sugar PIE!
By the time I got to my house, I was normal sized again.
OH BOY! Messages!
HI. This is your BOSS calling from Smoky-Joe's. I saw what you've done to my restaurant. I was going to FIRE you but then I thought that would be too NICE. Then I thought I'd SUE you but I figured that still wouldn't be treacherous enough. So I thought I'd just do a few Lines of CRANK and spend the night thinking up the cruelest thing I could do to you. So I'll call you in the morning and let you know what I've come up with. CIAO! (BEEP)
Hi, I'm calling for Gabrielle. This is the Police Department. We had a report that-
BEEP!

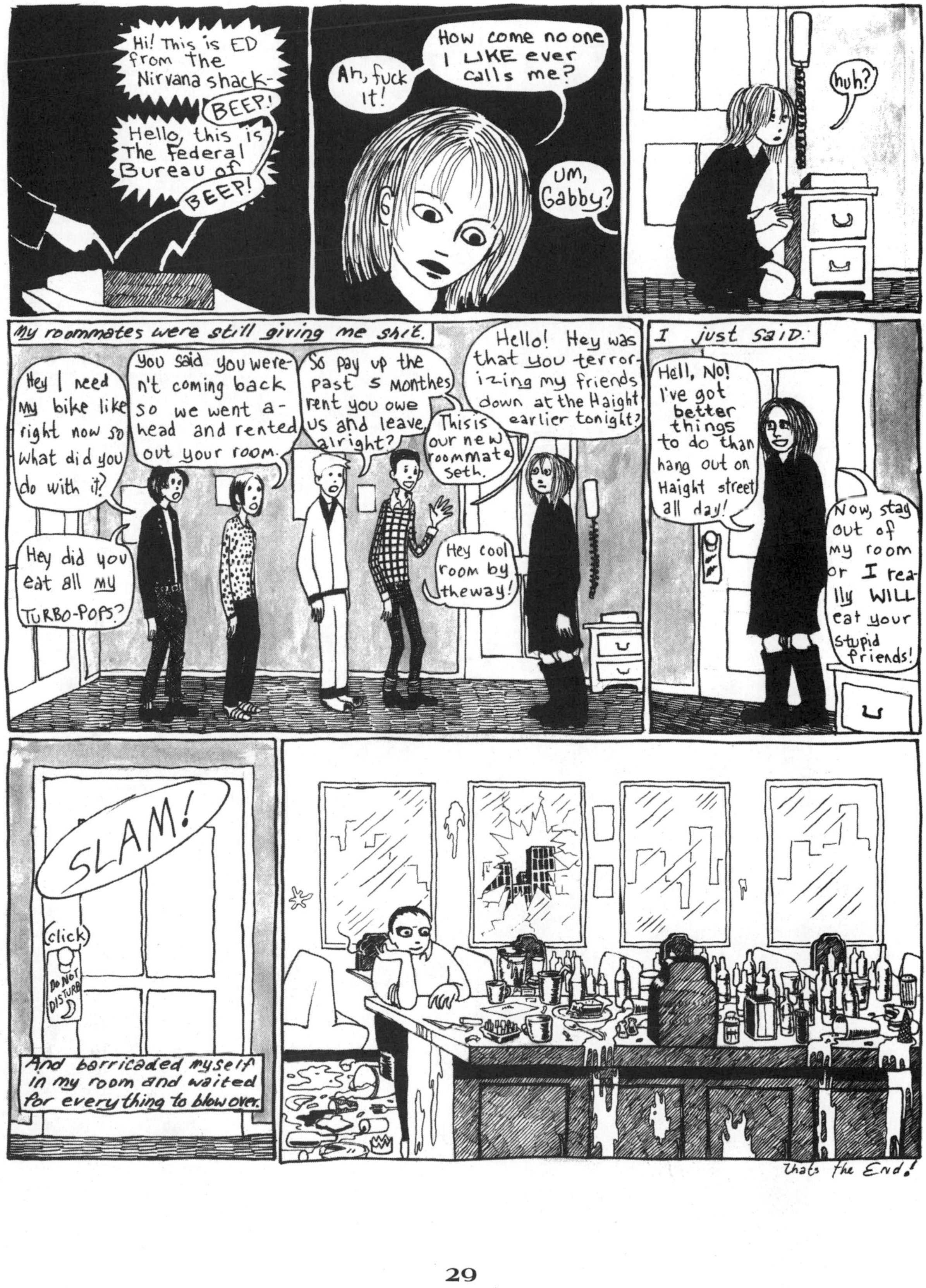

Hi! This is ED from the Nirvana shack-
BEEP!
Hello, this is The Federal Bureau of
BEEP!
How come no one I LIKE ever calls me?
Ah, fuck it!
UM, Gabby?
huh?
My roommates were still giving me shit.
Hey I need my bike like right now so what did you do with it?
Hey did you eat all my TURBO-POPS?
You said you weren't coming back so we went ahead and rented out your room.
So pay up the past 5 monthes rent you owe us and leave, alright?
This is our new roommate seth.
Hey cool room by the way!
Hello! Hey was that you terrorizing my friends down at the Haight earlier tonight?
I just said:
Hell, No! I've got better things to do than hang out on Haight street all day!
Now, stay out of my room or I really WILL eat your stupid friends!
SLAM!
click
Do NOT DISTURB
And barricaded myself in my room and waited for everything to blow over.

thats the End!

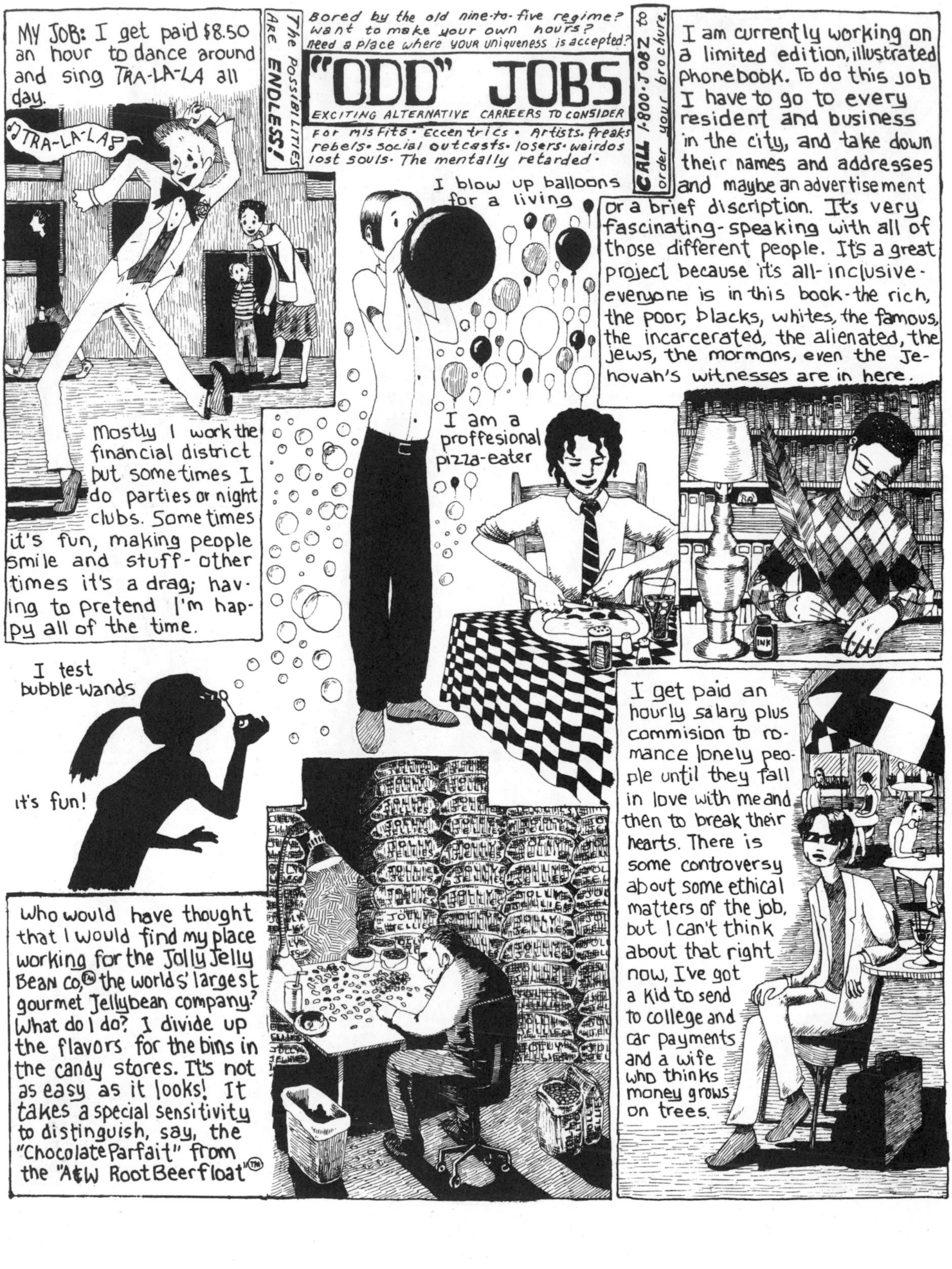

MY JOB: I get paid $8.50 an hour to dance around and sing TRA-LA-LA all day.
TRA-LA-LA
Mostly I work the financial district but sometimes I do parties or night clubs. Sometimes it's fun, making people smile and stuff- other times it's a drag; having to pretend I'm happy all of the time.
The POSSIBILITIES ARE ENDLESS!
Bored by the old nine-to-five regime? want to make your own hours? need a place where YOUR uniqueness is accepted?
"ODD" JOBS
EXCITING ALTERNATIVE CARREERS TO CONSIDER
For misfits • eccentrics • Artists • freaks rebels • social outcasts • losers • weirdos lost souls • The mentally retarded •
CALL 1-800-JOBZ to order your brochure.
I blow up balloons for a living
I am currently working on a limited edition, illustrated phonebook. To do this job I have to go to every resident and business in the city, and take down their names and addresses and maybe an advertisement or a brief discription. It's very fascinating- speaking with all of those different people. It's a great project because it's all-inclusive- everyone is in this book- the rich, the poor, blacks, whites, the famous, the incarcerated, the alienated, the jews, the mormons, even the Jehovah's witnesses are in here.
I am a proffesional pizza-eater
INK
I test bubble-wands
it's fun!
I get paid an hourly salary plus commision to romance lonely people until they fall in love with me and then to break their hearts. There is some controversy about some ethical matters of the job, but I can't think about that right now, I've got a kid to send to college and car payments and a wife who thinks money grows on trees.
Who would have thought that I would find my place working for the Jolly Jelly Bean Co.™ the world's largest gourmet Jellybean company? What do I do? I divide up the flavors for the bins in the candy stores. It's not as easy as it looks! It takes a special sensitivity to distinguish, say, the "Chocolate Parfait" from the "A&W Root Beer float"™

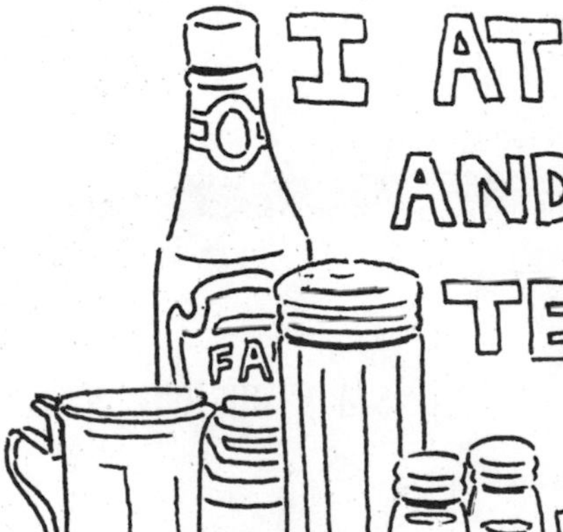

I ATE SHIT AND PRE-TENDED TO LIKE IT

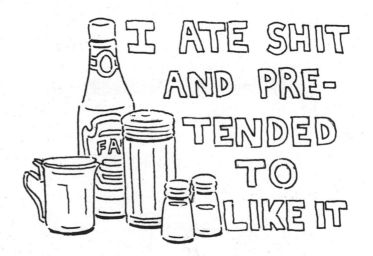

I ATE SHIT AND PRETENDED TO LIKE IT

When I was a child, I was a genius.

As I got older, I proved it by spending more time at the park reading than at school.

The school I went to was real liberal, but they didn't know how to deal with me. I didn't have many friends, and I never listened in class, unless I felt like it. In my senior year I was pretty much given up on, and allowed to do whatever I felt like, which they called independent study.

For example; For my government/economics class, I read Animal Farm, and that was it.

So... what'd think of it?

I liked it...

It was a good read.

It wasn't until years later that I realized that the book was about the russian revolution, and the animals symbolized the major figures like Marx and Lenin. I had no idea.

BARGAIN

CLEARANCE SALE

BACK TO SC

So, you probably assume, understandably, that I became something important, like a writer, right? Well you're wrong. I tried college for awhile, experimented with bad relationships, did some travelling. Fortunately, I've discovered in myself a remarkable talent for recovering from failure well.

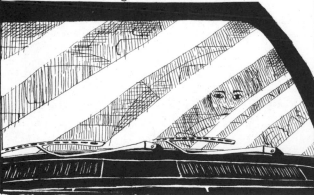

Right now I'm a waitress. It's not for everyone, but it is a challenging job, with many opportunities for self-expression and creativity.

One day I realized that I was no longer a genius. I had allowed myself to gradually erode into just an average person. But what was even worse was I was still hanging onto this conception of what I thought I once was. It was easier than taking responsibility for my fucked up life. In reality I was no better or worse than anyone else.
PSYCOLOGY
AN INTRODUCTION
This didn't make me glad, but it was a relief. My life wasn't so important anymore. It still left me wondering what I wanted to do with it, though. But I decided that, until I knew, I would distinguish myself as the best waitress in the world.
I smiled all of the time, even if I felt hateful. I apologized for things I didn't do, I washed things that were already clean, I did other peoples' chores when I ran out of my own to do, and I made each person who walked in the door feel like nobody more important ever existed.
It wasn't entirely unsatisfying. I got lots of compliments, And of course, the tips were good.
AR
R
Well I guess there was nothing going on anywhere in the world when this journalist wandered into the restaurant one day, because he decided to write an article about what a charming and polite waitress I was, and how I was part of a dying breed of decent, hardworking Americans. And how everyone should come see what a delight I was. It would have been flattering, if it weren't utter baloney.
There was even a photo of me, right there on the front page news.
Daily Headliner
DOWN TOWN
The owners were real pleased with this. It brought in business.
BURGER
DELICIOUS
PANC
WITH MAPL

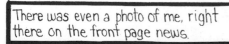

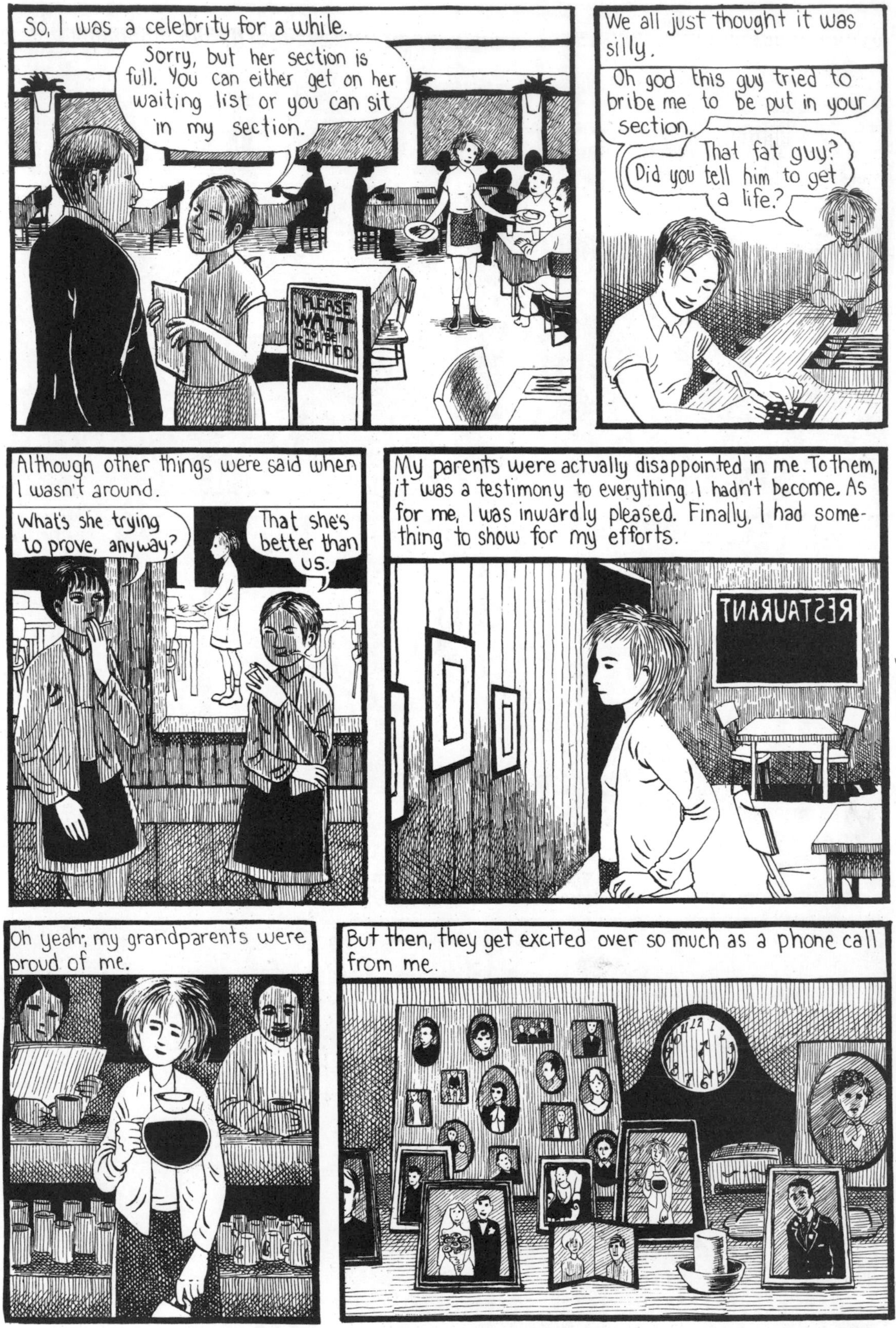
So, I was a celebrity for a while.
Sorry, but her section is full. You can either get on her waiting list or you can sit in my section.
PLEASE WAIT TO BE SEATED
We all just thought it was silly.
Oh god this guy tried to bribe me to be put in your section.
That fat guy? Did you tell him to get a life?
Although other things were said when I wasn't around.
What's she trying to prove, anyway?
That she's better than us.
My parents were actually disappointed in me. To them, it was a testimony to everything I hadn't become. As for me, I was inwardly pleased. Finally, I had something to show for my efforts.
RESTAURANT
Oh yeah; my grandparents were proud of me.
But then, they get excited over so much as a phone call from me.

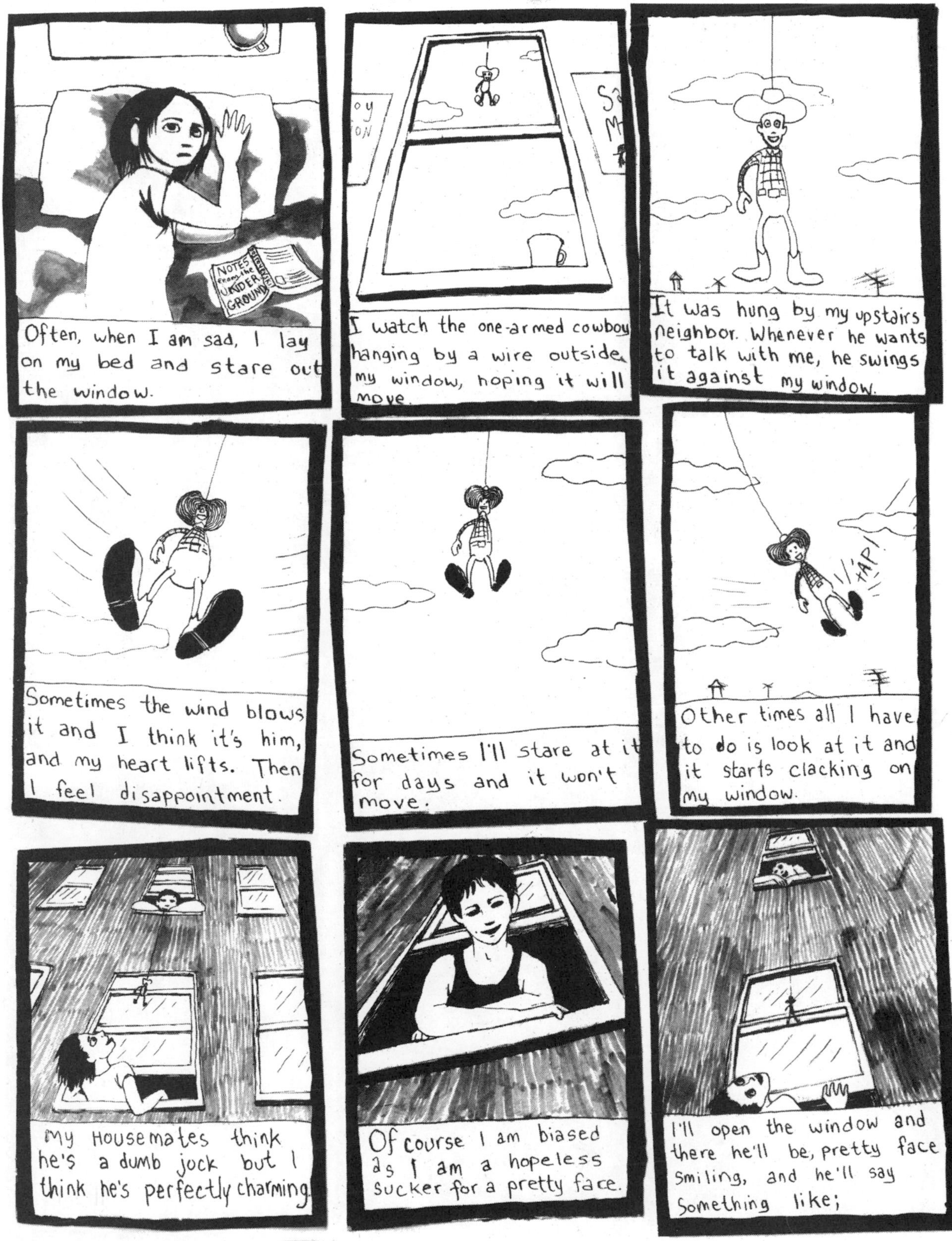
NOTES from the UNDERGROUND
Often, when I am sad, I lay on my bed and stare out the window.
I watch the one-armed cowboy hanging by a wire outside my window, hoping it will move.
It was hung by my upstairs neighbor. Whenever he wants to talk with me, he swings it against my window.
Sometimes the wind blows it and I think it's him, and my heart lifts. Then I feel disappointment.
Sometimes I'll stare at it for days and it won't move.
TAP!
Other times all I have to do is look at it and it starts clacking on my window.
My Housemates think he's a dumb jock but I think he's perfectly charming.
Of course I am biased as I am a hopeless sucker for a pretty face.
I'll open the window and there he'll be, pretty face smiling, and he'll say Something like;

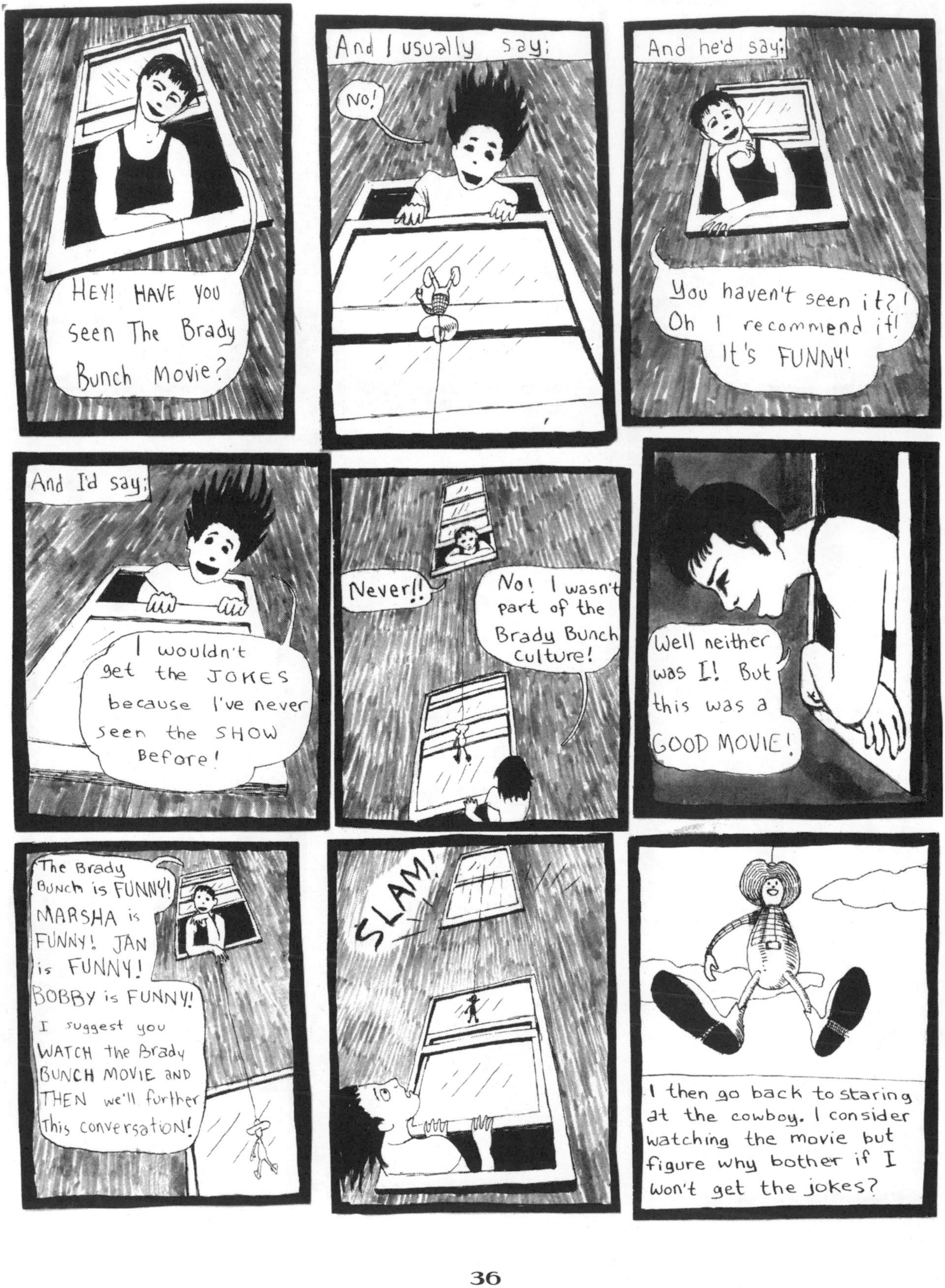
HEY! HAVE you seen The Brady Bunch Movie?
And I usually say;
No!
And he'd say;
You haven't seen it?! Oh I recommend it! It's FUNNY!
And I'd say;
I wouldn't get the JOKES because I've never seen the SHOW before!
Never!!
No! I wasn't part of the Brady Bunch culture!
Well neither was I! But this was a GOOD MOVIE!
The Brady Bunch is FUNNY! MARSHA is FUNNY! JAN is FUNNY! BOBBY is FUNNY! I suggest you WATCH the Brady BUNCH MOVIE and THEN we'll further this conversation!
SLAM!
I then go back to staring at the cowboy. I consider watching the movie but figure why bother if I won't get the jokes?

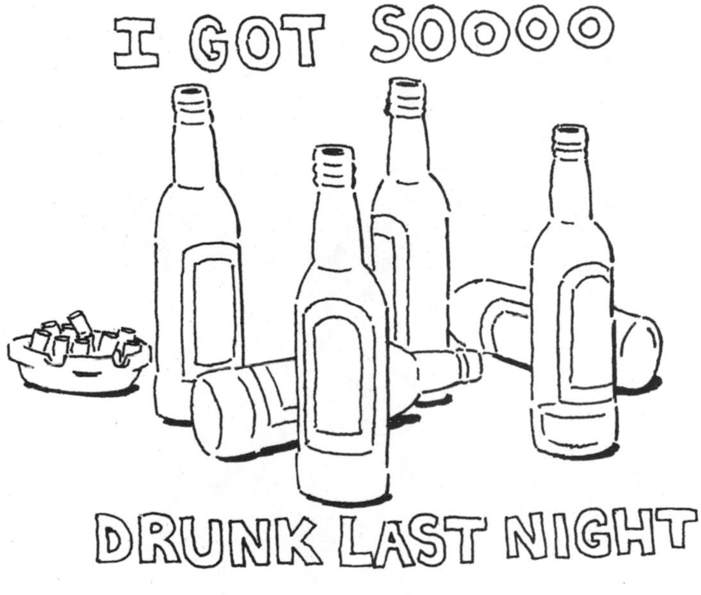
I GOT SOOOO
DRUNK LAST NIGHT

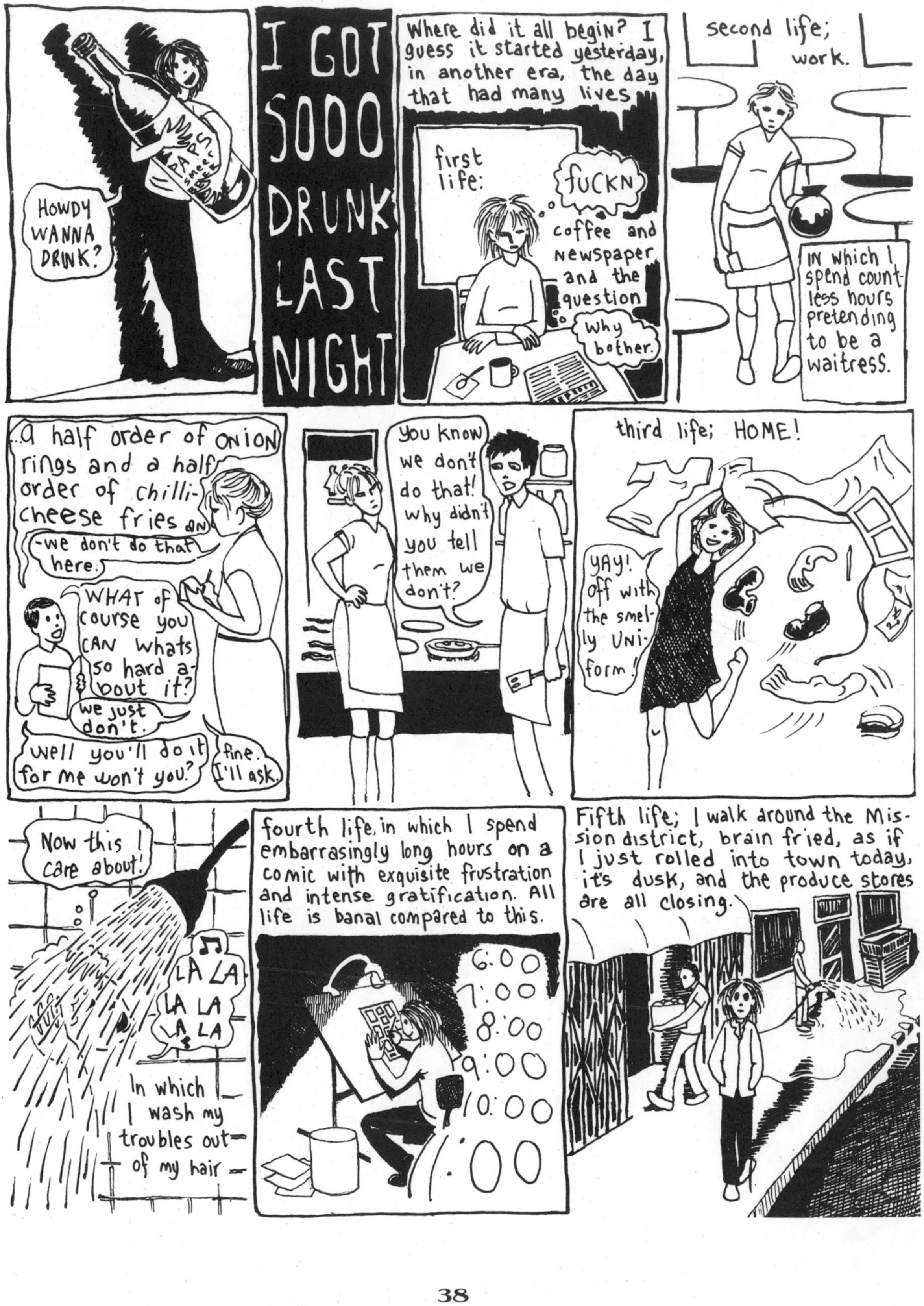
HOWDY WANNA DRINK?
PAPS
I GOT SOOO DRUNK LAST NIGHT
Where did it all begin? I guess it started yesterday, in another era, the day that had many lives
first life:
FUCKN
coffee and newspaper and the question
Why bother.
second life; work.
IN which I spend countless hours pretending to be a waitress.
...a half order of ONION rings and a half order of chilli-cheese fries an
-we don't do that here.
WHAT of course you CAN whats so hard about it?
we just don't.
well you'll do it for me won't you?
fine. I'll ask.
You know we don't do that! why didn't you tell them we don't?
third life; HOME!
YAY! off with the smelly UNIform!
Now this I care about!
LA LA LA LA LA LA
In which I wash my troubles out of my hair
fourth life, in which I spend embarrasingly long hours on a comic with exquisite frustration and intense gratification. All life is banal compared to this.
6:00
7:00
8:00
9:00
10:00
:00
Fifth life; I walk around the Mission district, brain fried, as if I just rolled into town today, it's dusk, and the produce stores are all closing.

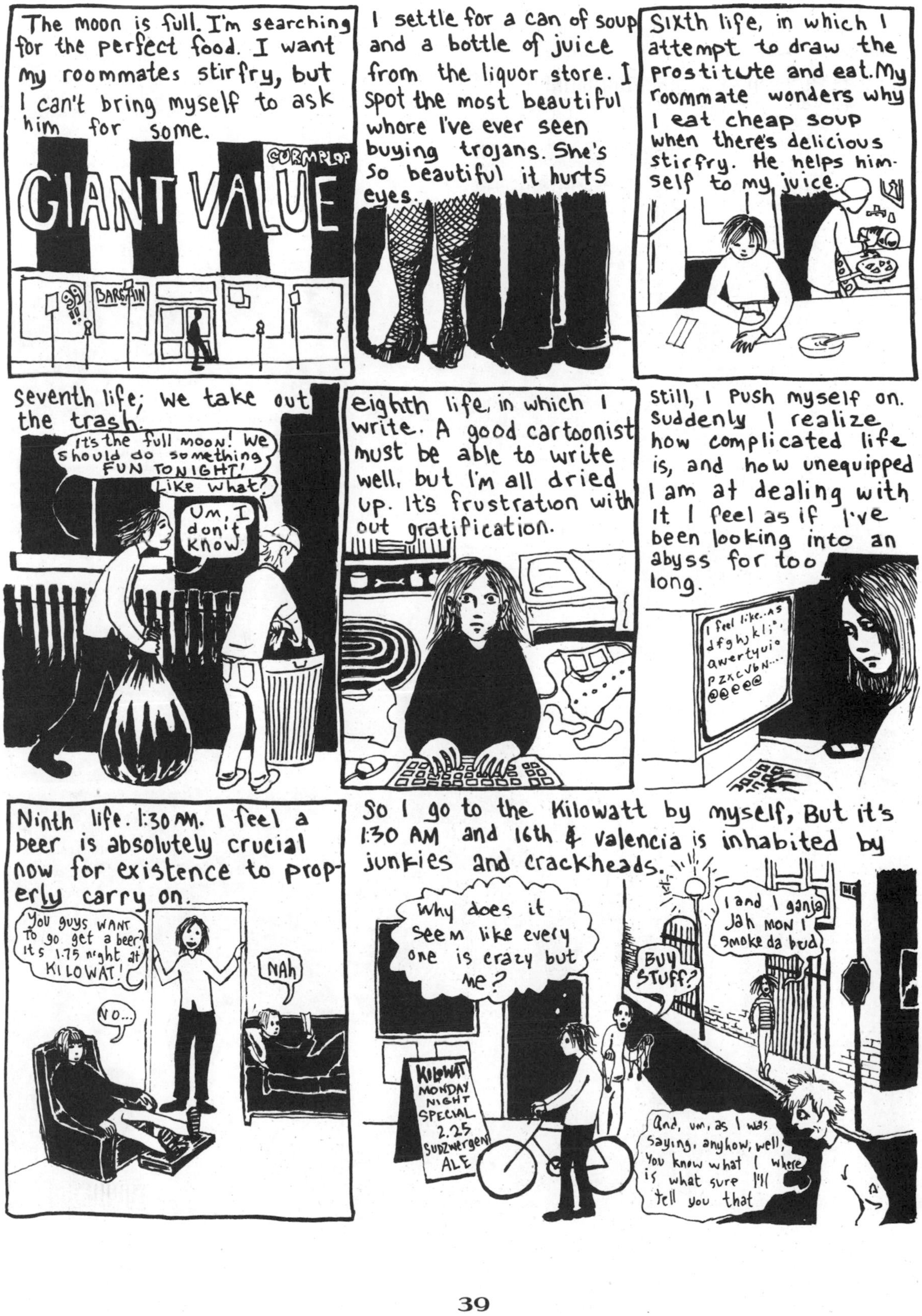

The moon is full. I'm searching for the perfect food. I want my roommates stirfry, but I can't bring myself to ask him for some.
GURMPLOP
GIANT VALUE
99
BARGAIN
I settle for a can of soup and a bottle of juice from the liquor store. I spot the most beautiful whore I've ever seen buying trojans. She's so beautiful it hurts eyes.
Sixth life, in which I attempt to draw the prostitute and eat. My roommate wonders why I eat cheap soup when there's delicious stirfry. He helps himself to my juice.
seventh life; we take out the trash.
It's the full moon! We should do something FUN TONIGHT!
Like what?
Um, I don't know.
eighth life, in which I write. A good cartoonist must be able to write well, but I'm all dried up. It's frustration without gratification.
Still, I push myself on. Suddenly I realize how complicated life is, and how unequipped I am at dealing with it. I feel as if I've been looking into an abyss for too long.
I feel like..as dfghjkl;" qwertyuio pzxcvbn.... @@e@@
Ninth life. 1:30 AM. I feel a beer is absolutely crucial now for existence to properly carry on.
You guys WANT To go get a beer? It's 1.75 night at KILOWAT!
NAh
NO...
So I go to the Kilowatt by myself, But it's 1:30 AM and 16th & valencia is inhabited by junkies and crackheads.
Why does it seem like every one is crazy but me?
BUY STUFF?
I and I ganja Jah MON I smoke da bud
KILOWAT MONDAY NIGHT SPECIAL 2.25 SUDZWERGEN ALE
And, um, as I was saying, anyhow, well, You know what I where is what sure I'll tell you that

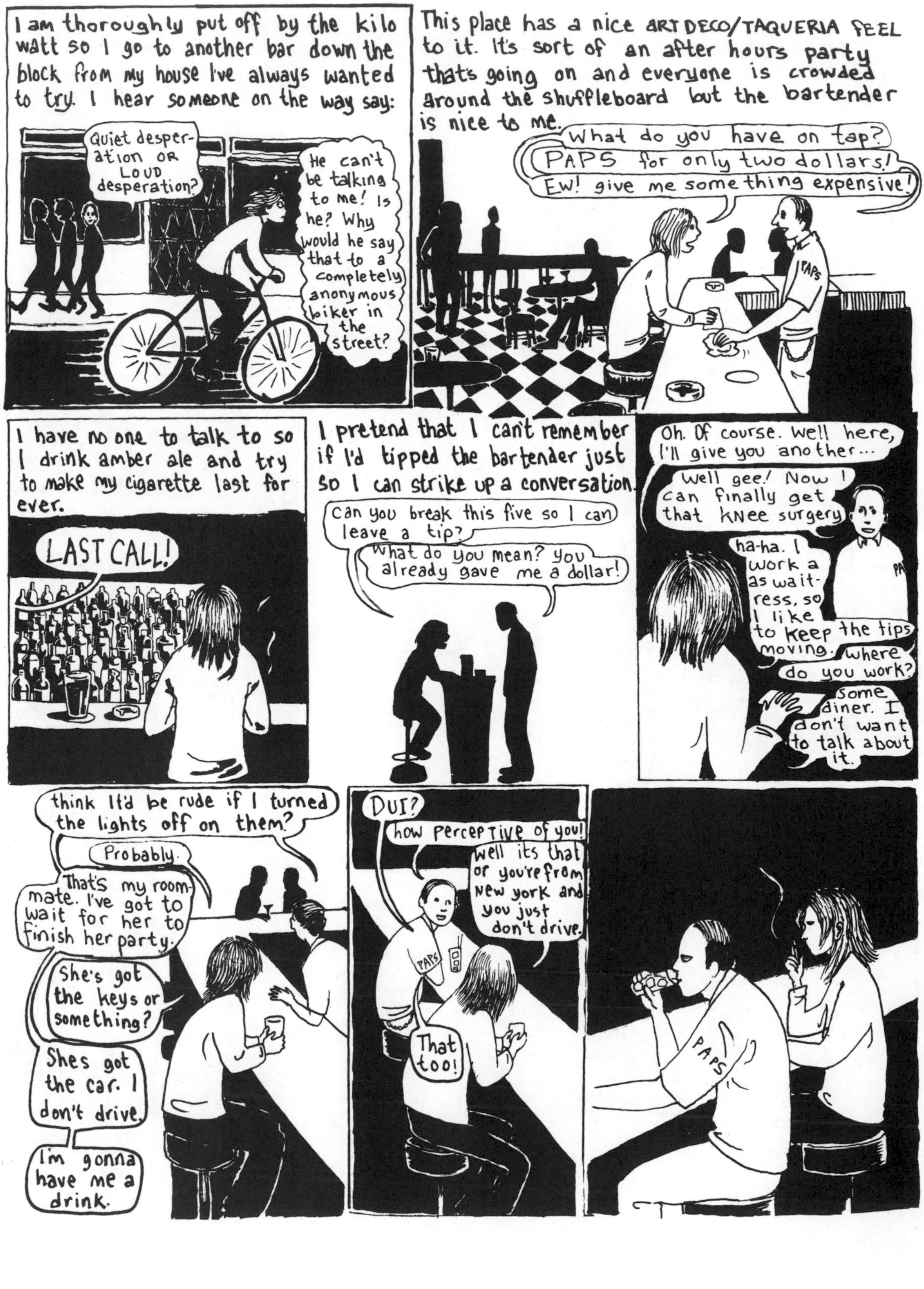
I am thoroughly put off by the kilo watt so I go to another bar down the block from my house I've always wanted to try. I hear someone on the way say:
Quiet desper-ation or LOUD desperation?
He can't be talking to me! Is he? Why would he say that to a completely anonymous biker in the street?
This place has a nice ART DECO/TAQUERIA FEEL to it. It's sort of an after hours party that's going on and everyone is crowded around the shuffleboard but the bartender is nice to me.
What do you have on tap?
PAPS for only two dollars!
Ew! give me something expensive!
PAPS
I have no one to talk to so I drink amber ale and try to make my cigarette last for ever.
LAST CALL!
I pretend that I can't remember if I'd tipped the bartender just so I can strike up a conversation.
Can you break this five so I can leave a tip?
What do you mean? You already gave me a dollar!
Oh. Of course. Well here, I'll give you another...
Well gee! Now I can finally get that knee surgery
ha-ha. I work as a wait-ress, so I like to keep the tips moving.
Where do you work?
Some diner. I don't want to talk about it.
think It'd be rude if I turned the lights off on them?
Probably.
That's my room-mate. I've got to wait for her to finish her party.
She's got the keys or something?
Shes got the car. I don't drive.
I'm gonna have me a drink.
DUI?
how perceptive of you!
well its that or you're from new york and you just don't drive.
That too!
PAPS

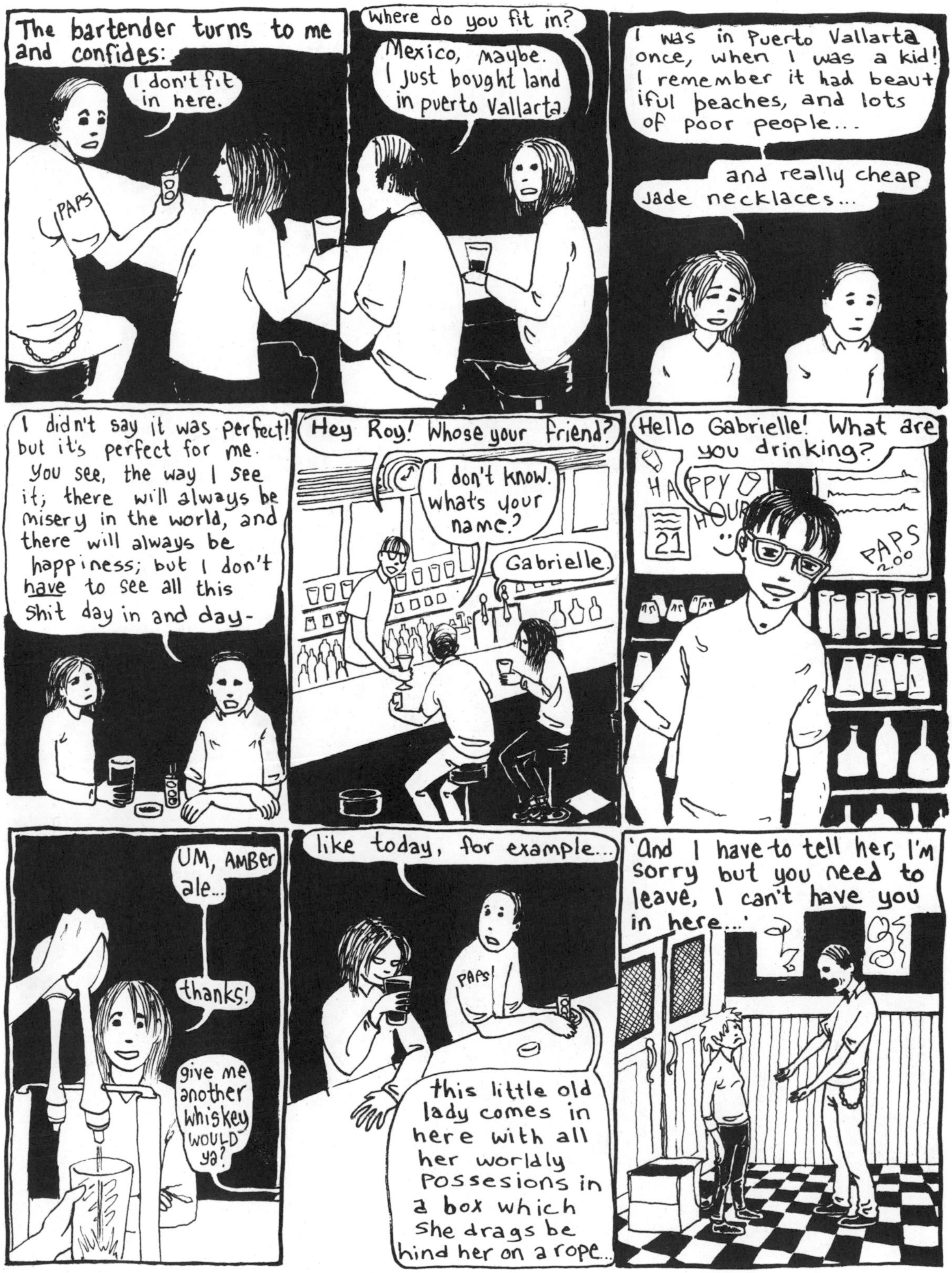

The bartender turns to me and confides:
I don't fit in here.
PAPS
Where do you fit in?
Mexico, maybe. I just bought land in puerto Vallarta.
I was in Puerto Vallarta once, when I was a kid! I remember it had beautiful beaches, and lots of poor people...
and really cheap jade necklaces...
I didn't say it was perfect! but it's perfect for me. You see, the way I see it; there will always be misery in the world, and there will always be happiness; but I don't have to see all this shit day in and day-
Hey Roy! Whose your friend?
I don't know. what's your name?
Gabrielle.
Hello Gabrielle! What are you drinking?
HAPPY HOUR
21
PAPS 200
UM, AMBER ale...
thanks!
give me another whiskey WOULD ya?
like today, for example...
PAPS
this little old lady comes in here with all her worldly possesions in a box which she drags be hind her on a rope...
'And I have to tell her, I'm sorry but you need to leave, I can't have you in here...'

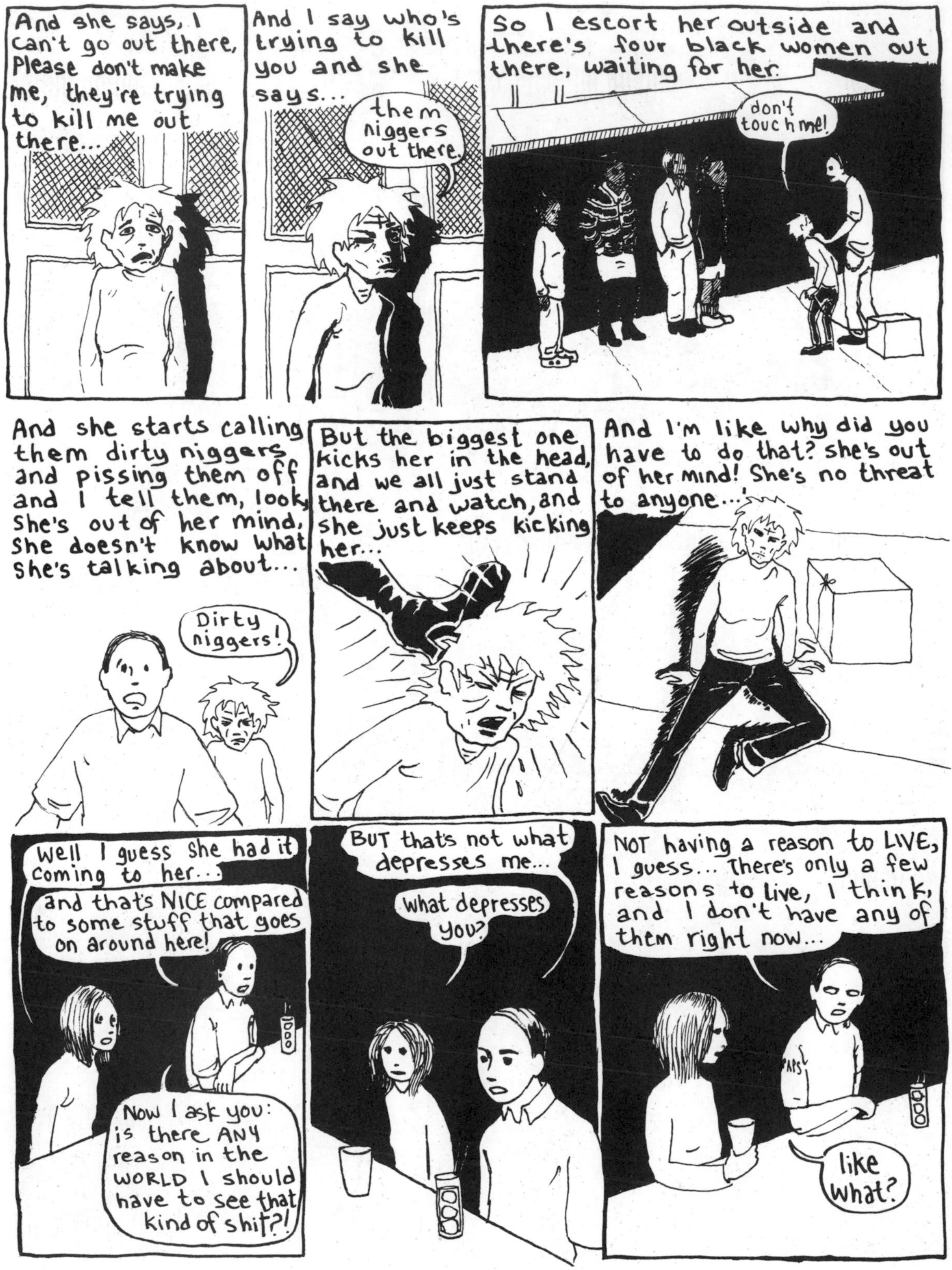
And she says, I can't go out there, Please don't make me, they're trying to kill me out there...
And I say who's trying to kill you and she says...
them niggers out there.
So I escort her outside and there's four black women out there, waiting for her.
don't touch me!
And she starts calling them dirty niggers and pissing them off and I tell them, look, She's out of her mind, She doesn't know what She's talking about...
Dirty niggers!
But the biggest one kicks her in the head, and we all just stand there and watch, and she just keeps kicking her...
And I'm like why did you have to do that? she's out of her mind! She's no threat to anyone...'
Well I guess she had it coming to her...
and that's NICE compared to some stuff that goes on around here!
Now I ask you: is there ANY reason in the WORLD I should have to see that kind of shit?!
BUT that's not what depresses me...
What depresses you?
NOT having a reason to LIVE, I guess... There's only a few reasons to live, I think, and I don't have any of them right now...
like what?

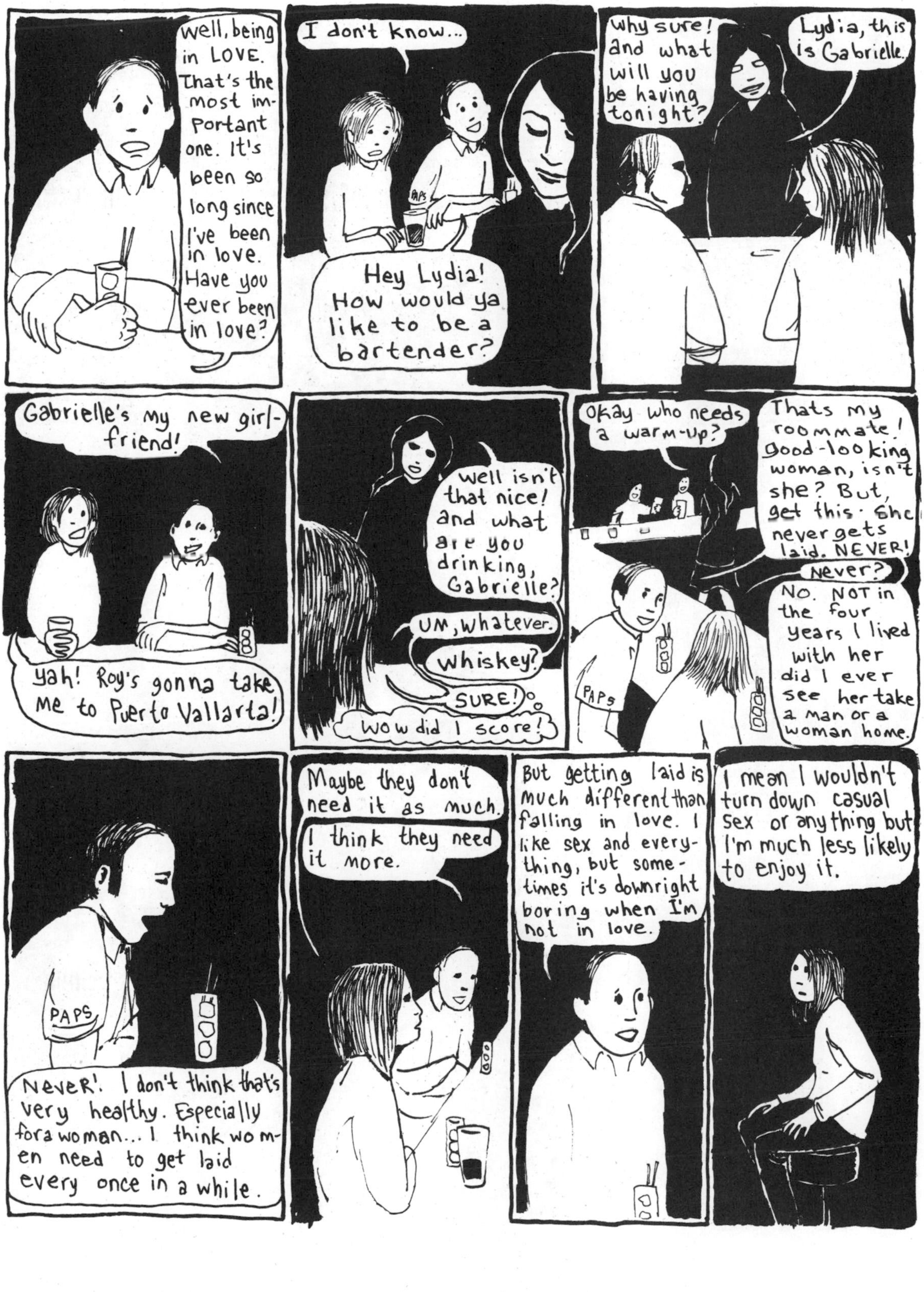
Well, being in LOVE. That's the most important one. It's been so long since I've been in love. Have you ever been in love?
I don't know...
Hey Lydia! How would ya like to be a bartender?
Why sure! and what will you be having tonight?
Lydia, this is Gabrielle.
Gabrielle's my new girlfriend!
yah! Roy's gonna take me to Puerto Vallarta!
Well isn't that nice! and what are you drinking, Gabrielle?
UM, whatever.
Whiskey?
SURE!
Wow did I score!
Okay who needs a warm-up?
Thats my roommate! good-looking woman, isn't she? But, get this. She never gets laid. NEVER!
Never?
NO. NOT in the four years I lived with her did I ever see her take a man or a woman home.
NEVER! I don't think that's very healthy. Especially for a woman... I think women need to get laid every once in a while.
Maybe they don't need it as much.
I think they need it more.
But getting laid is much different than falling in love. I like sex and everything, but sometimes it's downright boring when I'm not in love.
I mean I wouldn't turn down casual sex or anything but I'm much less likely to enjoy it.

And time keeps sliding on, and I get to feeling oddly attached to the bar stool.

I decide to see if I can't walk to the restroom.

excuse me.

sure.

The bar is suddenly empty. I head towards the restroom, in a roundabout sort of way.

WHOA HOW'D I GET SO DRUNK?!

In the bathroom I realize I am far more drunk than I thought. I hardly recognize myself. I look haggard and old.

feeling ill, I slide down the wall. Everything spins.

I consider puking, but I never puke, and I only had three drinks.

After awhile I get up and wander back.

where'd every body go?

I'm not sure what to do next so I sit back on the stool.

Suddenly I barf all over the bar.

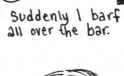

BLE TCH

In my drunken stupor I think maybe he won't notice.

44

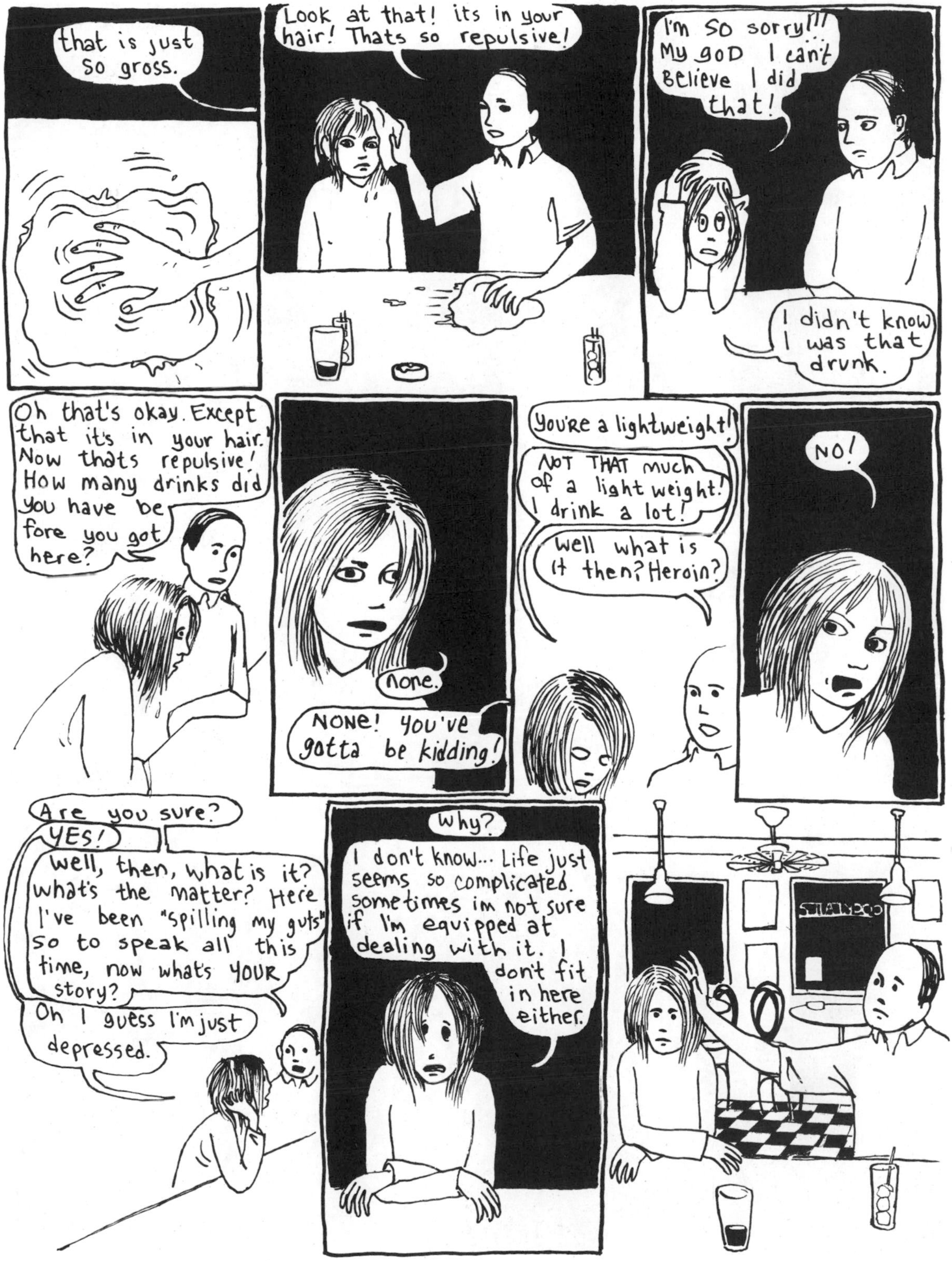
that is just so gross.
Look at that! its in your hair! Thats so repulsive!
I'm so sorry!!! My god I can't believe I did that!
I didn't know I was that drunk.
Oh that's okay. Except that it's in your hair. Now thats repulsive! How many drinks did you have be fore you got here?
None.
NONE! You've gotta be kidding!
You're a lightweight!
NOT THAT much of a light weight! I drink a lot!
Well what is it then? Heroin?
NO!
Are you sure?
YES!
Well, then, what is it? what's the matter? Here I've been "spilling my guts" so to speak all this time, now what's YOUR story?
Oh I guess I'm just depressed.
Why?
I don't know... Life just seems so complicated. Sometimes im not sure if I'm equipped at dealing with it. I don't fit in here either.

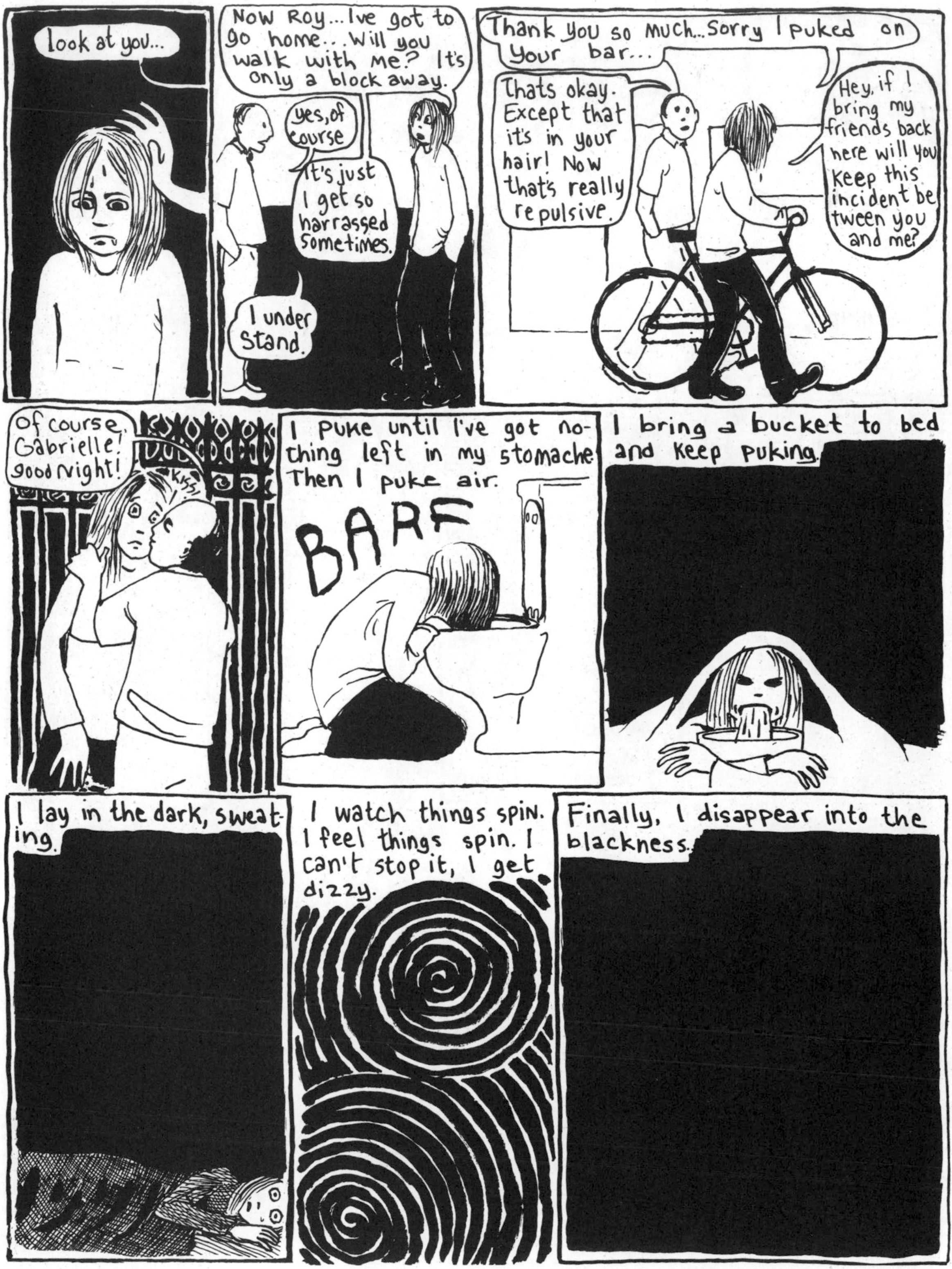
look at you...
Now Roy... Ive got to go home... Will you walk with me? It's only a block away.
yes, of course
It's just I get so harrassed sometimes.
I under stand.
Thank you so much... Sorry I puked on your bar...
Thats okay. Except that it's in your hair! Now that's really repulsive.
Hey, if I bring my friends back here will you keep this incident be tween you and me?
Of course, Gabrielle! good night!
I puke until I've got nothing left in my stomache. Then I puke air.
BARF
I bring a bucket to bed and keep puking.
I lay in the dark, sweating.
I watch things spin. I feel things spin. I can't stop it, I get dizzy.
Finally, I disappear into the blackness.

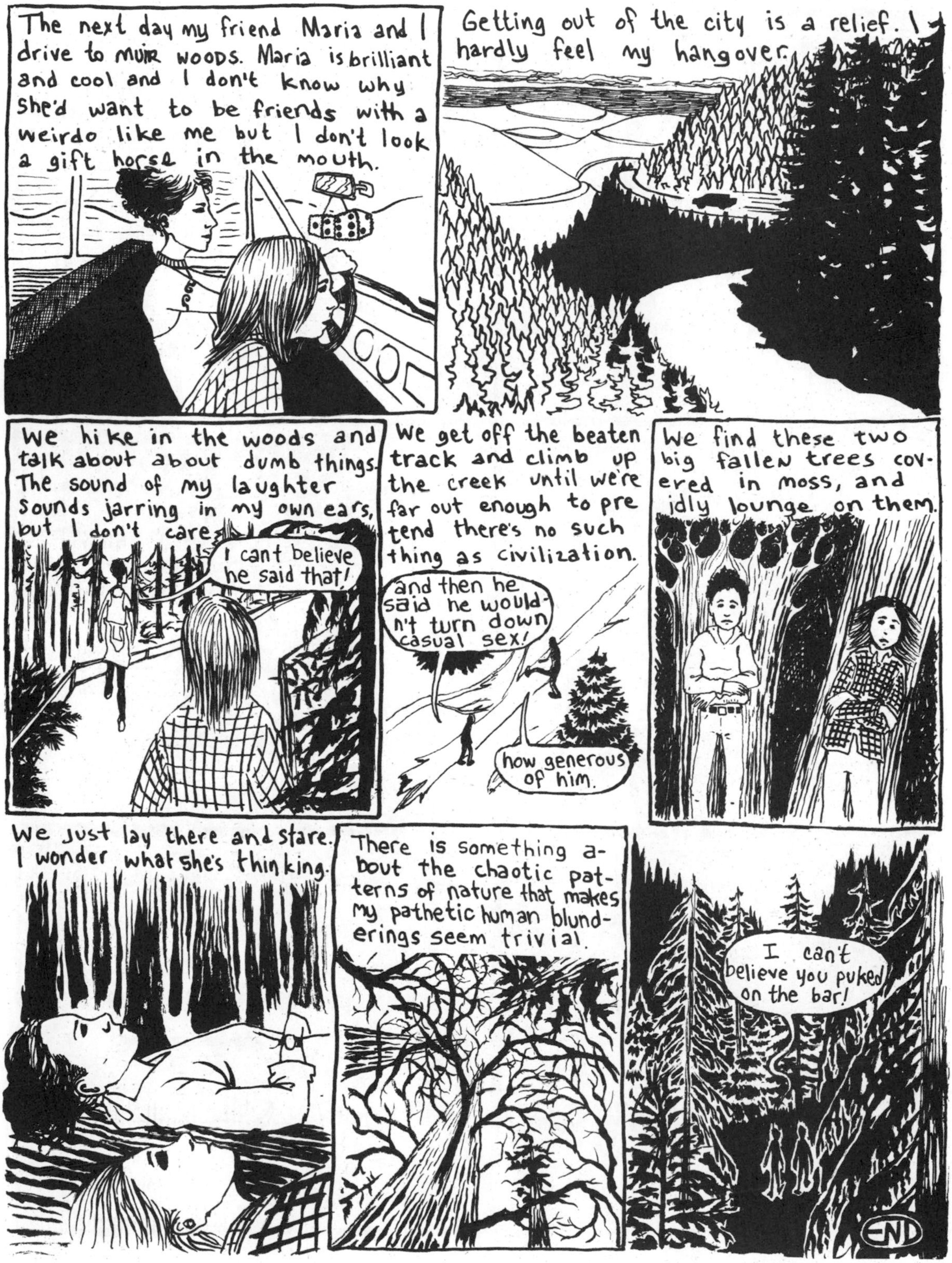

The next day my friend Maria and I drive to MUIR WOODS. Maria is brilliant and cool and I don't know why she'd want to be friends with a weirdo like me but I don't look a gift horse in the mouth.
Getting out of the city is a relief. I hardly feel my hangover.
We hike in the woods and talk about about dumb things. The sound of my laughter sounds jarring in my own ears, but I don't care.
I cant believe he said that!
We get off the beaten track and climb up the creek until we're far out enough to pretend there's no such thing as civilization.
and then he said he wouldn't turn down casual sex!
how generous of him.
We find these two big fallen trees covered in moss, and idly lounge on them.
We just lay there and stare. I wonder what she's thinking.
There is something about the chaotic patterns of nature that makes my pathetic human blunderings seem trivial.
I can't believe you puked on the bar!
END

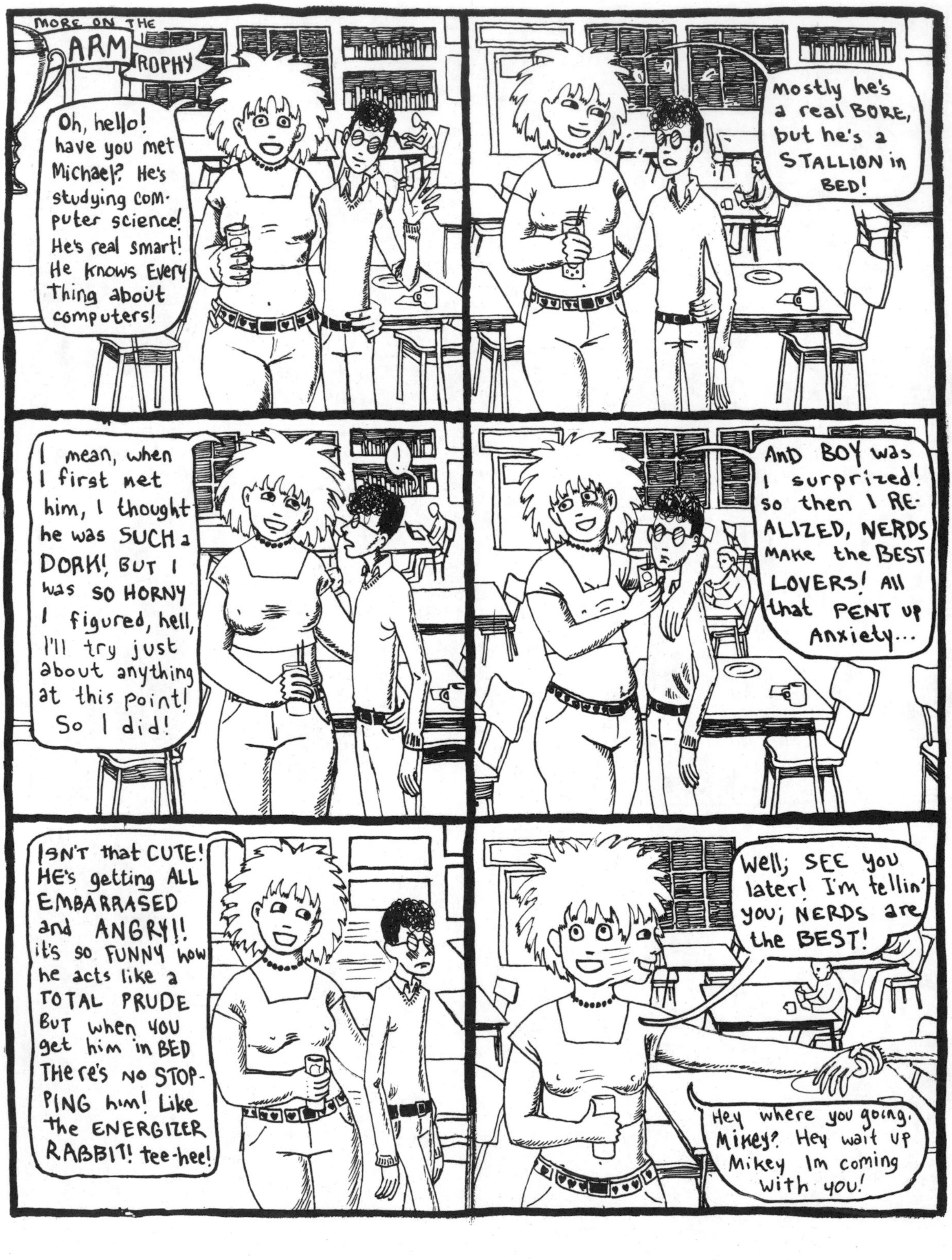
MORE ON THE ARM ROPHY
Oh, hello! have you met Michael? He's studying computer science! He's real smart! He knows Everything about computers!
Mostly he's a real BORE, but he's a STALLION in BED!
I mean, when I first met him, I thought he was SUCH a DORK! BUT I was SO HORNY I figured, hell, I'll try just about anything at this point! So I did!
!
AND BOY was I surprized! so then I REALIZED, NERDS MAKE the BEST LOVERS! All that PENT UP Anxiety...
ISN'T that CUTE! HE's getting ALL EMBARRASED and ANGRY!! it's so FUNNY how he acts like a TOTAL PRUDE BUT when YOU get him in BED THEre's NO STOPPING him! Like the ENERGIZER RABBIT! tee-hee!
Well; SEE YOU later! I'm tellin' you; NERDS are the BEST!
Hey where you going, Mikey? Hey wait up Mikey Im coming with you!

The Fairy Tale
About
the
Wicker
Chair

The Fairy-Tale about the WICKER CHAIR

BY HERMANN HESSE 1918 ILLUSTRATED by Gabrielle Bell ©1998

A young man sat in his solitary attic. His greatest desire was to become a painter, but first he had to overcome quite a few obstacles. To begin with, he lived peacefully in his attic, grew somewhat older, and became accustomed to sitting for hours in front of a small mirror and experimenting with painting self-portraits.

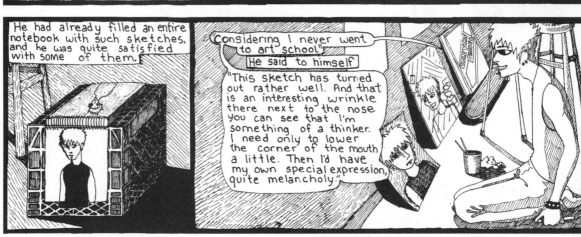

He had already filled an entire notebook with such sketches, and he was quite satisfied with some of them.

"Considering I never went to art school," He said to himself

"This sketch has turned out rather well. And that is an interesting wrinkle there next to the nose. You can see that I'm something of a thinker. I need only to lower the corner of the mouth a little. Then I'd have my own special expression, quite melancholy."

But when he reexamined them later, most of them no longer pleased him. That was irritating, but he concluded from this that he had made progress and was now placing greater demands on himself.

The young man did not live in the most desirable attic, nor did he have a very agreeable relationship with the things lying around this attic.

However, it was not a bad relationship. He did them no more or less harm than most people do.

He hardly noticed the objects and was not very familiar with them.

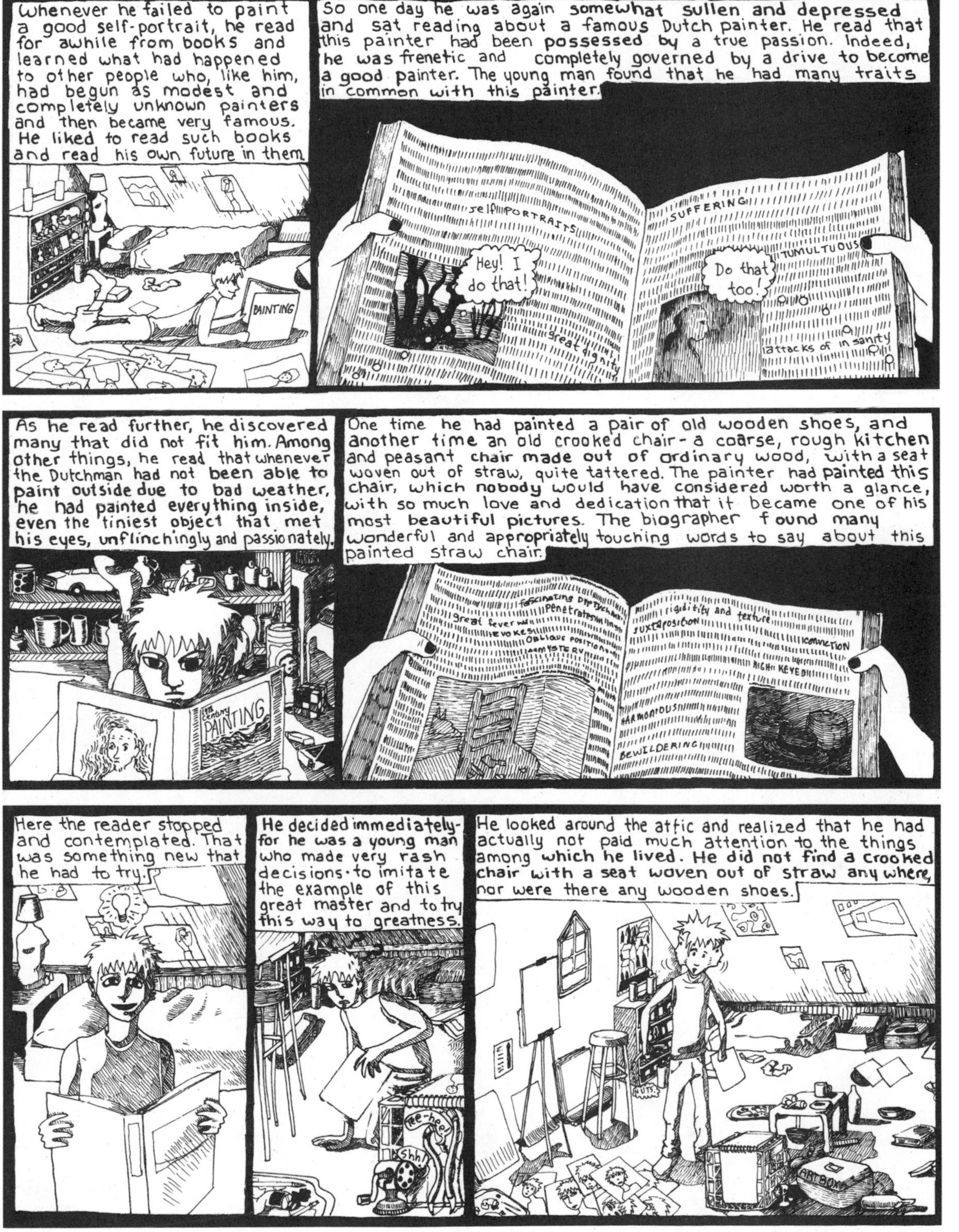
Whenever he failed to paint a good self-portrait, he read for awhile from books and learned what had happened to other people who, like him, had begun as modest and completely unknown painters and then became very famous. He liked to read such books and read his own future in them.
PAINTING
So one day he was again somewhat sullen and depressed and sat reading about a famous Dutch painter. He read that this painter had been possessed by a true passion. Indeed, he was frenetic and completely governed by a drive to become a good painter. The young man found that he had many traits in common with this painter.
self PORTRAITS
SUFFERING
TUMULTUOUS
Hey! I do that!
Do that too!
great dignity
attacks of insanity
As he read further, he discovered many that did not fit him. Among other things, he read that whenever the Dutchman had not been able to paint outside due to bad weather, he had painted everything inside, even the tiniest object that met his eyes, unflinchingly and passionately.
PAINTING
One time he had painted a pair of old wooden shoes, and another time an old crooked chair - a coarse, rough kitchen and peasant chair made out of ordinary wood, with a seat woven out of straw, quite tattered. The painter had painted this chair, which nobody would have considered worth a glance, with so much love and dedication that it became one of his most beautiful pictures. The biographer found many wonderful and appropriately touching words to say about this painted straw chair.
rigidity and texture
JUXTAPOSITION
HARMONIOUS
BEWILDERING
Here the reader stopped and contemplated. That was something new that he had to try.
He decided immediately - for he was a young man who made very rash decisions - to imitate the example of this great master and to try this way to greatness.
Tee-hee!
Shh!
He looked around the attic and realized that he had actually not paid much attention to the things among which he lived. He did not find a crooked chair with a seat woven out of straw anywhere, nor were there any wooden shoes.
NUTS
ART BOX

Therefore he was momentarily dejected and despondent, and he almost felt discouraged, as he had often felt whenever he read about the lives of great men.

At those times he realized that all the little indicators and remarkable coincidences that had played roles in the lives of the others had not become apparent in his life, and he would wait in vain for them to appear.

However, he soon pulled himself together and realized that it was now his task to be persistent and pursue his difficult path to fame. He examined all the objects in his room and discovered a wicker chair that could serve him very well as a model.

who, me?

He sharpened his art pencil, took his sketch pad on his knee, and began.

Wait, hold on, I've got to get comfortable!

After a couple of light first strokes, he seemed to have captured the form sufficiently

and now he inked in the thick outlines with a few firm and powerful strokes

Oh, waitamiNute, I've got an itch...

A deep triangular shadow in a corner attracted him, and he painted it in full strength, and so he continued until something began to disturb him.

He worked awhile longer. Then he held the sketch pad away from himself and examined his sketch carefully. His very first glance told him that he had completely failed to capture the wicker chair.

Lemme see...

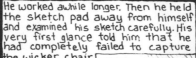

Angrily he drew a new line into the sketch and fixed his eyes grimly on the chair. The sketch was still not right. It made him mad.

Tra-LA LA!

Oh, SORRY!

YOU **DEMONIC** wicker chair! He screamed violently

I've never seen a beast as moody as you are!

The chair cracked a little and said with equanimity, Yes, take a look at me! I am as I am, and I won't change myself anymore!

The painter kicked it with his toe. The chair swerved backward to avoid the kick and now looked completely different.

You DUMB chair!
The young man exclaimed
Everything is crooked and wrong about you!
The wicker chair smiled a little and said softly;
That's what's called perspective, young man!
The painter jumped up
Perspective!
He yelled furiously
now this clown of a chair wants to play Schoolteacher!
perspective is my affair, not yours, remember that!
The chair said nothing more. The painter stomped loudly back and forth a few times until someone began pounding beneath the floor with a cane. An elderly man, a scholar, lived under him and could not bear the noise.
STOMP STOMP
THUD THUD!
The young man sat down and looked at his last self-portrait. It did not please him. He found that he looked more handsome and interesting in reality.
and that was the truth.
Now he wanted to read his book again, but there was more about the Dutch straw chair, which irritated him.
PAINTING
He now felt that the writer had made too much of it, and after all...
eek!
The young man looked for his hat and decided to go out. He remembered that he had long ago been struck by the fact that painting was not very fulfilling. One had nothing but bother and disappointments, and in the end even the best painter in the world could portray only the simple surface of objects.
Hey! Watch it!
Quick! in here!
ARTBOX

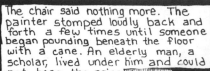

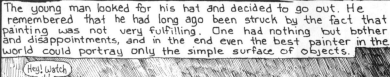

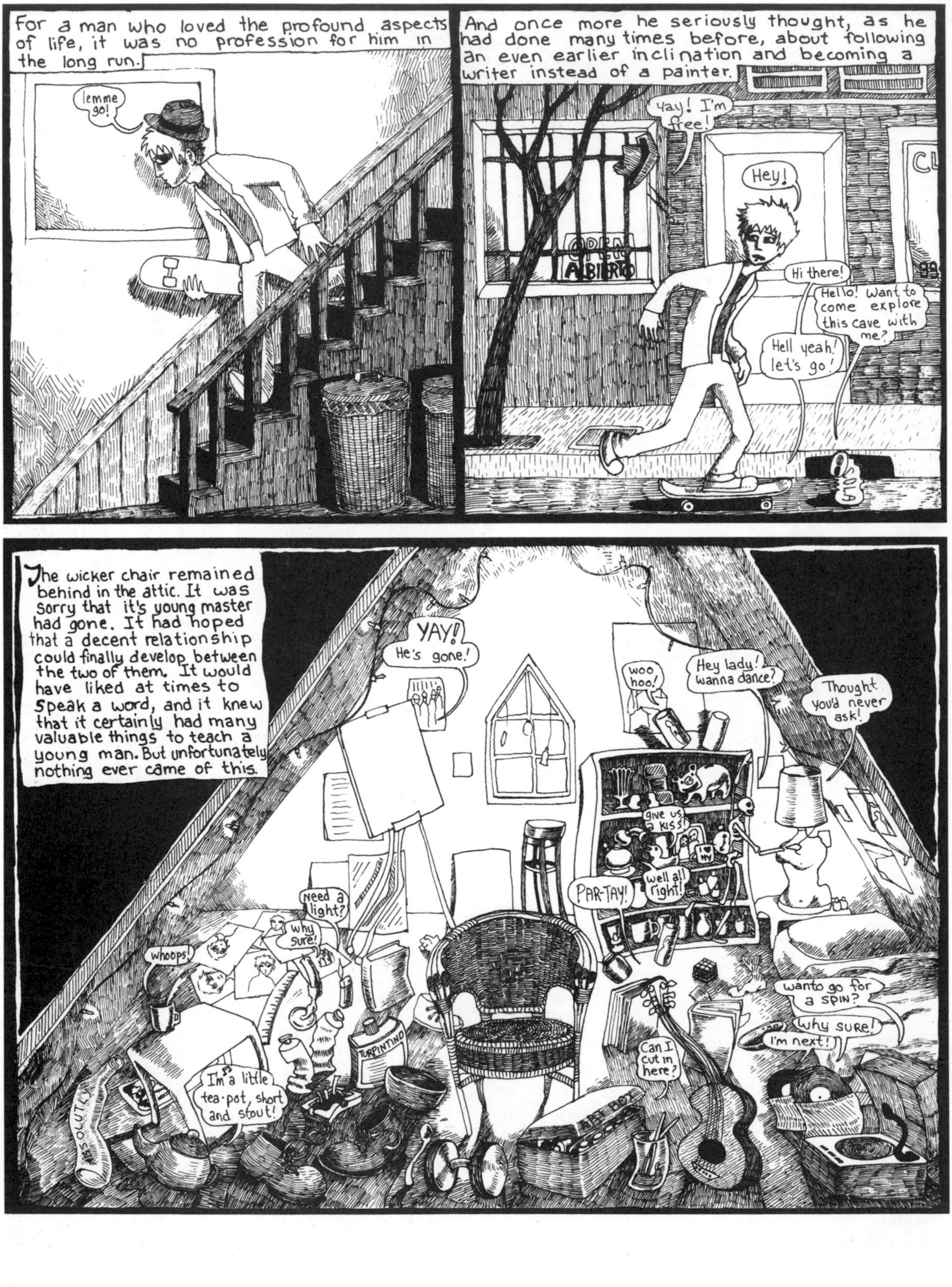
For a man who loved the profound aspects of life, it was no profession for him in the long run.
lemme go!
And once more he seriously thought, as he had done many times before, about following an even earlier inclination and becoming a writer instead of a painter.
Yay! I'm free!
OPEN
ABIERTO
Hey!
Hi there!
Hello! Want to come explore this cave with me?
Hell yeah! let's go!
The wicker chair remained behind in the attic. It was sorry that it's young master had gone. It had hoped that a decent relationship could finally develop between the two of them. It would have liked at times to speak a word, and it knew that it certainly had many valuable things to teach a young man. But unfortunately nothing ever came of this.
YAY! He's gone!
woo hoo!
Hey lady! wanna dance?
Thought you'd never ask!
give us a kiss!
PAR-TAY!
well all right!
Need a light?
why sure!
whoops!
wanto go for a SPIN?
Why SURE!
I'm next!
Can I cut in here?
I'm a little tea-pot, short and stout!

ON
THE
SEA-SHORE

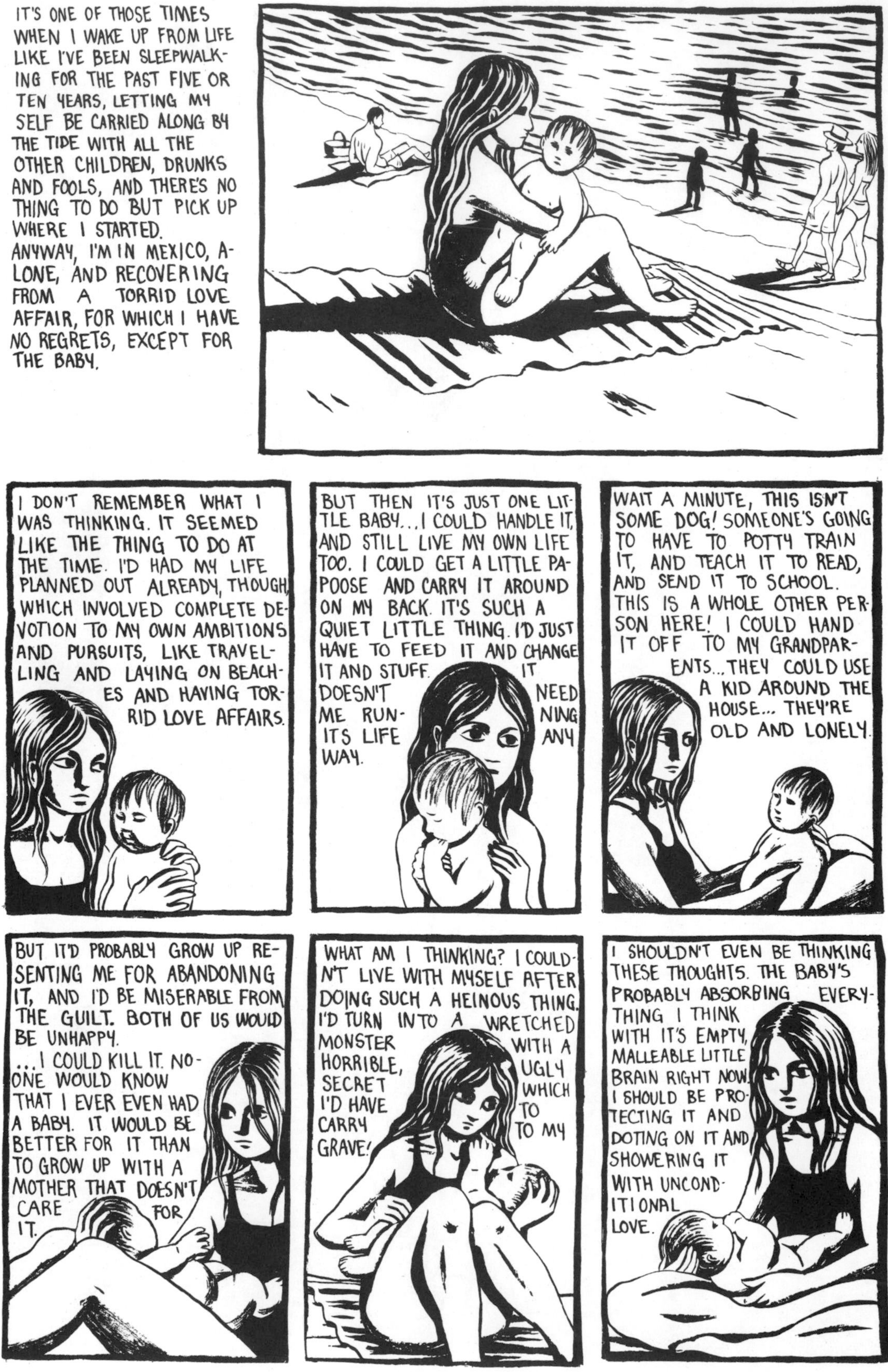
IT'S ONE OF THOSE TIMES WHEN I WAKE UP FROM LIFE LIKE I'VE BEEN SLEEPWALK-ING FOR THE PAST FIVE OR TEN YEARS, LETTING MY SELF BE CARRIED ALONG BY THE TIDE WITH ALL THE OTHER CHILDREN, DRUNKS AND FOOLS, AND THERE'S NO THING TO DO BUT PICK UP WHERE I STARTED.
ANYWAY, I'M IN MEXICO, A-LONE, AND RECOVERING FROM A TORRID LOVE AFFAIR, FOR WHICH I HAVE NO REGRETS, EXCEPT FOR THE BABY.
I DON'T REMEMBER WHAT I WAS THINKING. IT SEEMED LIKE THE THING TO DO AT THE TIME. I'D HAD MY LIFE PLANNED OUT ALREADY, THOUGH, WHICH INVOLVED COMPLETE DE-VOTION TO MY OWN AMBITIONS AND PURSUITS, LIKE TRAVEL-LING AND LAYING ON BEACH-ES AND HAVING TOR-RID LOVE AFFAIRS.
BUT THEN IT'S JUST ONE LIT-TLE BABY... I COULD HANDLE IT, AND STILL LIVE MY OWN LIFE TOO. I COULD GET A LITTLE PA-POOSE AND CARRY IT AROUND ON MY BACK. IT'S SUCH A QUIET LITTLE THING. I'D JUST HAVE TO FEED IT AND CHANGE IT AND STUFF. IT DOESN'T NEED ME RUN-NING ITS LIFE ANY WAY.
WAIT A MINUTE, THIS ISN'T SOME DOG! SOMEONE'S GOING TO HAVE TO POTTY TRAIN IT, AND TEACH IT TO READ, AND SEND IT TO SCHOOL. THIS IS A WHOLE OTHER PER-SON HERE! I COULD HAND IT OFF TO MY GRANDPAR-ENTS... THEY COULD USE A KID AROUND THE HOUSE... THEY'RE OLD AND LONELY.
BUT IT'D PROBABLY GROW UP RE-SENTING ME FOR ABANDONING IT, AND I'D BE MISERABLE FROM THE GUILT. BOTH OF US WOULD BE UNHAPPY.
...I COULD KILL IT. NO-ONE WOULD KNOW THAT I EVER EVEN HAD A BABY. IT WOULD BE BETTER FOR IT THAN TO GROW UP WITH A MOTHER THAT DOESN'T CARE FOR IT.
WHAT AM I THINKING? I COULD-N'T LIVE WITH MYSELF AFTER DOING SUCH A HEINOUS THING. I'D TURN INTO A WRETCHED MONSTER WITH A HORRIBLE, UGLY SECRET WHICH I'D HAVE TO CARRY TO MY GRAVE!
I SHOULDN'T EVEN BE THINKING THESE THOUGHTS. THE BABY'S PROBABLY ABSORBING EVERY-THING I THINK WITH IT'S EMPTY, MALLEABLE LITTLE BRAIN RIGHT NOW. I SHOULD BE PRO-TECTING IT AND DOTING ON IT AND SHOWERING IT WITH UNCOND-ITIONAL LOVE.

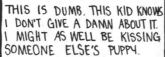

 SWEET LITTLE DARLING BABY

HOW I LOVE YOU MY DEAR LITTLE ONE...

-KISS KISS

 THIS IS DUMB. THIS KID KNOWS I DON'T GIVE A DAMN ABOUT IT. I MIGHT AS WELL BE KISSING SOMEONE ELSE'S PUPPY.

 I'M SORRY, LITTLE ONE. I JUST DON'T HAVE ANY LOVE FOR YOU. YOU ARE VERY CUTE, BUT I'M AFRAID I'M TOO SELFISH TO HAVE MATERNAL FEELINGS.

 OH, I'M SO DEPRESSED. MAYBE I'LL FEEL BETTER IF I TAKE A SHOWER.

 UGH. CAN'T THEY AFFORD SHOWER CURTAINS?

 PARDON US?

 SORRY TO INTERRUPT YOU, SEÑORITA, THERE'S NO MORE SHOWER STALLS LEFT, SO MY BROTHER AND I WERE WONDERING IF WE COULD SHARE YOURS

NO! WAIT YOUR TURN LIKE EVERY ONE ELSE! NOW GET OUT!

 WHAT'D SHE SAY?

SHE SAID NO. BUT THATS ALL RIGHT. SHE'S A SNOB ANYWAY.

 THIS IS MUCH BETTER! WHAT A NICE IDEA, TO HAVE MUSIC IN A PUBLIC SHOWER!

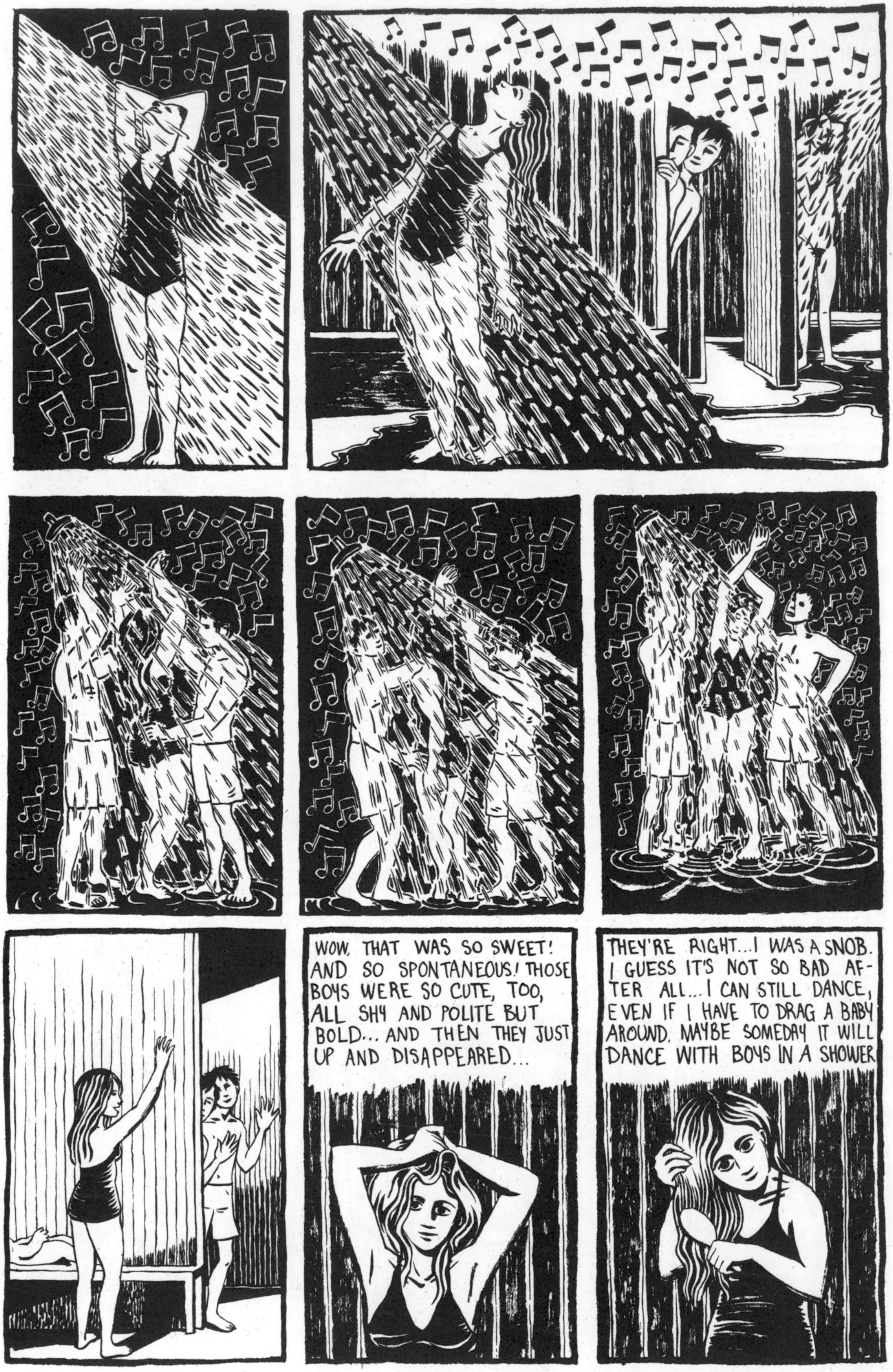
WOW, THAT WAS SO SWEET! AND SO SPONTANEOUS! THOSE BOYS WERE SO CUTE, TOO, ALL SHY AND POLITE BUT BOLD... AND THEN THEY JUST UP AND DISAPPEARED...
THEY'RE RIGHT... I WAS A SNOB. I GUESS IT'S NOT SO BAD AFTER ALL... I CAN STILL DANCE, EVEN IF I HAVE TO DRAG A BABY AROUND. MAYBE SOMEDAY IT WILL DANCE WITH BOYS IN A SHOWER

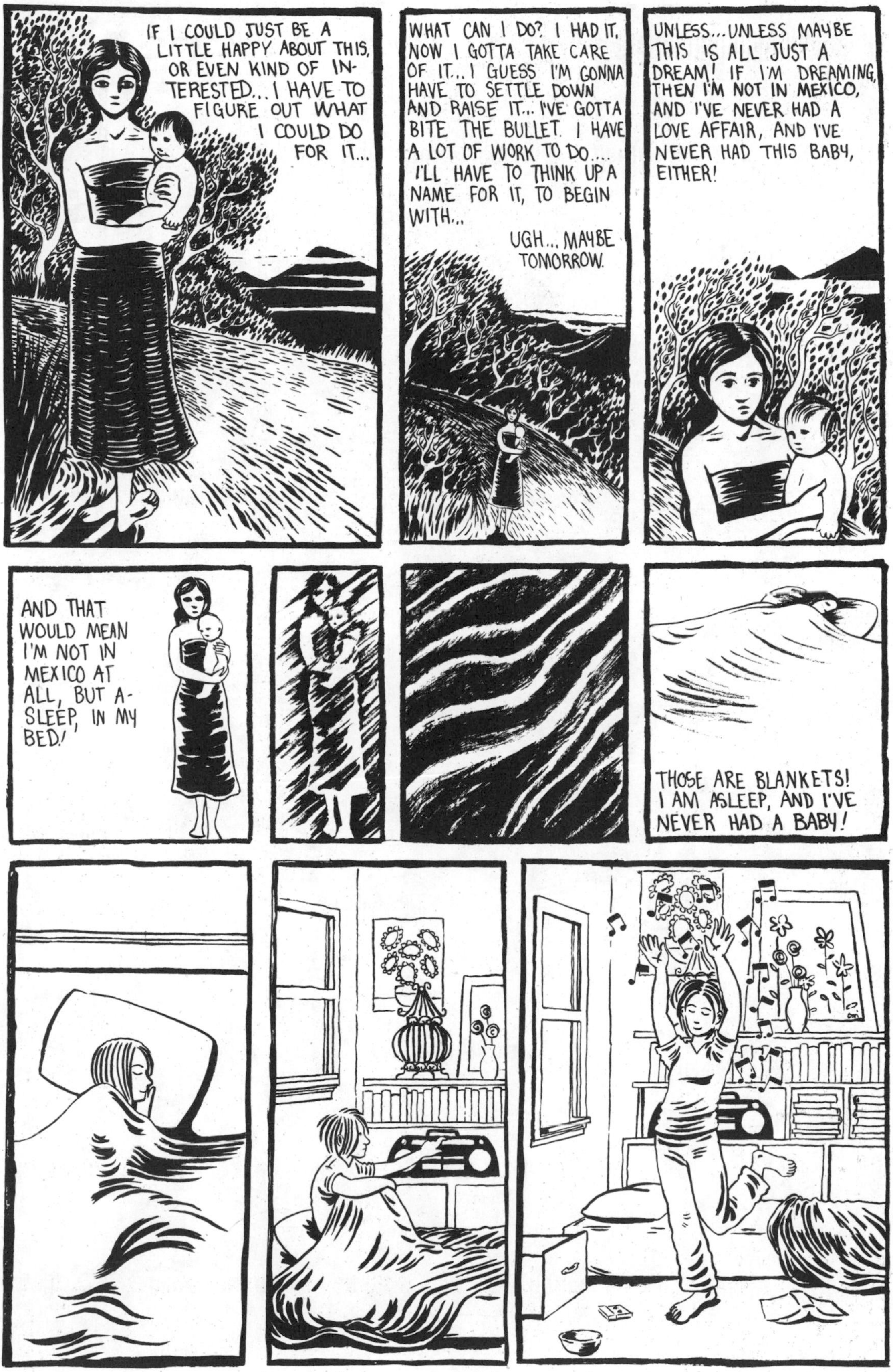
IF I COULD JUST BE A LITTLE HAPPY ABOUT THIS, OR EVEN KIND OF INTERESTED... I HAVE TO FIGURE OUT WHAT I COULD DO FOR IT...
WHAT CAN I DO? I HAD IT, NOW I GOTTA TAKE CARE OF IT... I GUESS I'M GONNA HAVE TO SETTLE DOWN AND RAISE IT... I'VE GOTTA BITE THE BULLET. I HAVE A LOT OF WORK TO DO.... I'LL HAVE TO THINK UP A NAME FOR IT, TO BEGIN WITH...
UGH... MAYBE TOMORROW.
UNLESS... UNLESS MAYBE THIS IS ALL JUST A DREAM! IF I'M DREAMING, THEN I'M NOT IN MEXICO, AND I'VE NEVER HAD A LOVE AFFAIR, AND I'VE NEVER HAD THIS BABY, EITHER!
AND THAT WOULD MEAN I'M NOT IN MEXICO AT ALL, BUT ASLEEP, IN MY BED!
THOSE ARE BLANKETS! I AM ASLEEP, AND I'VE NEVER HAD A BABY!

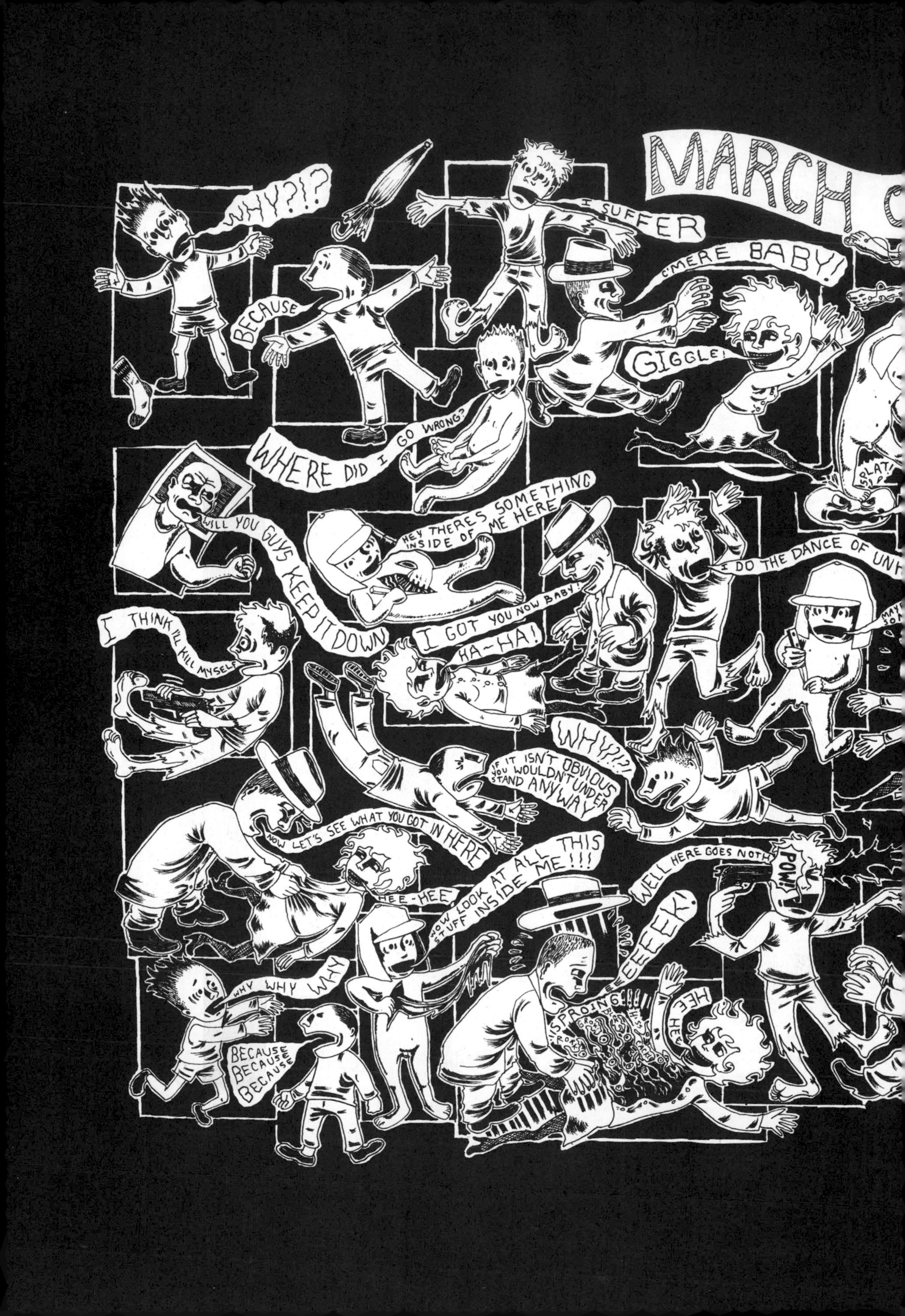

MARCH
WHY?!?
BECAUSE
I SUFFER
C'MERE BABY!
GIGGLE!
WHERE DID I GO WRONG?
WILL YOU GUYS KEEP IT DOWN
HEY THERES SOMETHING INSIDE OF ME HERE
I DO THE DANCE OF
I THINK I'LL KILL MYSELF
I GOT YOU NOW BABY!
HA-HA!
WHY?!?!
IF IT ISN'T OBVIOUS YOU WOULDN'T UNDERSTAND ANYWAY
NOW LET'S SEE WHAT YOU GOT IN HERE
HEE-HEE
NOW LOOK AT ALL THIS STUFF INSIDE ME!!!
WELL HERE GOES
POW!
EEEEK!
WHY WHY WHY
BECAUSE BECAUSE BECAUSE
SPROING!
HEE HEE

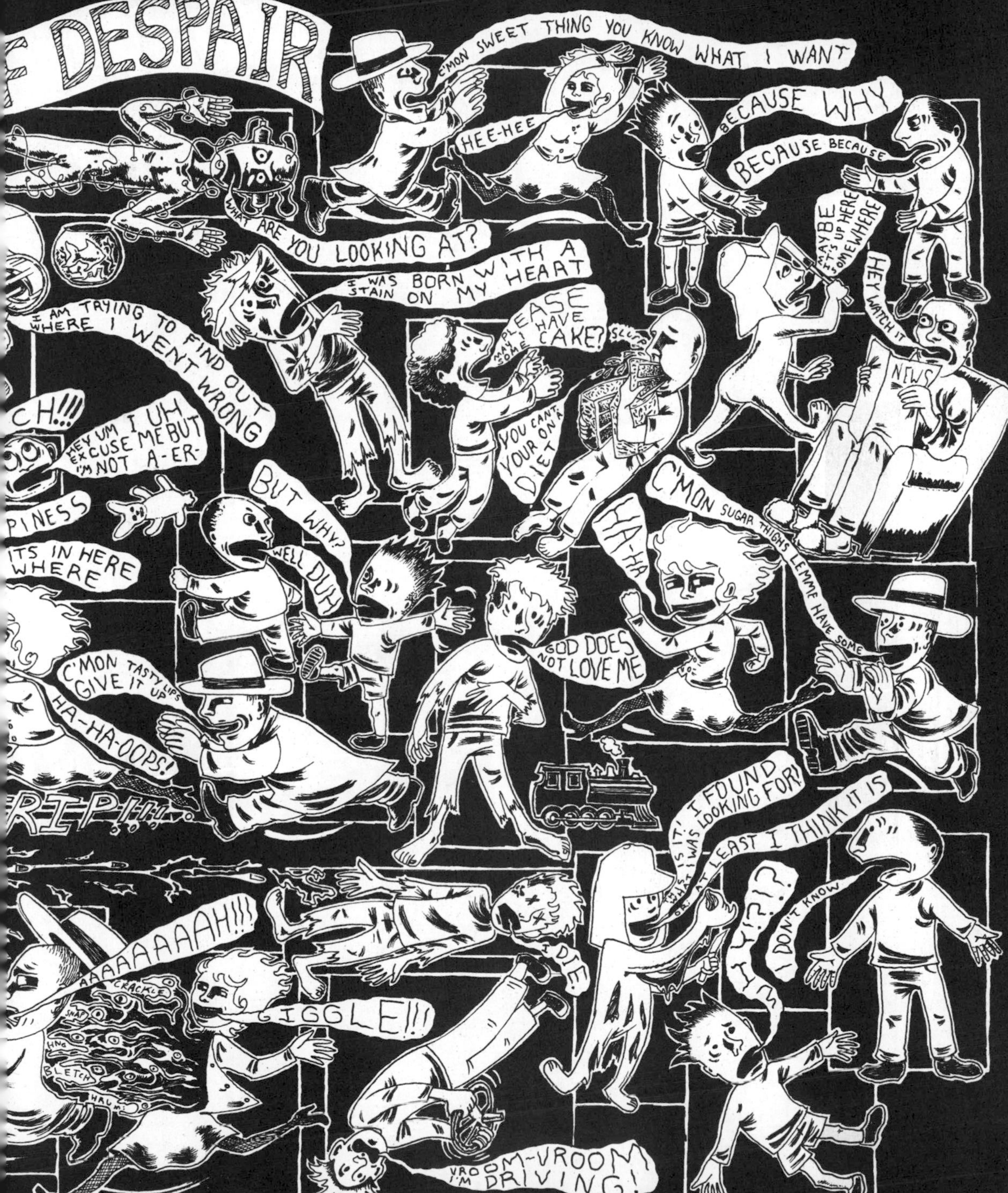

F DESPAIR
C'MON SWEET THING YOU KNOW WHAT I WANT
HEE-HEE
BECAUSE WHY
BECAUSE BECAUSE
WHAT ARE YOU LOOKING AT?
MAYBE IT'S UP HERE SOMEWHERE
I WAS BORN WITH A STAIN ON MY HEART
I AM TRYING TO FIND OUT WHERE I WENT WRONG
PLEASE MAY I HAVE SOME CAKE?
HEY WATCH IT
NEWS
CH!!!
HEY UM I UH EXCUSE ME BUT I'M NOT A-ER-
YOU CAN'T YOUR ON A DIET
PINESS
BUT WHY?
WELL DUH
ITS IN HERE WHERE
C'MON SUGAR THIGHS LEMME HAVE SOME
HA-HA
GOD DOES NOT LOVE ME
C'MON TASTY LIPS GIVE IT UP
HA-HA-OOPS!
RIP!!!!
IS IT? I FOUND WHAT I WAS LOOKING FOR!
OR AT LEAST I THINK IT IS
WHY?!?!
I DON'T KNOW
AAAAAAAAH!!!
I DIE.
CRACKLE
SNAP
BLETCH
GIGGLE!!!
VROOM-VROOM I'M DRIVING!

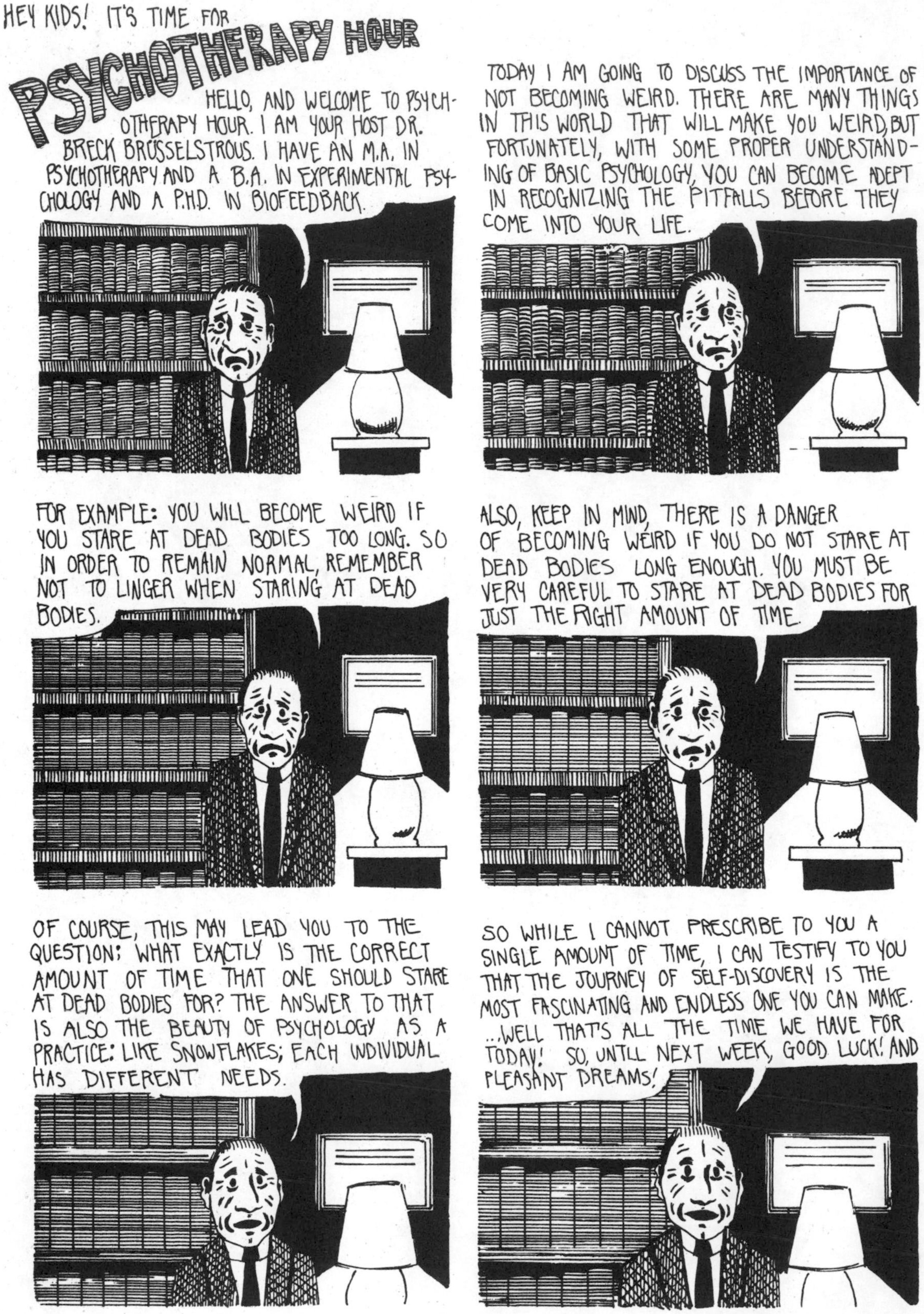
HEY KIDS! IT'S TIME FOR
PSYCHOTHERAPY HOUR
HELLO, AND WELCOME TO PSYCHOTHERAPY HOUR. I AM YOUR HOST DR. BRECK BRUSSELSTROUS. I HAVE AN M.A. IN PSYCHOTHERAPY AND A B.A. IN EXPERIMENTAL PSYCHOLOGY AND A P.H.D. IN BIOFEEDBACK.
TODAY I AM GOING TO DISCUSS THE IMPORTANCE OF NOT BECOMING WEIRD. THERE ARE MANY THINGS IN THIS WORLD THAT WILL MAKE YOU WEIRD, BUT FORTUNATELY, WITH SOME PROPER UNDERSTANDING OF BASIC PSYCHOLOGY, YOU CAN BECOME ADEPT IN RECOGNIZING THE PITFALLS BEFORE THEY COME INTO YOUR LIFE.
FOR EXAMPLE: YOU WILL BECOME WEIRD IF YOU STARE AT DEAD BODIES TOO LONG. SO IN ORDER TO REMAIN NORMAL, REMEMBER NOT TO LINGER WHEN STARING AT DEAD BODIES.
ALSO, KEEP IN MIND, THERE IS A DANGER OF BECOMING WEIRD IF YOU DO NOT STARE AT DEAD BODIES LONG ENOUGH. YOU MUST BE VERY CAREFUL TO STARE AT DEAD BODIES FOR JUST THE RIGHT AMOUNT OF TIME.
OF COURSE, THIS MAY LEAD YOU TO THE QUESTION: WHAT EXACTLY IS THE CORRECT AMOUNT OF TIME THAT ONE SHOULD STARE AT DEAD BODIES FOR? THE ANSWER TO THAT IS ALSO THE BEAUTY OF PSYCHOLOGY AS A PRACTICE: LIKE SNOWFLAKES; EACH INDIVIDUAL HAS DIFFERENT NEEDS.
SO WHILE I CANNOT PRESCRIBE TO YOU A SINGLE AMOUNT OF TIME, I CAN TESTIFY TO YOU THAT THE JOURNEY OF SELF-DISCOVERY IS THE MOST FASCINATING AND ENDLESS ONE YOU CAN MAKE. ...WELL THAT'S ALL THE TIME WE HAVE FOR TODAY! SO, UNTILL NEXT WEEK, GOOD LUCK! AND PLEASANT DREAMS!

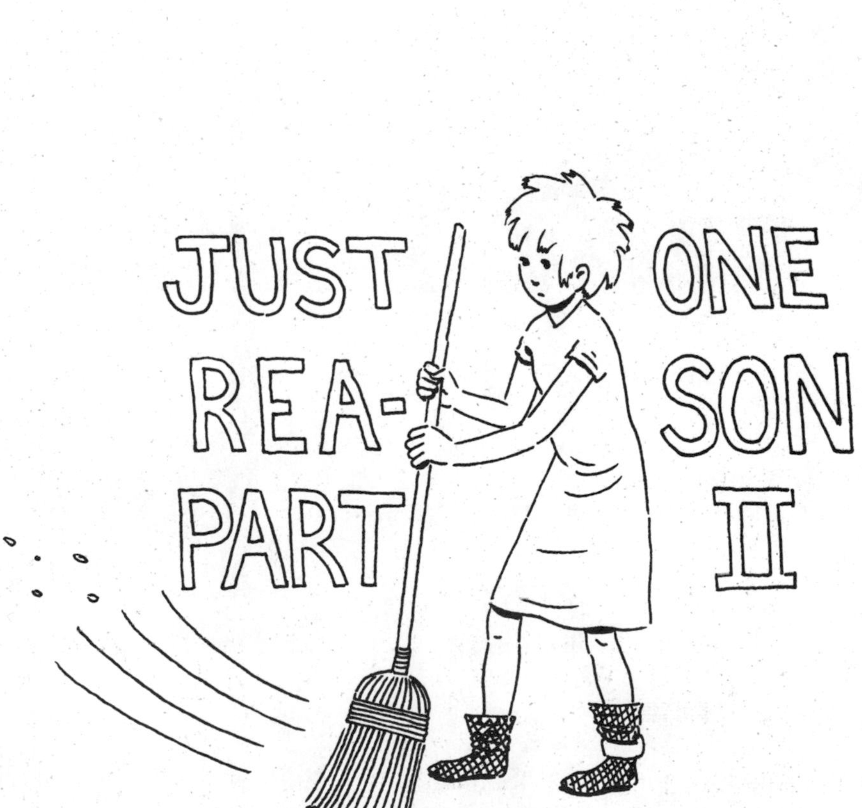
JUST ONE
REA- SON
PART II

JUST ONE REASON

PART II

©1999 GABRIELLE BELL

KATE SPENT MOST OF HER TEENAGE YEARS IN A PRISON FOR GIRLS, BUT ON HER EIGHTEENTH BIRTHDAY WAS RELEASED WITH A HOMETRACKING DEVICE, AND CONFINED TO A SHABBY LITTLE APARTMENT WHICH SHE COULD LEAVE ONLY TO WALK TO WORK, AND A SHORT DISTANCE AROUND THE OUTSIDE OF HER HOUSE. TO HER, THIS WAS AN ABUNDANCE OF FREEDOM, AND THE THOUGHT OF MORE MADE HER NERVOUS.

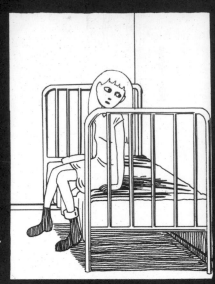

SHE GOT HERSELF A ROOMMATE, A BUSY AND POPULAR GIRL, WHO FOUND KATE BORING.

BYE BYE!

HAVE FUN

INDEED, KATE'S LIFE WAS BORING, AND SHE LIKED IT THAT WAY.

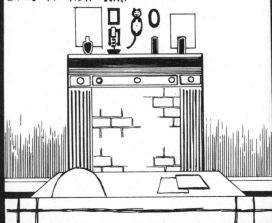

AT WORK SHE KEPT TO HERSELF, AND TUNED OUT THE GOSSIP AND IDLE CHIT-CHAT OF HER COWORKERS.

SO I TOLD SANDRA LIKE TWO WEEKS AGO THAT I COULDN'T WORK THE THIRD, RIGHT BECAUSE I HAD THIS BIG IMPORTANT DATE AND SHE'S ALL, 'OH TRACY I'M SO EXCITED FOR YOU'

AND THEN ON THE SECOND I WAS LIKE REMEMBER I CAN'T WORK TOMORROW BECAUSE OF MY DATE AND SHE GOES, WHAT?

SHE FORGOT ALL ABOUT IT BUT I SAID WELL REGARDLESS I GAVE YOU NOTICE SO I'M NOT COMING TO WORK AND SHE'S LIKE BUT YOU HAVE TO I DON'T HAVE ANY ONE TO COVER FOR YOU, TRYING TO GUILT-TRIP ME, RIGHT...

SO WHEN I STILL SAID NO SHE STARTED SCREAMING AT ME, RIGHT, TRYING TO INTIMIDATE ME, AND WHEN SHE SAW THAT IT WASN'T WORKING EITHER SHE STARTED BEGGING, WHICH WAS TOTALLY DISGUSTING BUT THE WEIRDEST THING WAS THAT SHE DIDN'T STOP SMILING ONCE. AND THEN I REALIZED I DON'T RECALL HER EVER CHANGING HER EXPRESSION. HAVE YOU EVER SEEN HER FROWN, KATE?

DR. SANDRA RHODES
RHINOPLASTY

HEY YO, KATE? HELLO? EARTH TO KATE?

SHE SHOOK OFF ALL ATTEMPTS AT FRIENDSHIP AND WALKED HOME ALONE EACH DAY.

HEY BABY!

OCCASIONALLY, SHE WOULD STOP AT THE CAFE FOR A STEAMED MILK.

IN THE EVENINGS SHE WOULD COOK DINNER, AND LISTEN TO HER HOUSEMATE TALK ABOUT HER LAST DATE.

SO THEN HE TAKES ME OUT TO DINNER AND I'M STILL PISSED OFF ABOUT HIM TEASING ME IN THE CAR SO HE GOES AND BUYS A FLOWER FROM SOMEWHERE AND PUTS IT IN MY MINT JULEP.

BUT I JUST PRETENDED NOT TO NOTICE SO HE GRABS TWO FORKS AND STICKS THEM INTO TWO DINNER ROLLS AND MAKES THEM DANCE, AND I JUST STARTED CRACKING UP. I KNEW RIGHT THEN I JUST HAD TO FUCK HIM.

HE DIDN'T MAKE THAT UP, TRISHA! THATS AN OLD CHARLIE CHAPLIN JOKE!

IT IS? OH, I FEEL SO CHEAP.

OH WELL! I GOT EVERYTHING I NEEDED FROM HIM ANYWAY. BESIDES I GOT ANOTHER DATE TONIGHT HE'S A MUSICIAN...

AFTERWARDS, TRISHA WOULD USUALLY GO OUT AND KATE WOULD STARE OUT THE WINDOW FOR A WHILE.

IF SHE DIDN'T LIKE WHAT SHE SAW OUT THE WINDOW SHE WOULD STARE AT THE WALL.

SHE LIKED THE WALLPAPER THE FLOWERS ON IT WERE UNIFORM AND SOOTHING.

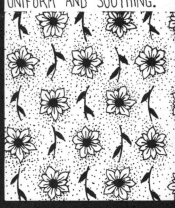

ON THE WEEKENDS SHE WOULD GO TO THE PARK OUTSIDE OF HER HOUSE. SHE COULD ONLY GO INTO A SMALL PORTION OF IT, BECAUSE OF HER HOME TRACKING DEVICE.

SHE DIDN'T MIND. SHE LIKED HER LIFE TO BE SMALL AND UNEXCITING, SO THAT SHE WOULDN'T KNOW DISAPPOINTMENT OR DESPAIR.

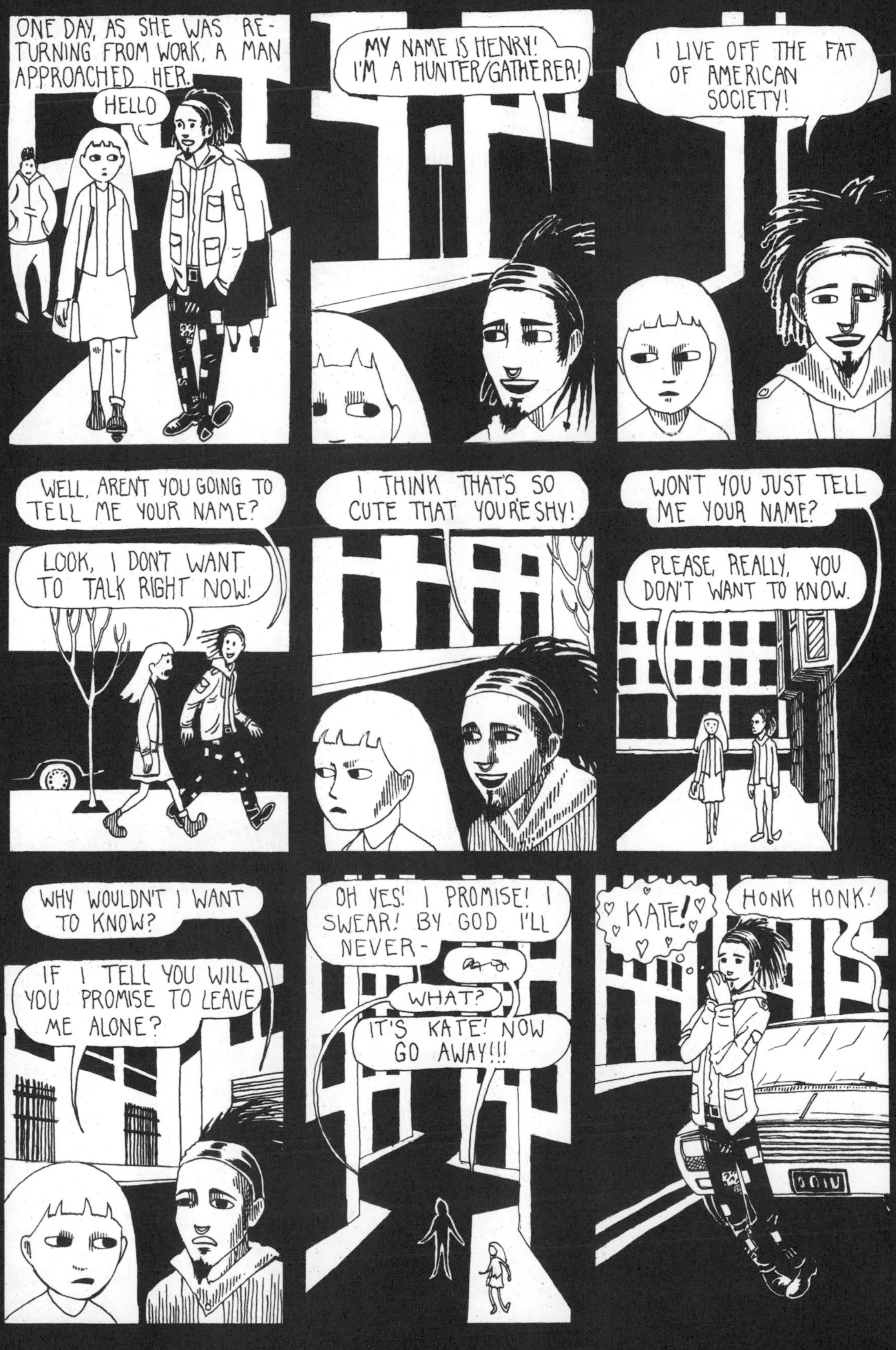
ONE DAY, AS SHE WAS RETURNING FROM WORK, A MAN APPROACHED HER.
HELLO
MY NAME IS HENRY! I'M A HUNTER/GATHERER!
I LIVE OFF THE FAT OF AMERICAN SOCIETY!
WELL, AREN'T YOU GOING TO TELL ME YOUR NAME?
LOOK, I DON'T WANT TO TALK RIGHT NOW!
I THINK THAT'S SO CUTE THAT YOU'RE SHY!
WON'T YOU JUST TELL ME YOUR NAME?
PLEASE, REALLY, YOU DON'T WANT TO KNOW.
WHY WOULDN'T I WANT TO KNOW?
IF I TELL YOU WILL YOU PROMISE TO LEAVE ME ALONE?
OH YES! I PROMISE! I SWEAR! BY GOD I'LL NEVER-
WHAT?
IT'S KATE! NOW GO AWAY!!!
KATE!
HONK HONK!

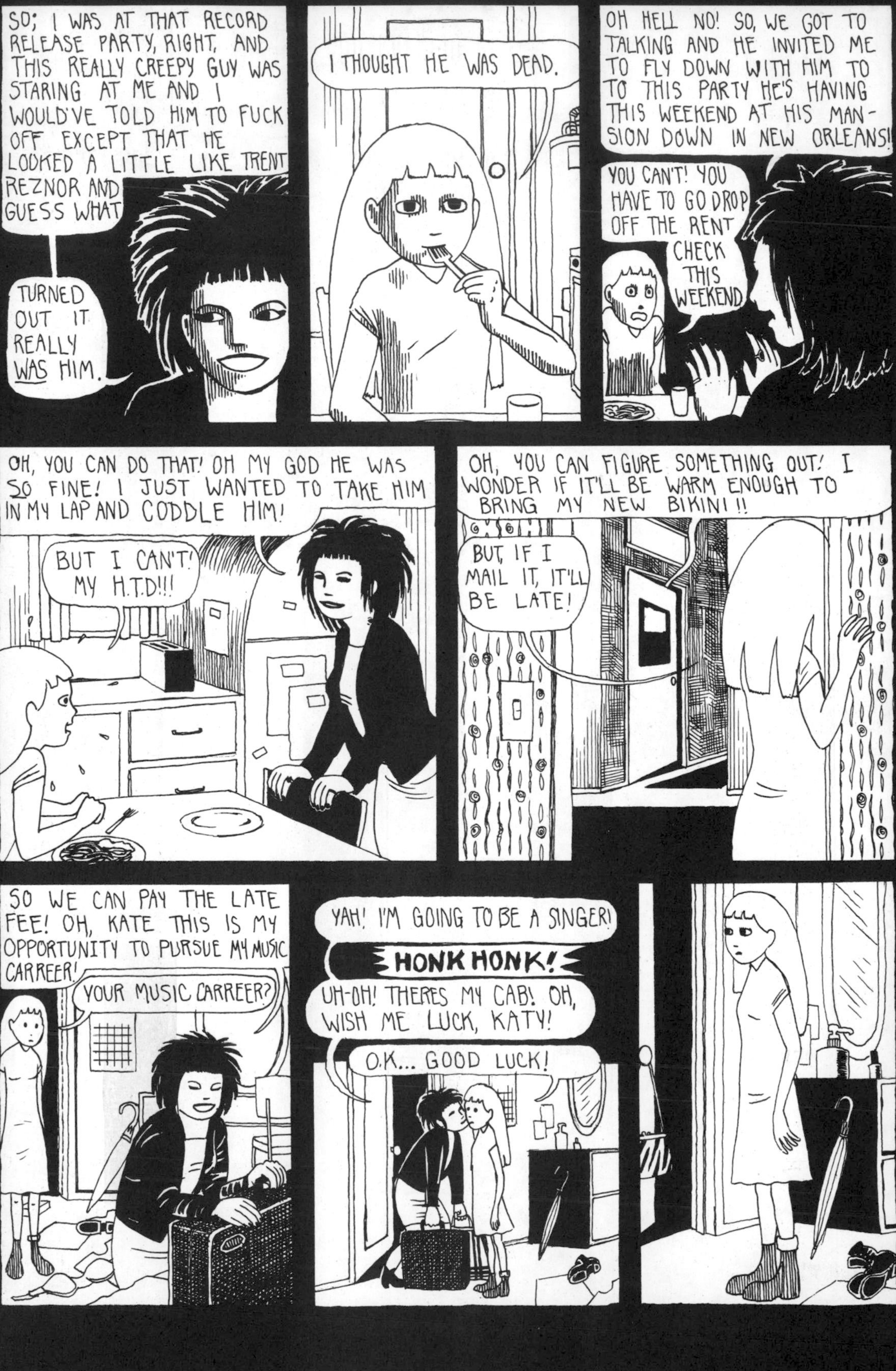
SO; I WAS AT THAT RECORD RELEASE PARTY, RIGHT, AND THIS REALLY CREEPY GUY WAS STARING AT ME AND I WOULD'VE TOLD HIM TO FUCK OFF EXCEPT THAT HE LOOKED A LITTLE LIKE TRENT REZNOR AND GUESS WHAT
TURNED OUT IT REALLY WAS HIM.
I THOUGHT HE WAS DEAD.
OH HELL NO! SO, WE GOT TO TALKING AND HE INVITED ME TO FLY DOWN WITH HIM TO TO THIS PARTY HE'S HAVING THIS WEEKEND AT HIS MAN-SION DOWN IN NEW ORLEANS!
YOU CAN'T! YOU HAVE TO GO DROP OFF THE RENT CHECK THIS WEEKEND.
OH, YOU CAN DO THAT! OH MY GOD HE WAS SO FINE! I JUST WANTED TO TAKE HIM IN MY LAP AND CODDLE HIM!
BUT I CAN'T! MY H.T.D!!!
OH, YOU CAN FIGURE SOMETHING OUT! I WONDER IF IT'LL BE WARM ENOUGH TO BRING MY NEW BIKINI!!
BUT, IF I MAIL IT, IT'LL BE LATE!
SO WE CAN PAY THE LATE FEE! OH, KATE THIS IS MY OPPORTUNITY TO PURSUE MY MUSIC CARREER!
YOUR MUSIC CARREER?
YAH! I'M GOING TO BE A SINGER!
HONK HONK!
UH-OH! THERES MY CAB! OH, WISH ME LUCK, KATY!
O.K... GOOD LUCK!

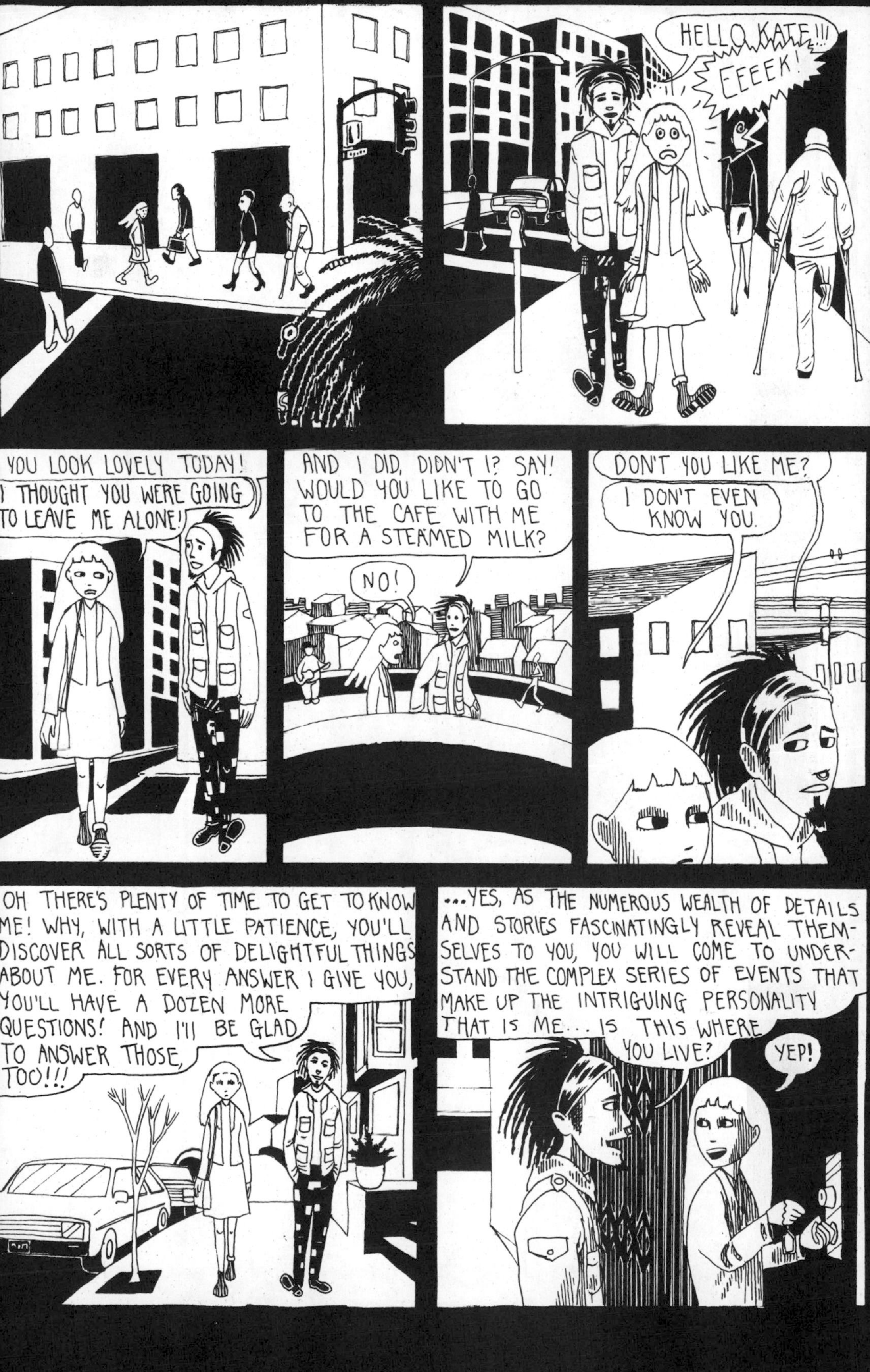
HELLO KATE!!!
EEEEK!
YOU LOOK LOVELY TODAY!
I THOUGHT YOU WERE GOING TO LEAVE ME ALONE!
AND I DID, DIDN'T I? SAY! WOULD YOU LIKE TO GO TO THE CAFE WITH ME FOR A STEAMED MILK?
NO!
DON'T YOU LIKE ME?
I DON'T EVEN KNOW YOU.
OH THERE'S PLENTY OF TIME TO GET TO KNOW ME! WHY, WITH A LITTLE PATIENCE, YOU'LL DISCOVER ALL SORTS OF DELIGHTFUL THINGS ABOUT ME. FOR EVERY ANSWER I GIVE YOU, YOU'LL HAVE A DOZEN MORE QUESTIONS! AND I'LL BE GLAD TO ANSWER THOSE, TOO!!!
...YES, AS THE NUMEROUS WEALTH OF DETAILS AND STORIES FASCINATINGLY REVEAL THEMSELVES TO YOU, YOU WILL COME TO UNDERSTAND THE COMPLEX SERIES OF EVENTS THAT MAKE UP THE INTRIGUING PERSONALITY THAT IS ME... IS THIS WHERE YOU LIVE?
YEP!

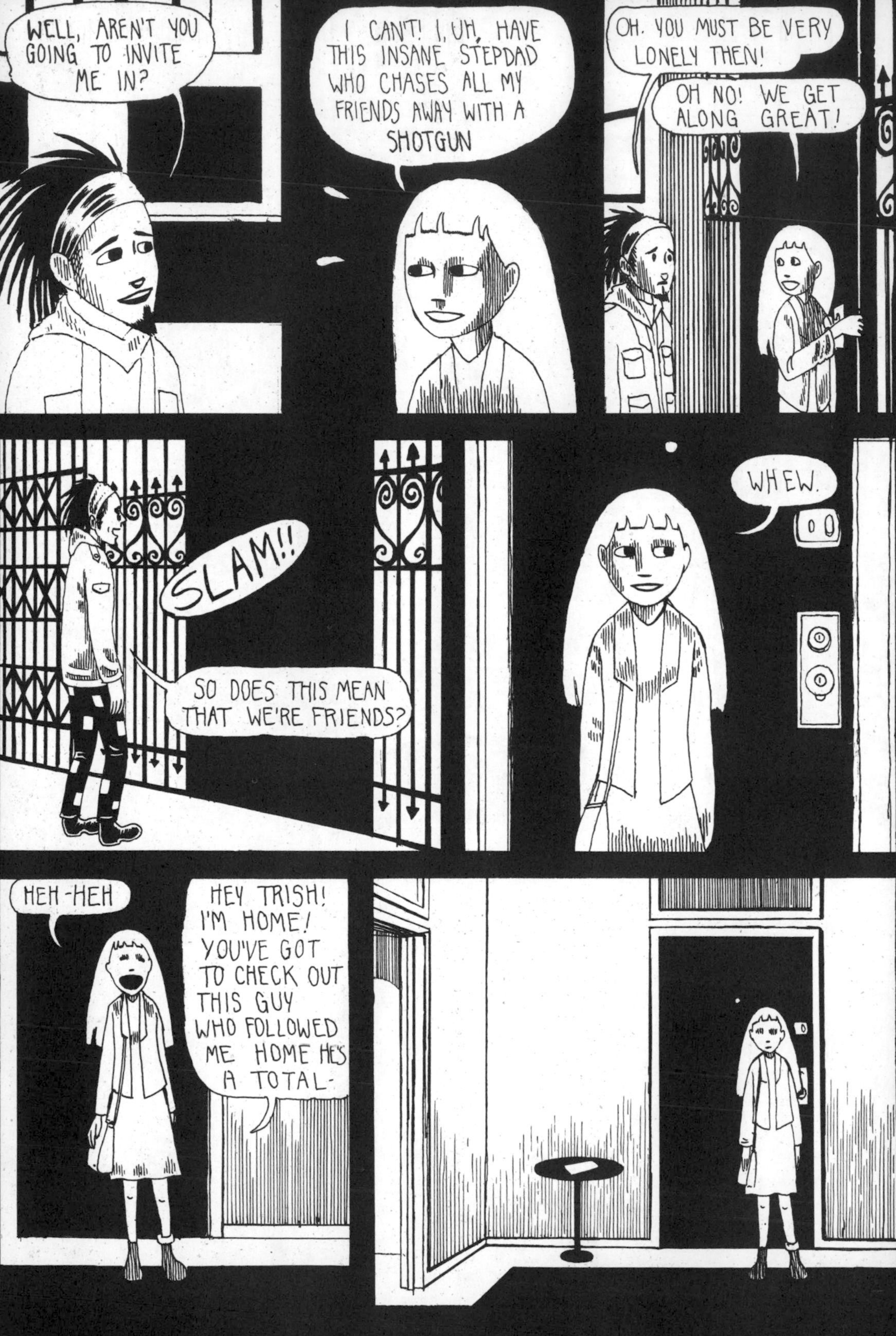
WELL, AREN'T YOU GOING TO INVITE ME IN?
I CAN'T! I, UH, HAVE THIS INSANE STEPDAD WHO CHASES ALL MY FRIENDS AWAY WITH A SHOTGUN
OH. YOU MUST BE VERY LONELY THEN!
OH NO! WE GET ALONG GREAT!
SLAM!!
SO DOES THIS MEAN THAT WE'RE FRIENDS?
WHEW.
HEH-HEH
HEY TRISH! I'M HOME! YOU'VE GOT TO CHECK OUT THIS GUY WHO FOLLOWED ME HOME HE'S A TOTAL-

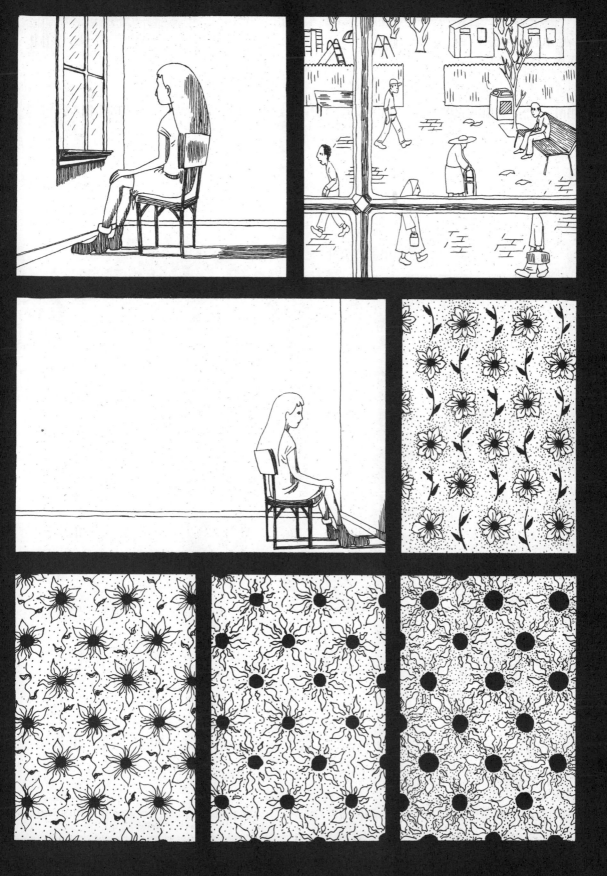

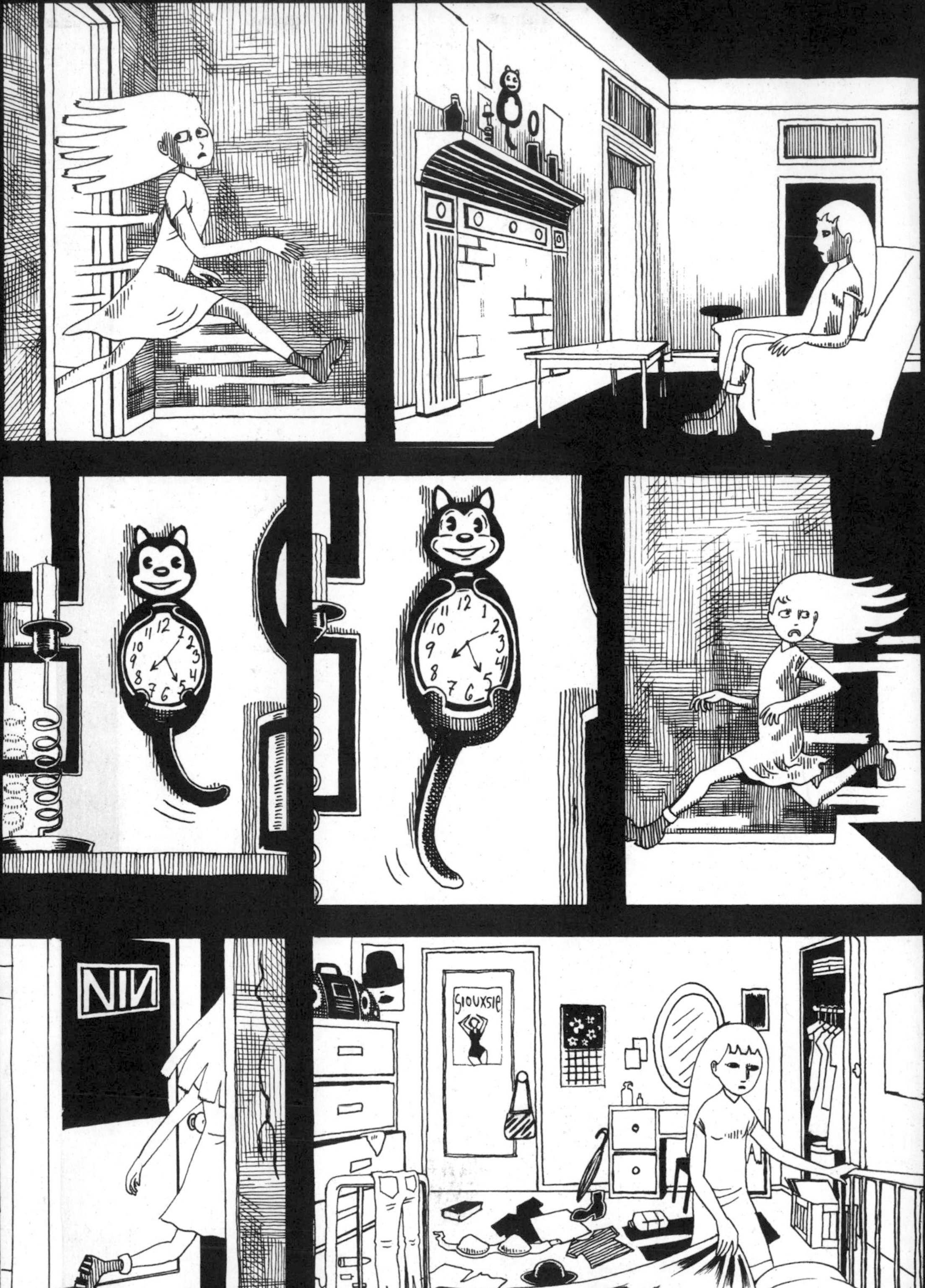
NIN
Siouxsie

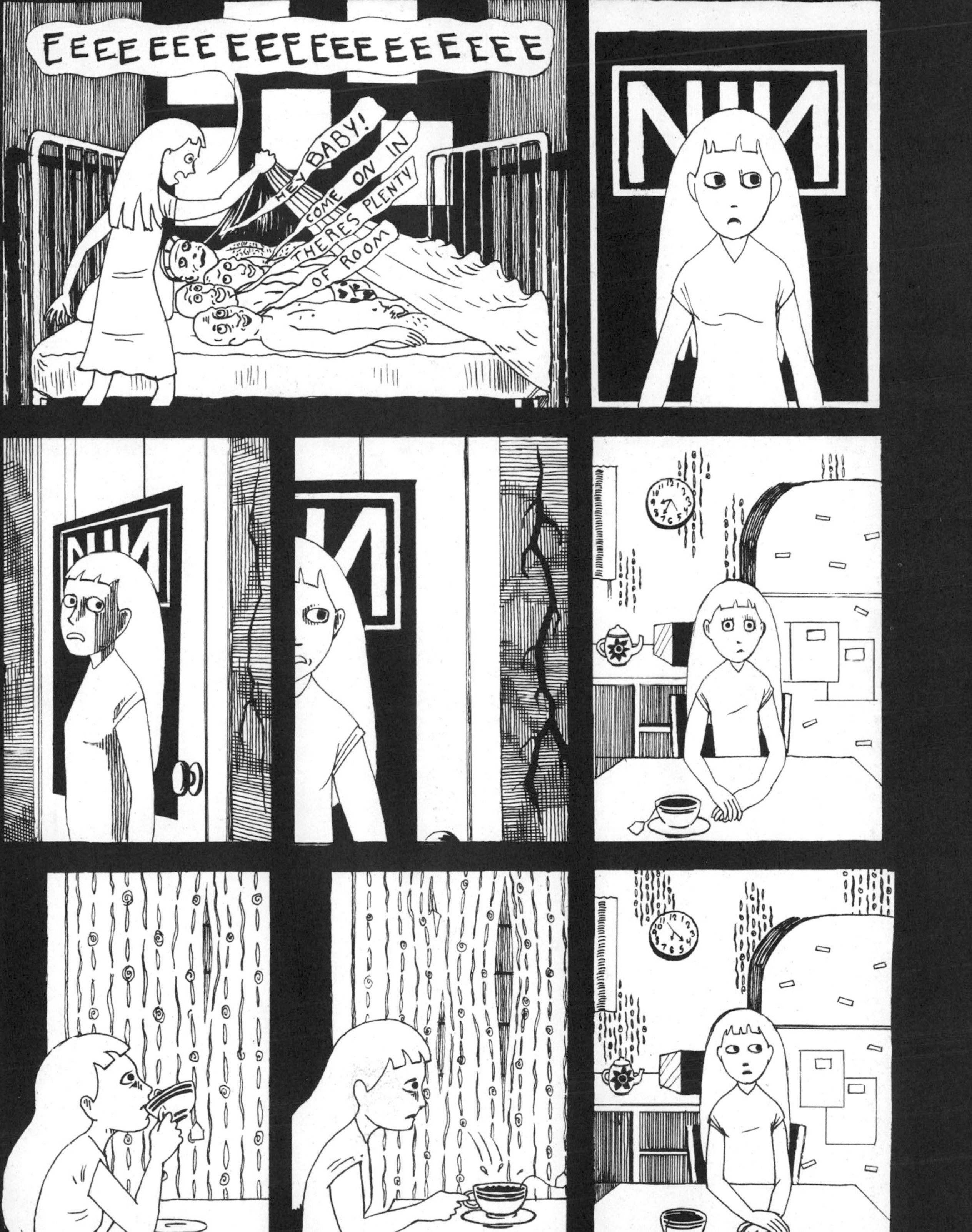
EEEEEEEEEEEEEEEEEEEE
HEY BABY!
COME ON IN
THERES PLENTY
OF ROOM

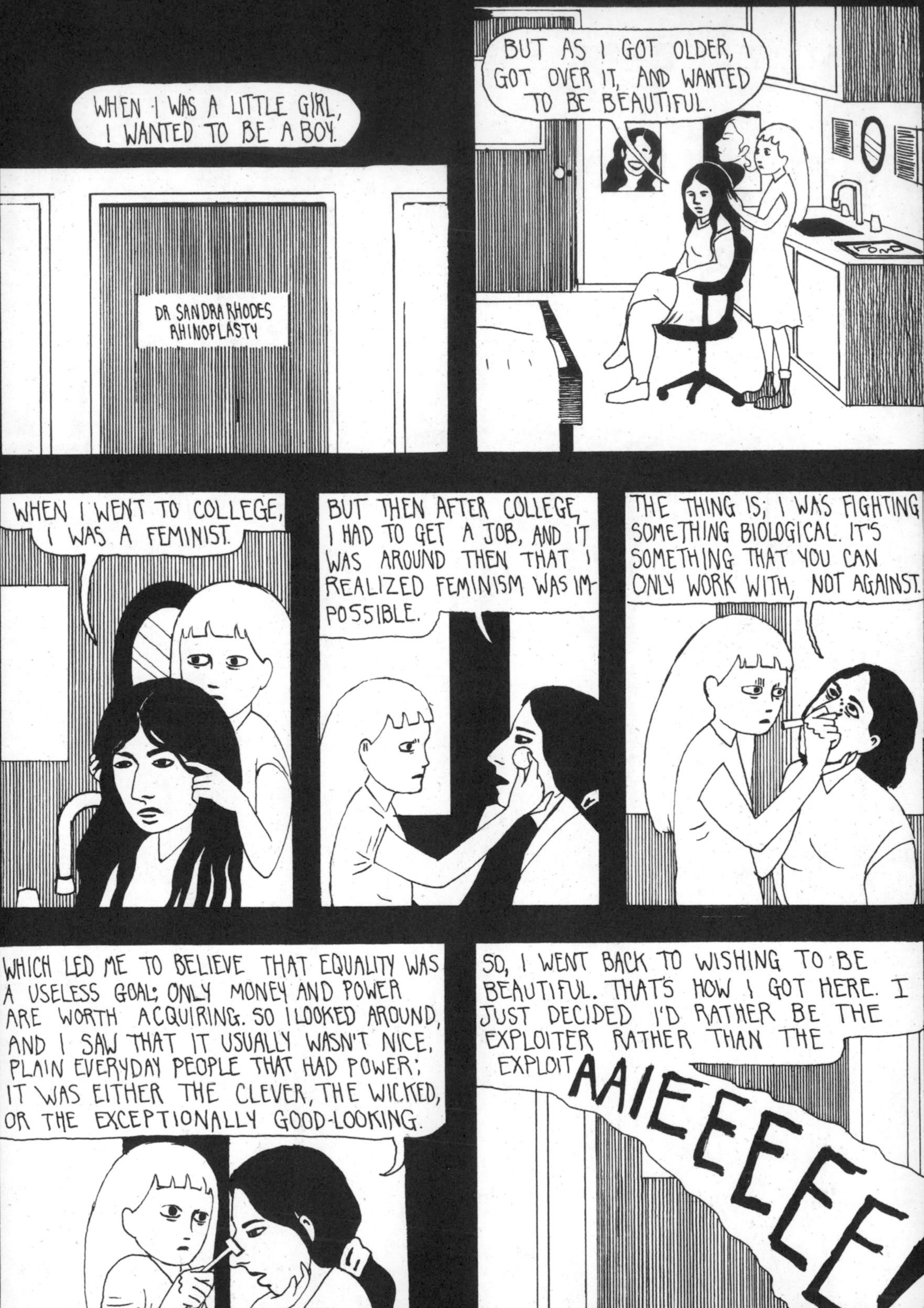
WHEN I WAS A LITTLE GIRL, I WANTED TO BE A BOY.
DR SANDRA RHODES RHINOPLASTY
BUT AS I GOT OLDER, I GOT OVER IT, AND WANTED TO BE BEAUTIFUL.
WHEN I WENT TO COLLEGE, I WAS A FEMINIST.
BUT THEN AFTER COLLEGE, I HAD TO GET A JOB, AND IT WAS AROUND THEN THAT I REALIZED FEMINISM WAS IMPOSSIBLE.
THE THING IS; I WAS FIGHTING SOMETHING BIOLOGICAL. IT'S SOMETHING THAT YOU CAN ONLY WORK WITH, NOT AGAINST.
WHICH LED ME TO BELIEVE THAT EQUALITY WAS A USELESS GOAL; ONLY MONEY AND POWER ARE WORTH ACQUIRING. SO I LOOKED AROUND, AND I SAW THAT IT USUALLY WASN'T NICE, PLAIN EVERYDAY PEOPLE THAT HAD POWER; IT WAS EITHER THE CLEVER, THE WICKED, OR THE EXCEPTIONALLY GOOD-LOOKING.
SO, I WENT BACK TO WISHING TO BE BEAUTIFUL. THAT'S HOW I GOT HERE. I JUST DECIDED I'D RATHER BE THE EXPLOITER RATHER THAN THE EXPLOIT
AAIEEEEE!!

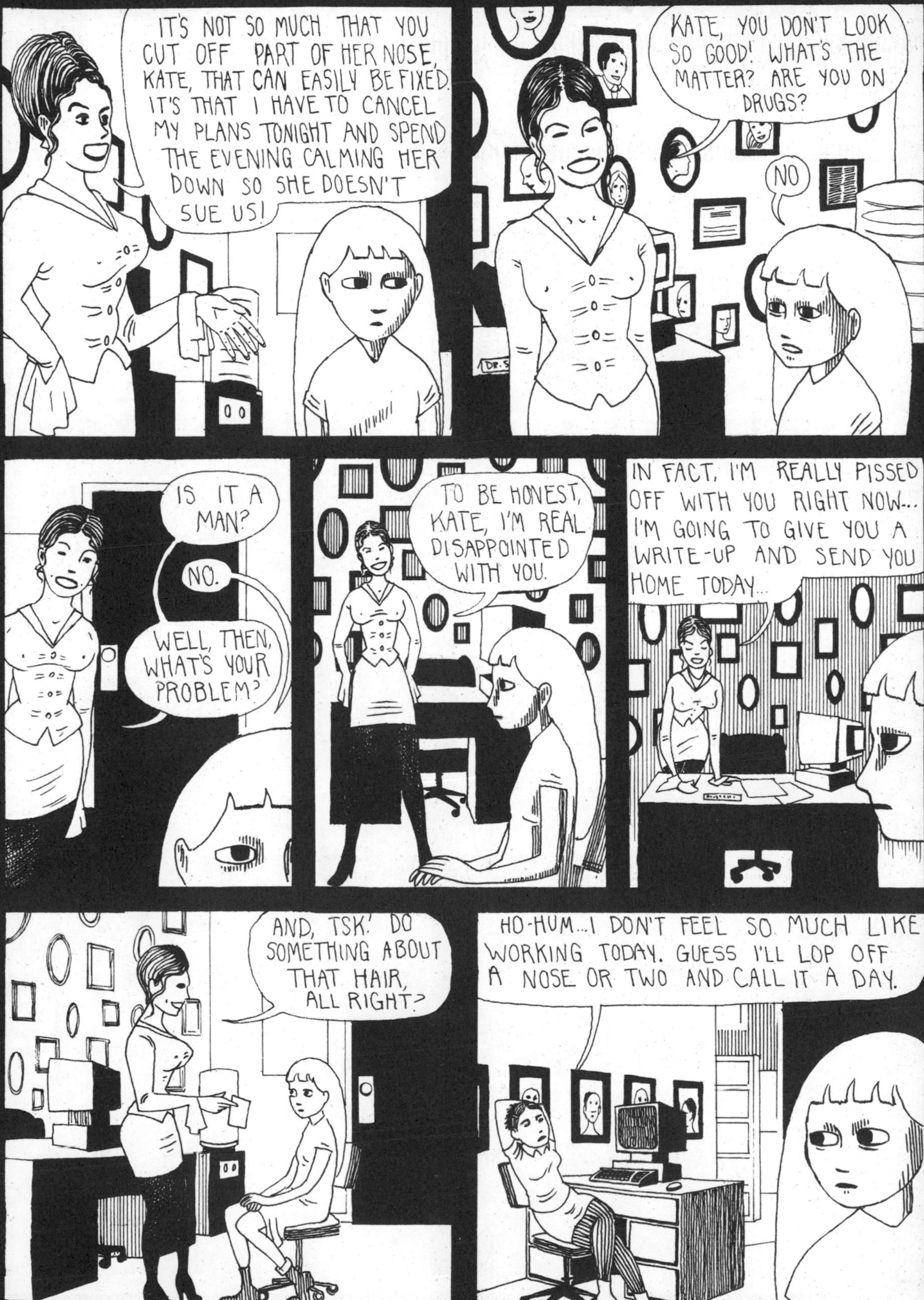
IT'S NOT SO MUCH THAT YOU CUT OFF PART OF HER NOSE, KATE, THAT CAN EASILY BE FIXED. IT'S THAT I HAVE TO CANCEL MY PLANS TONIGHT AND SPEND THE EVENING CALMING HER DOWN SO SHE DOESN'T SUE US!
KATE, YOU DON'T LOOK SO GOOD! WHAT'S THE MATTER? ARE YOU ON DRUGS?
NO
IS IT A MAN?
NO.
WELL, THEN, WHAT'S YOUR PROBLEM?
TO BE HONEST, KATE, I'M REAL DISAPPOINTED WITH YOU.
IN FACT, I'M REALLY PISSED OFF WITH YOU RIGHT NOW... I'M GOING TO GIVE YOU A WRITE-UP AND SEND YOU HOME TODAY...
AND, TSK! DO SOMETHING ABOUT THAT HAIR, ALL RIGHT?
HO-HUM...I DON'T FEEL SO MUCH LIKE WORKING TODAY. GUESS I'LL LOP OFF A NOSE OR TWO AND CALL IT A DAY.

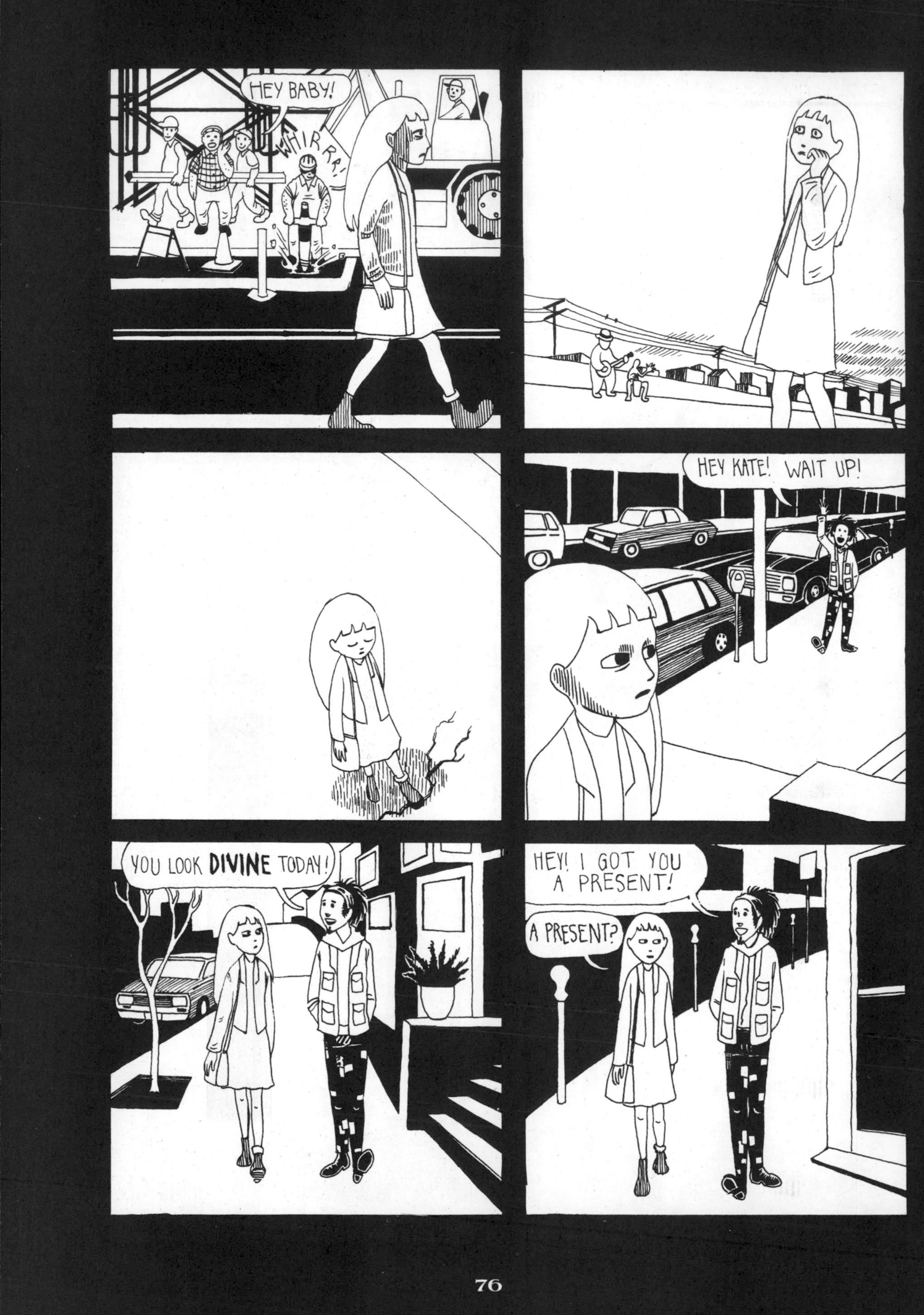
HEY BABY!
WHIRRR!
HEY KATE! WAIT UP!
YOU LOOK **DIVINE** TODAY!
HEY! I GOT YOU A PRESENT!
A PRESENT?

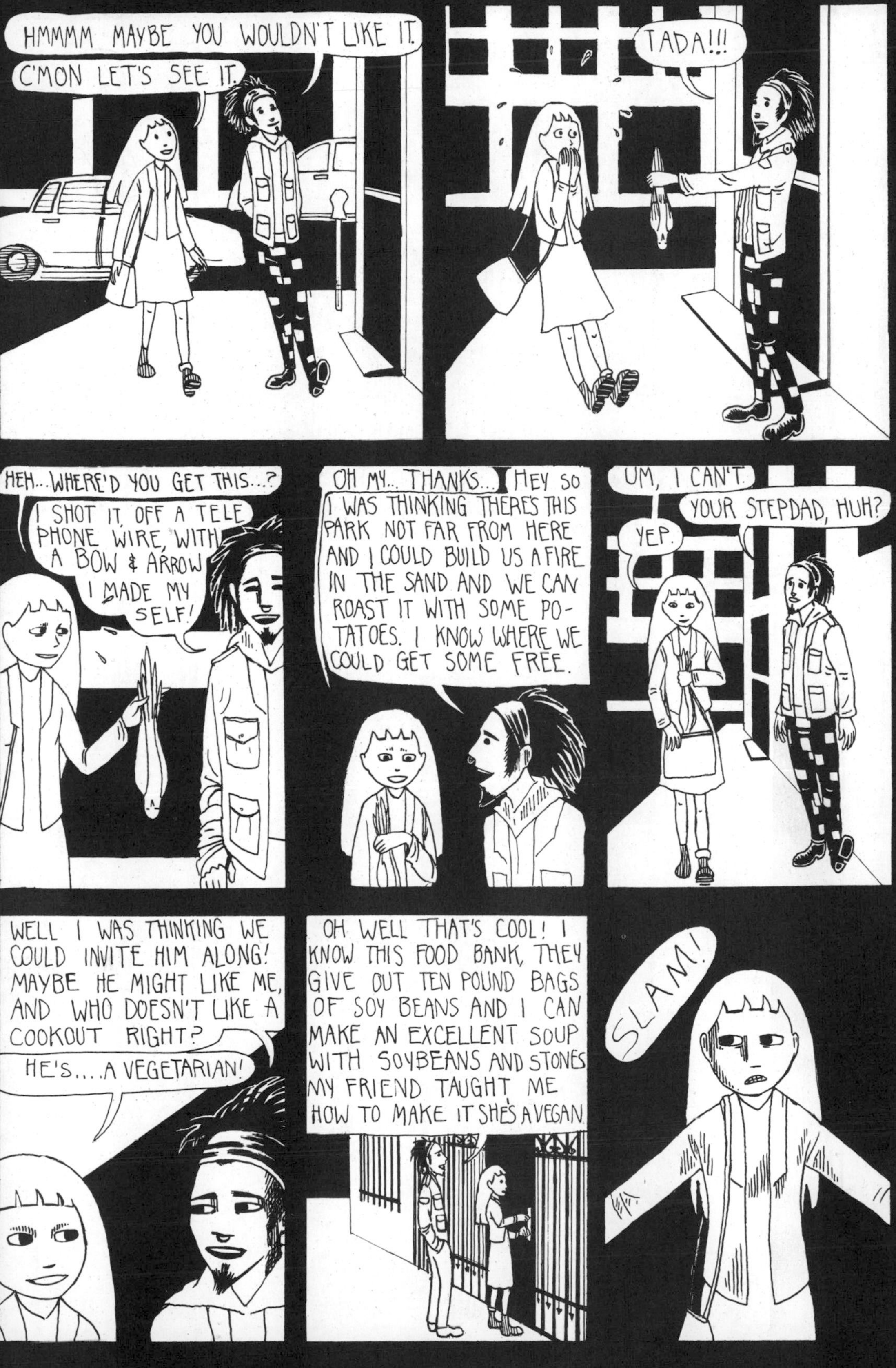
HMMMM MAYBE YOU WOULDN'T LIKE IT.
C'MON LET'S SEE IT.
TADA!!!
HEH... WHERE'D YOU GET THIS...?
I SHOT IT OFF A TELE PHONE WIRE, WITH A BOW & ARROW I MADE MY SELF!
OH MY... THANKS...
HEY SO I WAS THINKING THERE'S THIS PARK NOT FAR FROM HERE AND I COULD BUILD US A FIRE IN THE SAND AND WE CAN ROAST IT WITH SOME PO-TATOES. I KNOW WHERE WE COULD GET SOME FREE.
UM, I CAN'T.
YOUR STEPDAD, HUH?
YEP.
WELL I WAS THINKING WE COULD INVITE HIM ALONG! MAYBE HE MIGHT LIKE ME, AND WHO DOESN'T LIKE A COOKOUT RIGHT?
HE'S.... A VEGETARIAN!
OH WELL THAT'S COOL! I KNOW THIS FOOD BANK, THEY GIVE OUT TEN POUND BAGS OF SOY BEANS AND I CAN MAKE AN EXCELLENT SOUP WITH SOYBEANS AND STONES MY FRIEND TAUGHT ME HOW TO MAKE IT SHE'S A VEGAN.
SLAM!

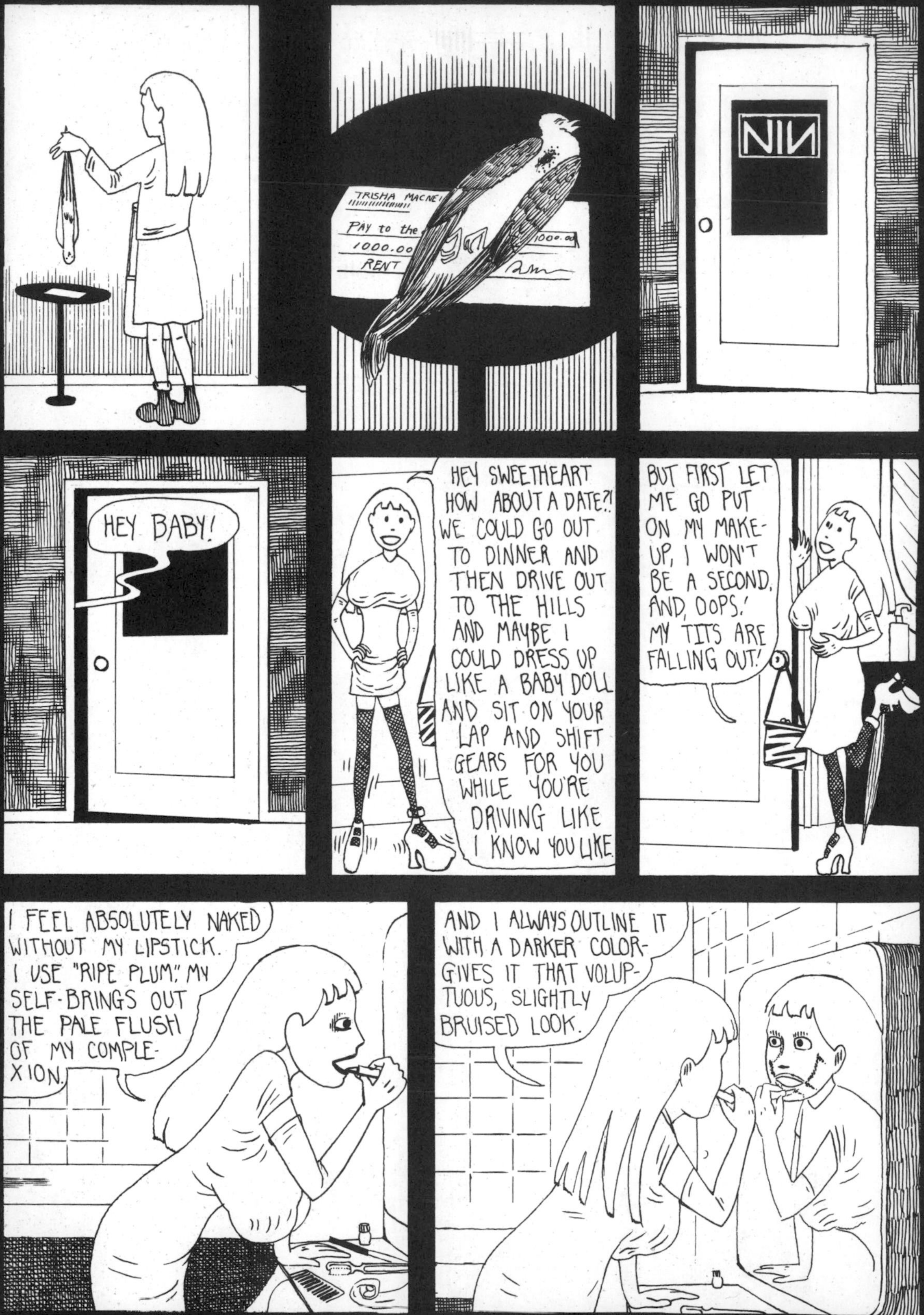
TRISHA MACNE
PAY to the
1000.00
RENT
1000.00
NIN
HEY BABY!
HEY SWEETHEART HOW ABOUT A DATE?! WE COULD GO OUT TO DINNER AND THEN DRIVE OUT TO THE HILLS AND MAYBE I COULD DRESS UP LIKE A BABY DOLL AND SIT ON YOUR LAP AND SHIFT GEARS FOR YOU WHILE YOU'RE DRIVING LIKE I KNOW YOU LIKE.
BUT FIRST LET ME GO PUT ON MY MAKE-UP, I WON'T BE A SECOND, AND, OOPS! MY TITS ARE FALLING OUT!
I FEEL ABSOLUTELY NAKED WITHOUT MY LIPSTICK. I USE "RIPE PLUM," MY SELF-BRINGS OUT THE PALE FLUSH OF MY COMPLE-XION.
AND I ALWAYS OUTLINE IT WITH A DARKER COLOR-GIVES IT THAT VOLUP-TUOUS, SLIGHTLY BRUISED LOOK.

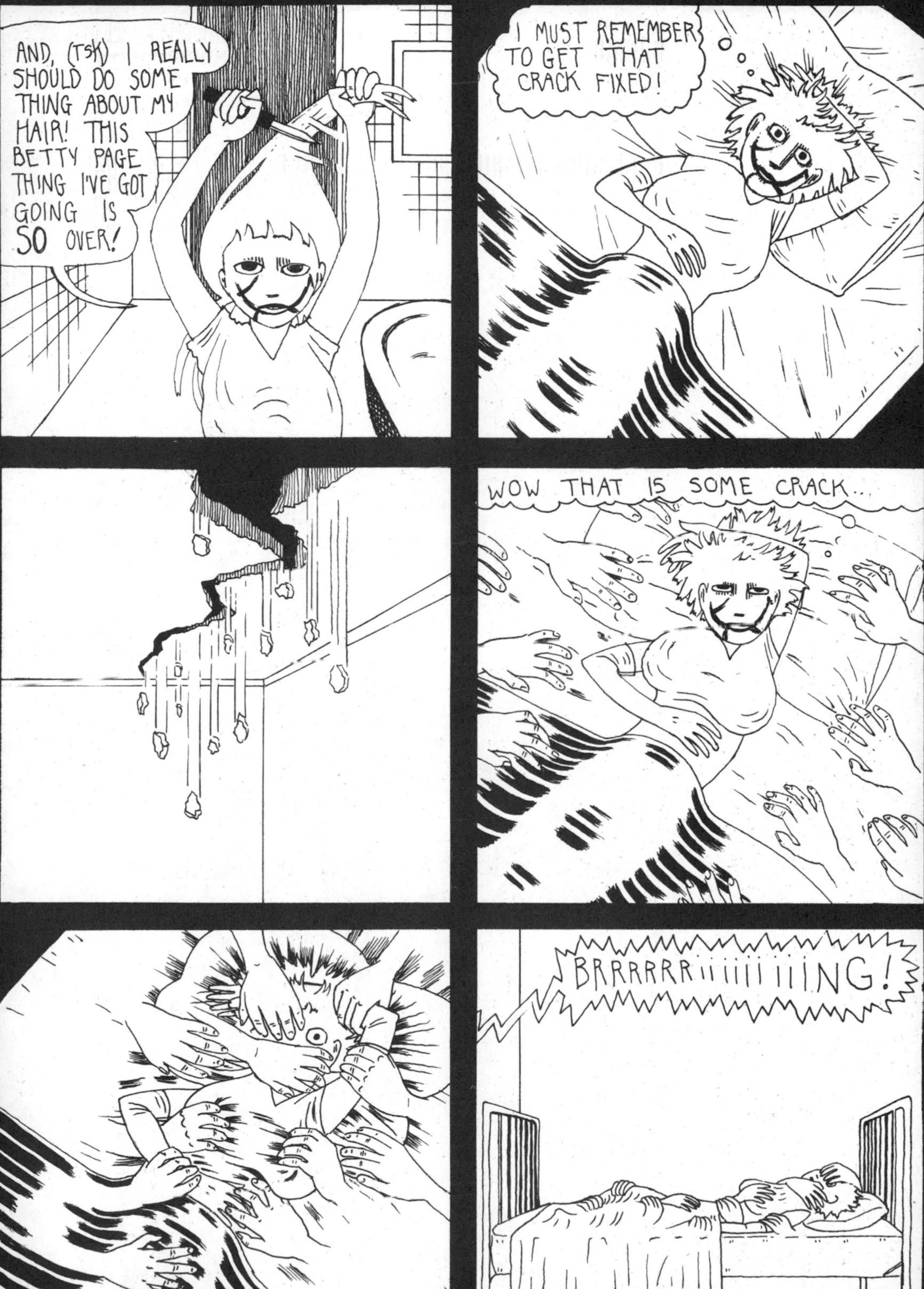
AND, (TSK) I REALLY SHOULD DO SOME THING ABOUT MY HAIR! THIS BETTY PAGE THING I'VE GOT GOING IS SO OVER!
I MUST REMEMBER TO GET THAT CRACK FIXED!
WOW THAT IS SOME CRACK...
BRRRRRRiiiiiiiiiNG!

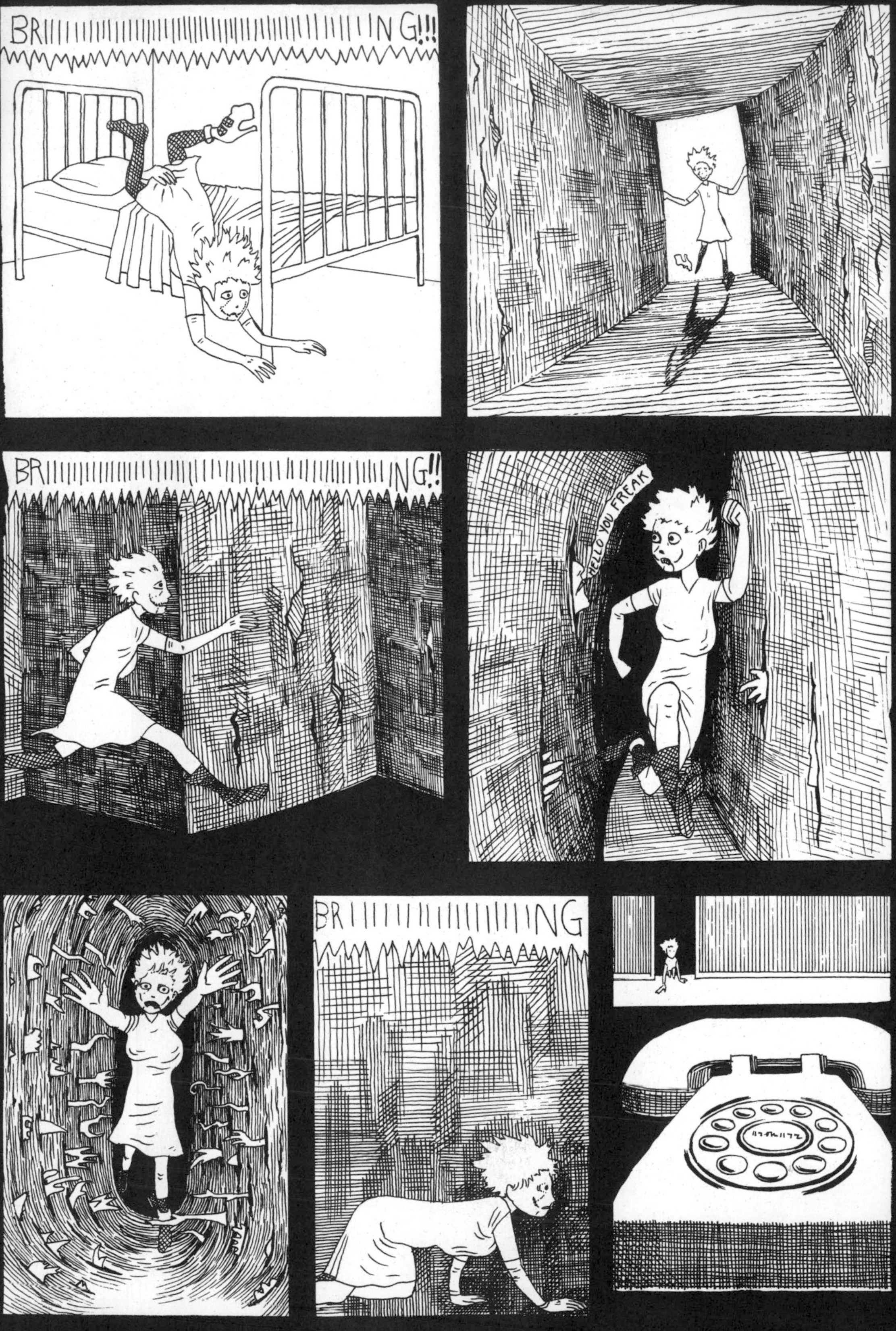
BRIIIIIIIIIIIIIIIIIIIIIIIIIIIIIIIIING!!!
BRIIIIIIIIIIIIIIIIIIIIIIIIIIIIIIIIIIIIIIIIING!!
HELLO YOU FREAK
BRIIIIIIIIIIIIIIING

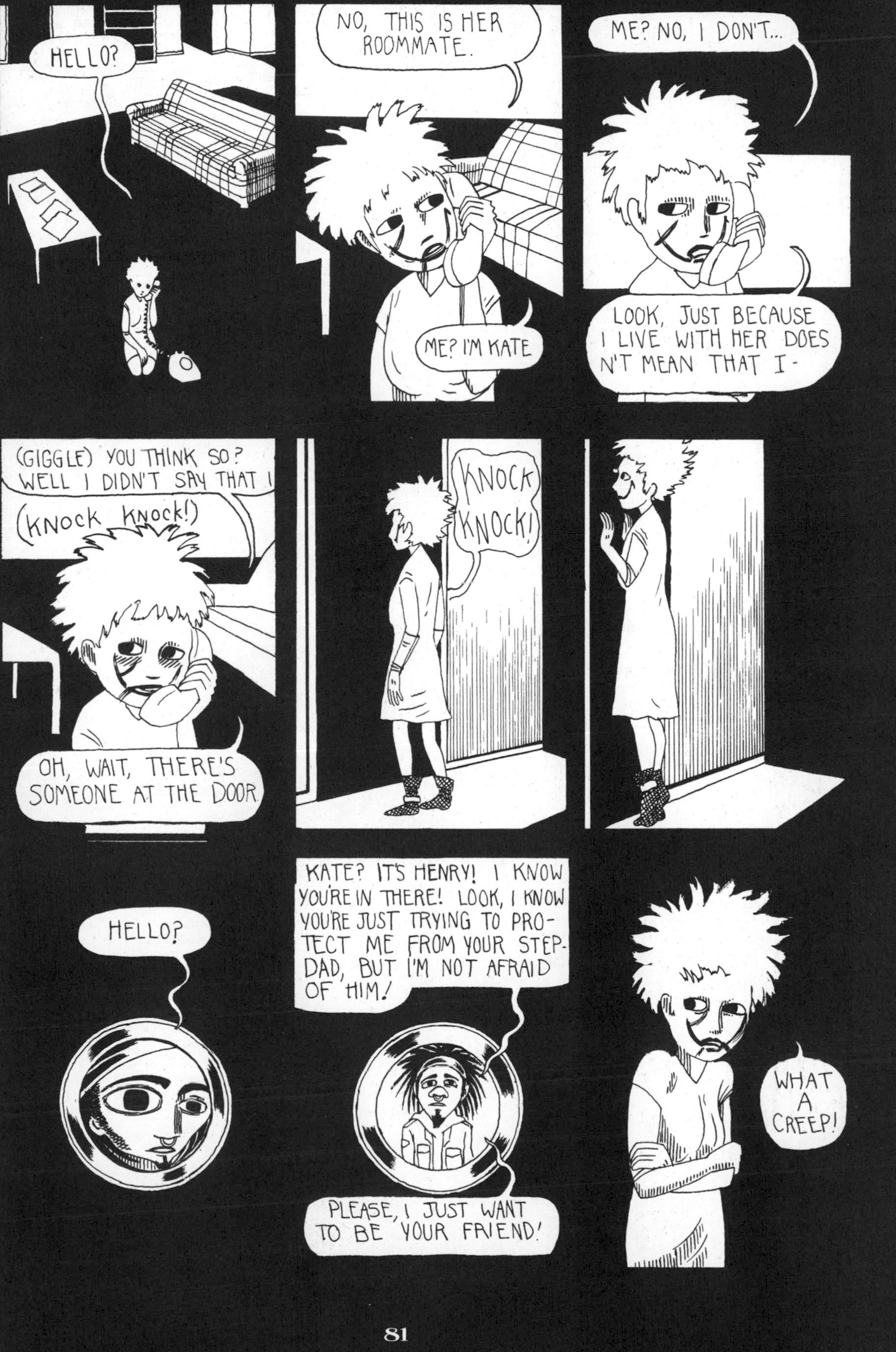
HELLO?
NO, THIS IS HER ROOMMATE.
ME? I'M KATE
ME? NO, I DON'T...
LOOK, JUST BECAUSE I LIVE WITH HER DOES N'T MEAN THAT I-
(GIGGLE) YOU THINK SO? WELL I DIDN'T SAY THAT!
(KNOCK KNOCK!)
OH, WAIT, THERE'S SOMEONE AT THE DOOR.
KNOCK KNOCK!
HELLO?
KATE? IT'S HENRY! I KNOW YOU'RE IN THERE! LOOK, I KNOW YOU'RE JUST TRYING TO PROTECT ME FROM YOUR STEP-DAD, BUT I'M NOT AFRAID OF HIM!
PLEASE, I JUST WANT TO BE YOUR FRIEND!
WHAT A CREEP!

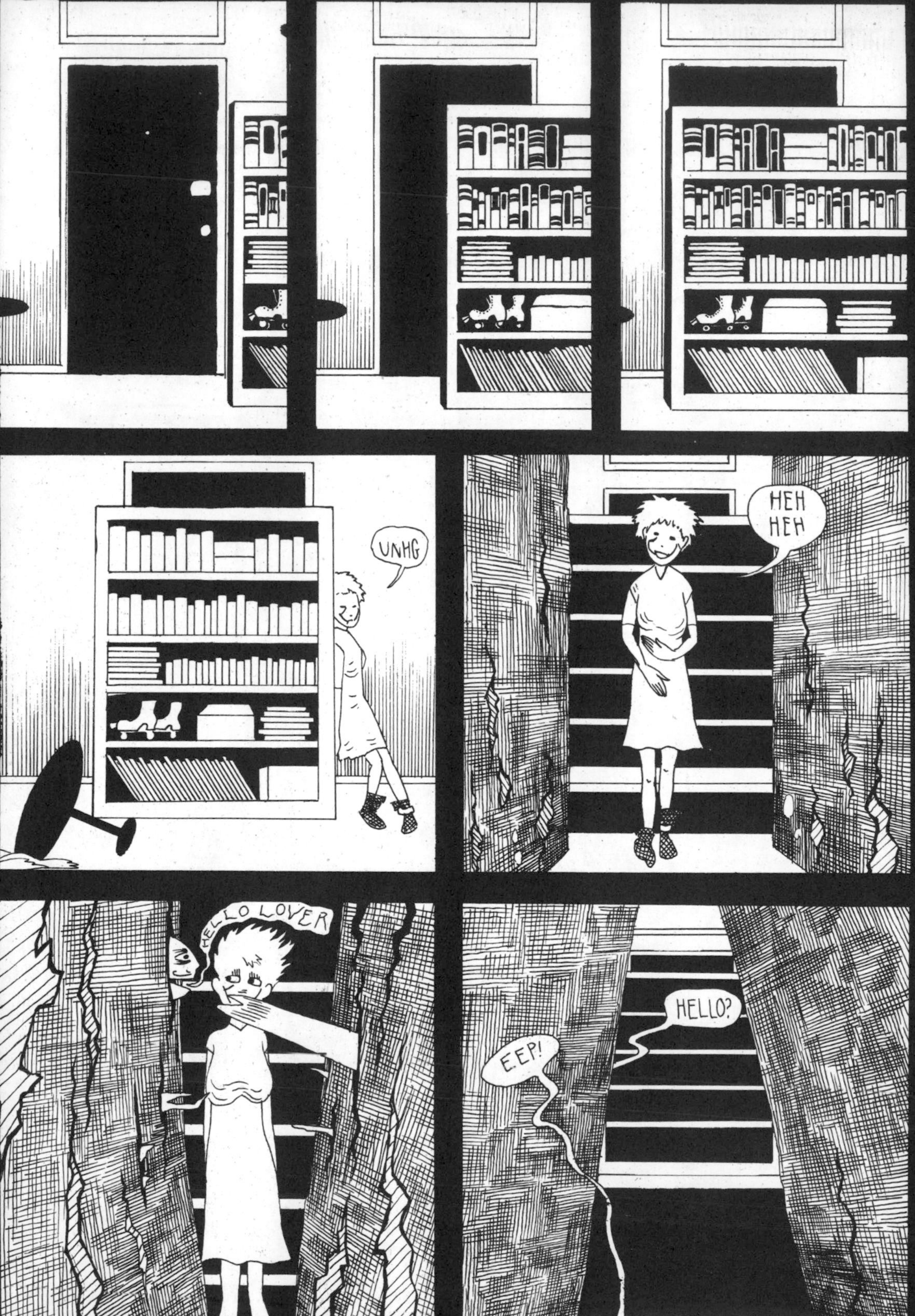
UNHG
HEH HEH
HELLO LOVER
HELLO?
EEP!

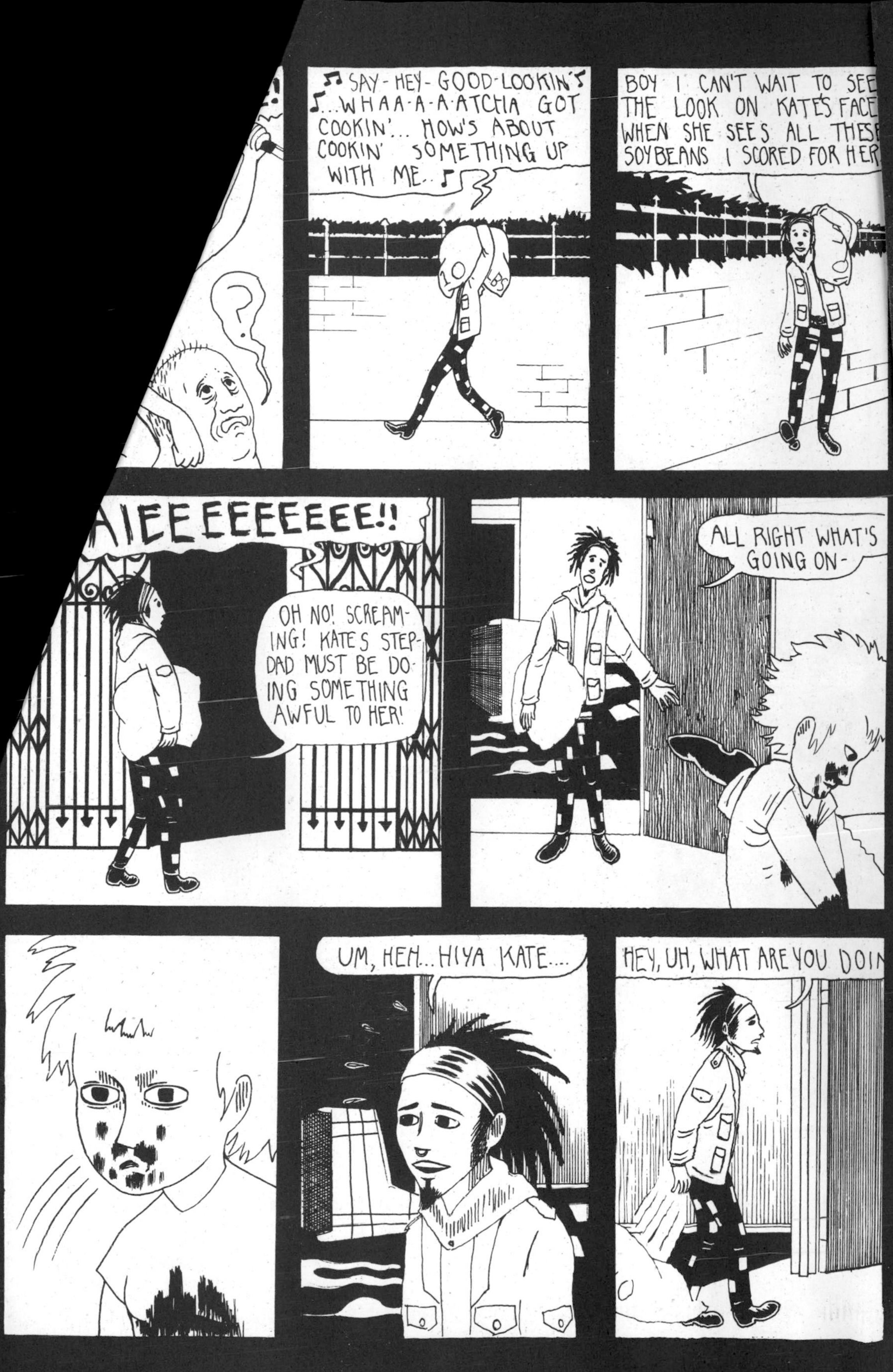
SAY-HEY-GOOD-LOOKIN' ...WHAA-A-A-ATCHA GOT COOKIN'... HOW'S ABOUT COOKIN' SOMETHING UP WITH ME..
BOY I CAN'T WAIT TO SEE THE LOOK ON KATE'S FACE WHEN SHE SEES ALL THESE SOYBEANS I SCORED FOR HER
AIEEEEEEEEE!!
OH NO! SCREAMING! KATE'S STEP-DAD MUST BE DOING SOMETHING AWFUL TO HER!
ALL RIGHT WHAT'S GOING ON-
UM, HEH...HIYA KATE....
HEY, UH, WHAT ARE YOU DOIN

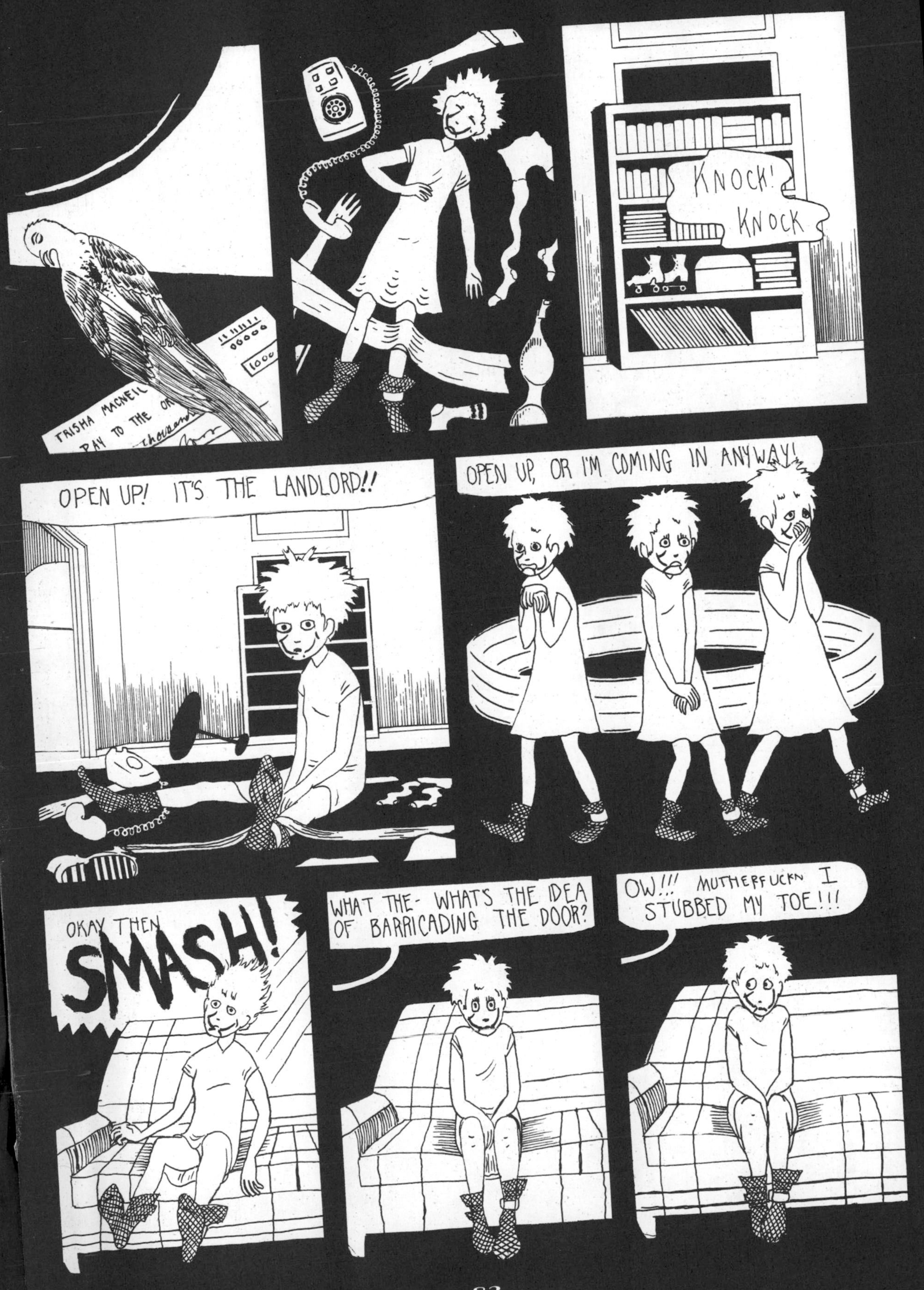
KNOCK! KNOCK
OPEN UP! IT'S THE LANDLORD!!
OPEN UP, OR I'M COMING IN ANYWAY!
OKAY THEN
SMASH!
WHAT THE- WHAT'S THE IDEA OF BARRICADING THE DOOR?
OW!!! MUTHERFUCKN I STUBBED MY TOE!!!

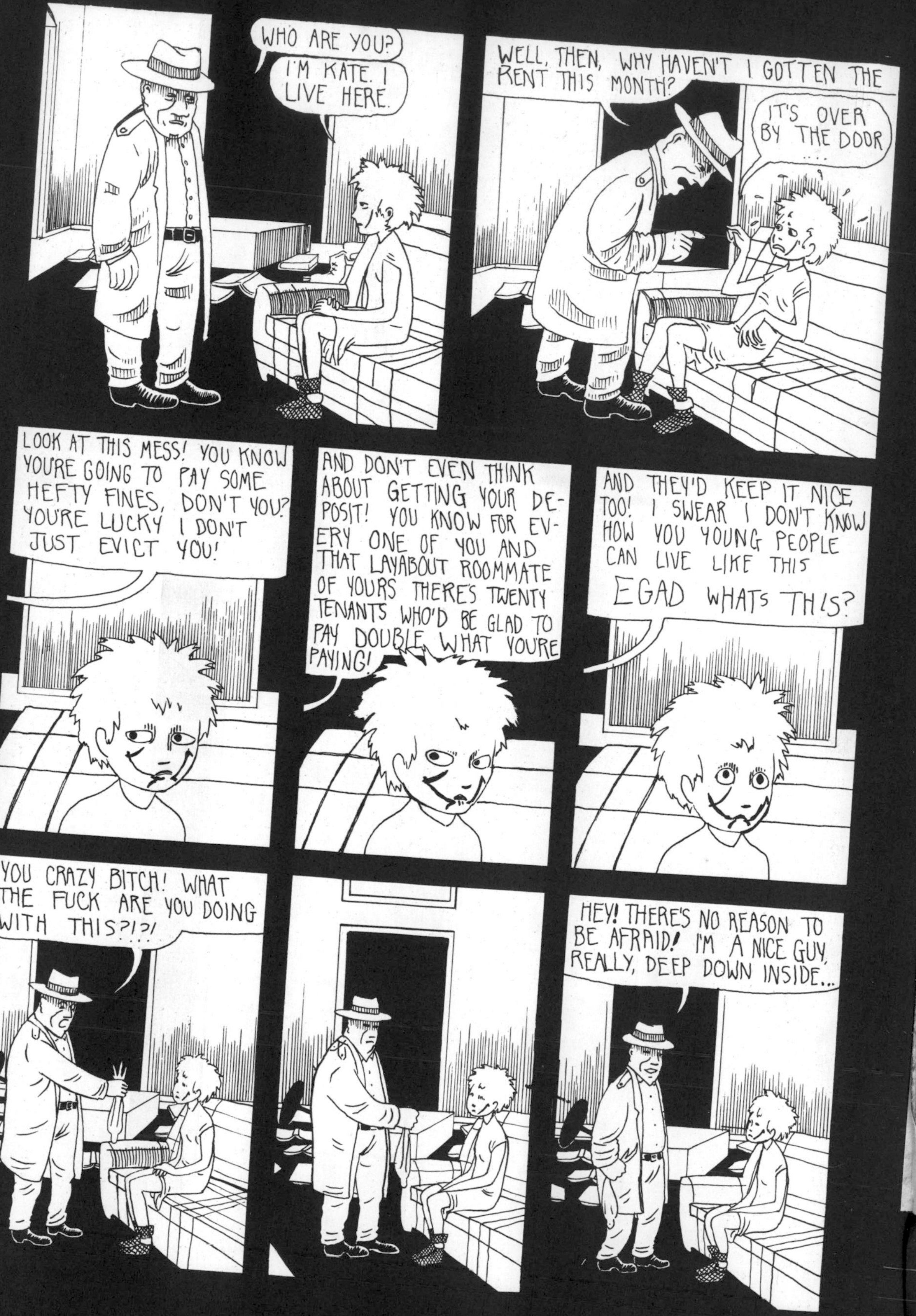
WHO ARE YOU?
I'M KATE. I LIVE HERE.
WELL, THEN, WHY HAVEN'T I GOTTEN THE RENT THIS MONTH?
IT'S OVER BY THE DOOR ...
LOOK AT THIS MESS! YOU KNOW YOU'RE GOING TO PAY SOME HEFTY FINES, DON'T YOU? YOU'RE LUCKY I DON'T JUST EVICT YOU!
AND DON'T EVEN THINK ABOUT GETTING YOUR DEPOSIT! YOU KNOW FOR EVERY ONE OF YOU AND THAT LAYABOUT ROOMMATE OF YOURS THERE'S TWENTY TENANTS WHO'D BE GLAD TO PAY DOUBLE WHAT YOU'RE PAYING!
AND THEY'D KEEP IT NICE TOO! I SWEAR I DON'T KNOW HOW YOU YOUNG PEOPLE CAN LIVE LIKE THIS
EGAD WHATS THIS?
YOU CRAZY BITCH! WHAT THE FUCK ARE YOU DOING WITH THIS?!?!
HEY! THERE'S NO REASON TO BE AFRAID! I'M A NICE GUY, REALLY, DEEP DOWN INSIDE...

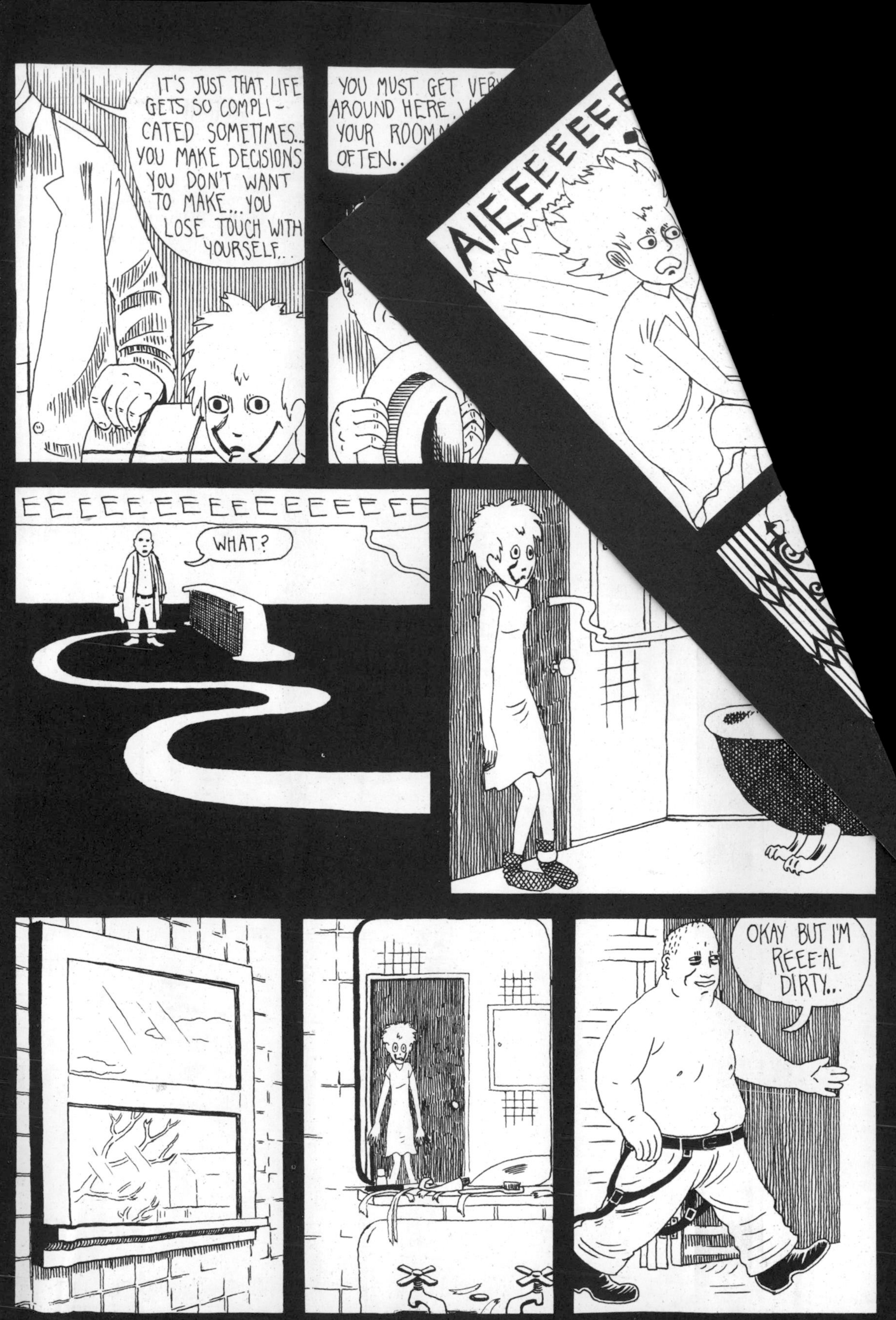
IT'S JUST THAT LIFE GETS SO COMPLICATED SOMETIMES.. YOU MAKE DECISIONS YOU DON'T WANT TO MAKE...YOU LOSE TOUCH WITH YOURSELF..
YOU MUST GET VER
AROUND HERE.
YOUR ROOM
OFTEN..
AIEEEEEEE
EEEEEEEEEEEEEEEEE
WHAT?
OKAY BUT I'M REEE-AL DIRTY...

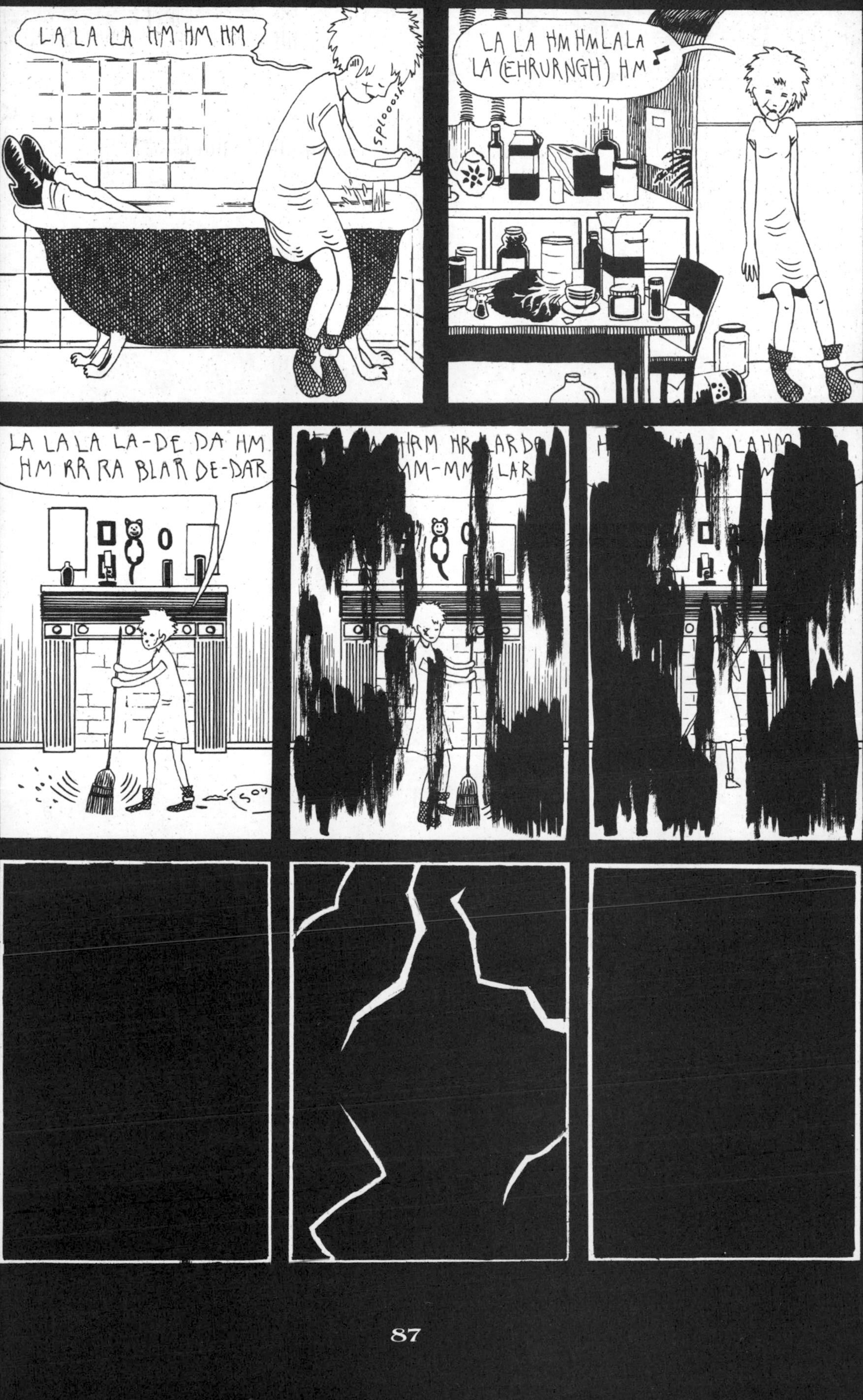
LA LA LA HM HM HM
SPLOOOSH
LA LA HM HM LA LA
LA (EHRURNGH) HM
LA LA LA LA-DE DA HM
HM RR RA BLAR DE-DAR
SOY
HRM HR LARDE
MM-MM LAR
LA LA HM

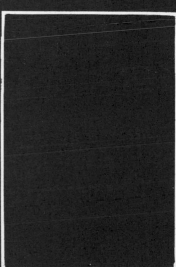

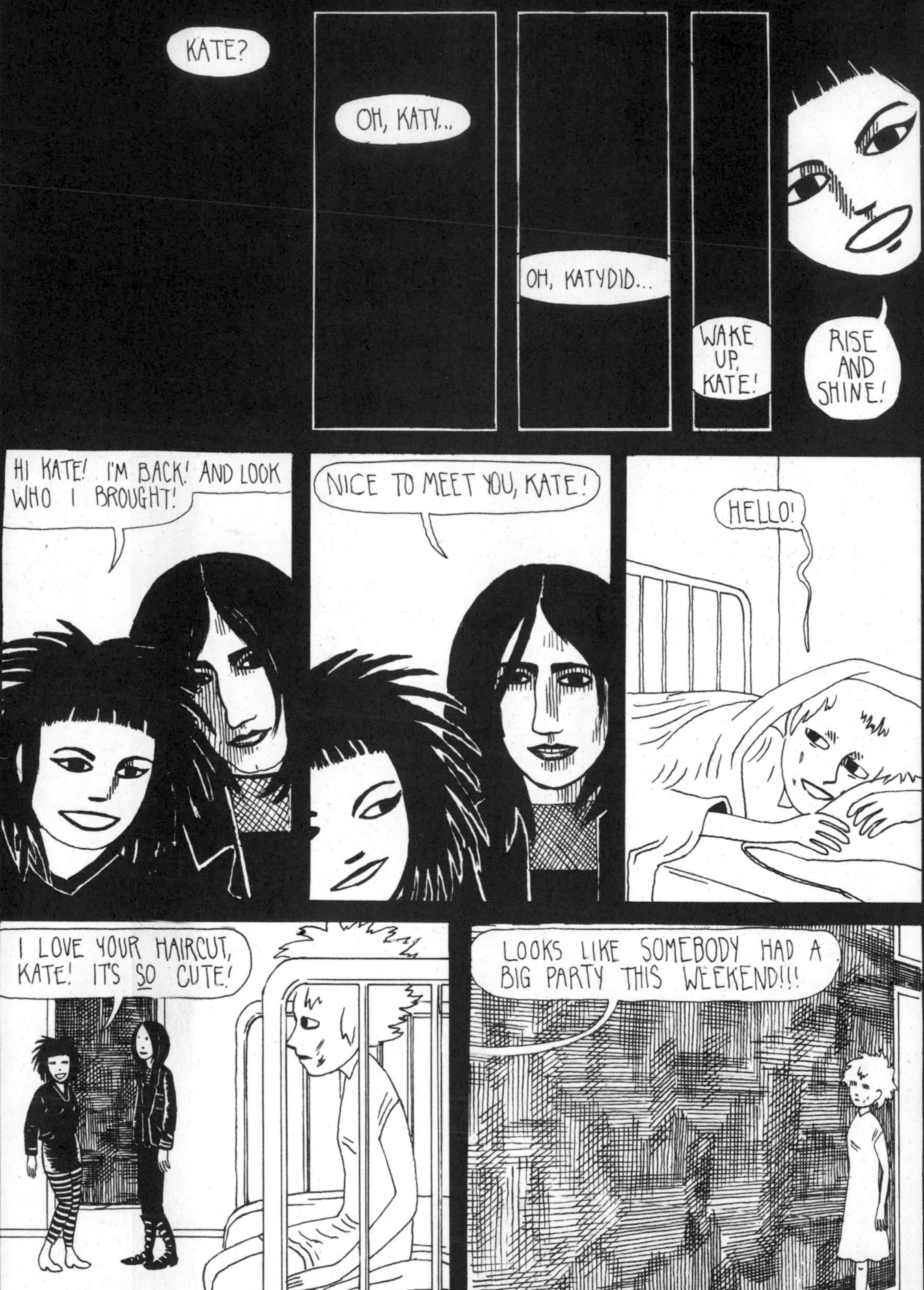
KATE?
OH, KATY...
OH, KATYDID...
WAKE UP, KATE!
RISE AND SHINE!
HI KATE! I'M BACK! AND LOOK WHO I BROUGHT!
NICE TO MEET YOU, KATE!
HELLO!
I LOVE YOUR HAIRCUT, KATE! IT'S SO CUTE!
LOOKS LIKE SOMEBODY HAD A BIG PARTY THIS WEEKEND!!!

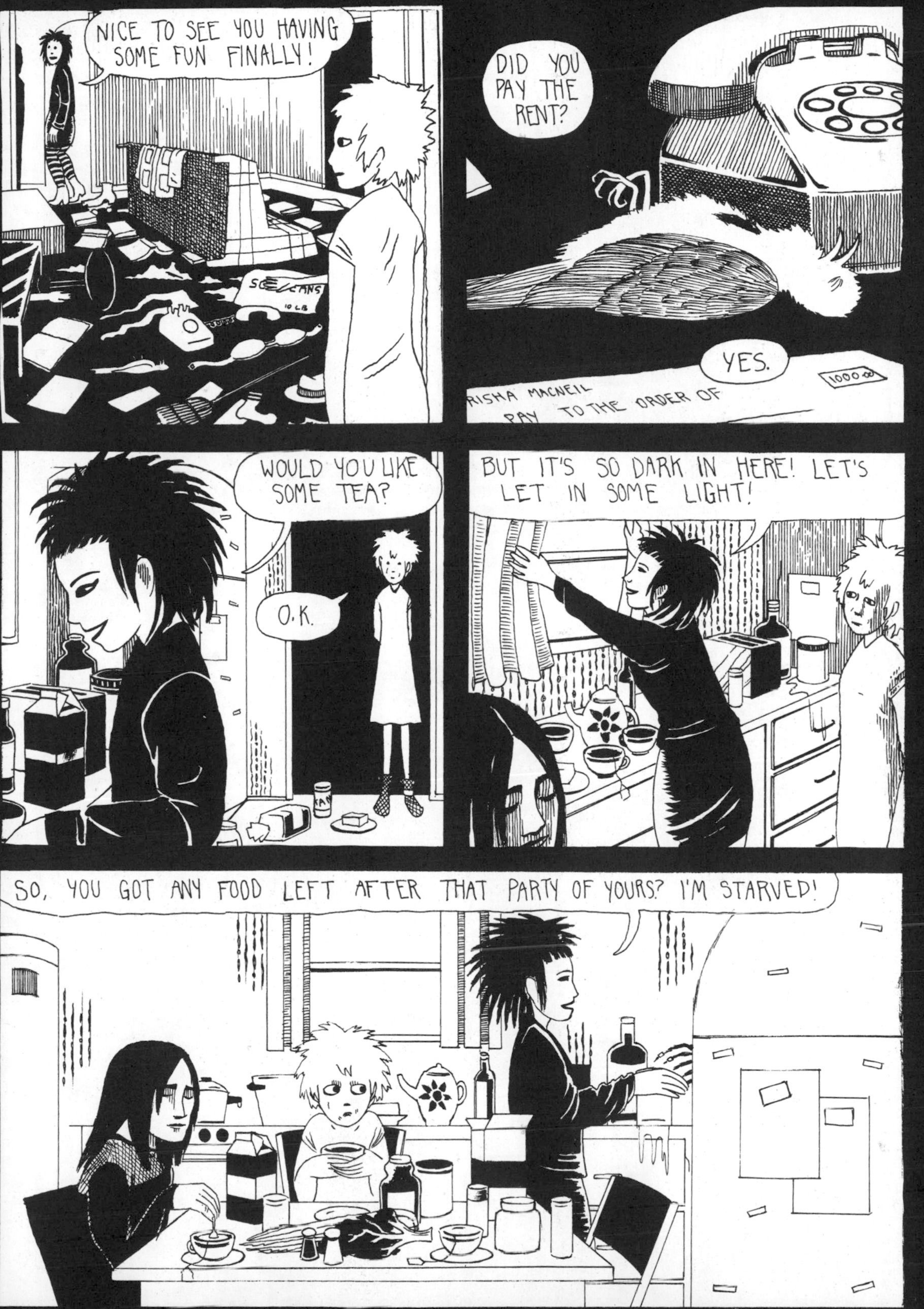
NICE TO SEE YOU HAVING SOME FUN FINALLY!
DID YOU PAY THE RENT?
YES.
RISHA MACNEIL
PAY TO THE ORDER OF
1000.00
WOULD YOU LIKE SOME TEA?
O.K.
BUT IT'S SO DARK IN HERE! LET'S LET IN SOME LIGHT!
SO, YOU GOT ANY FOOD LEFT AFTER THAT PARTY OF YOURS? I'M STARVED!
END

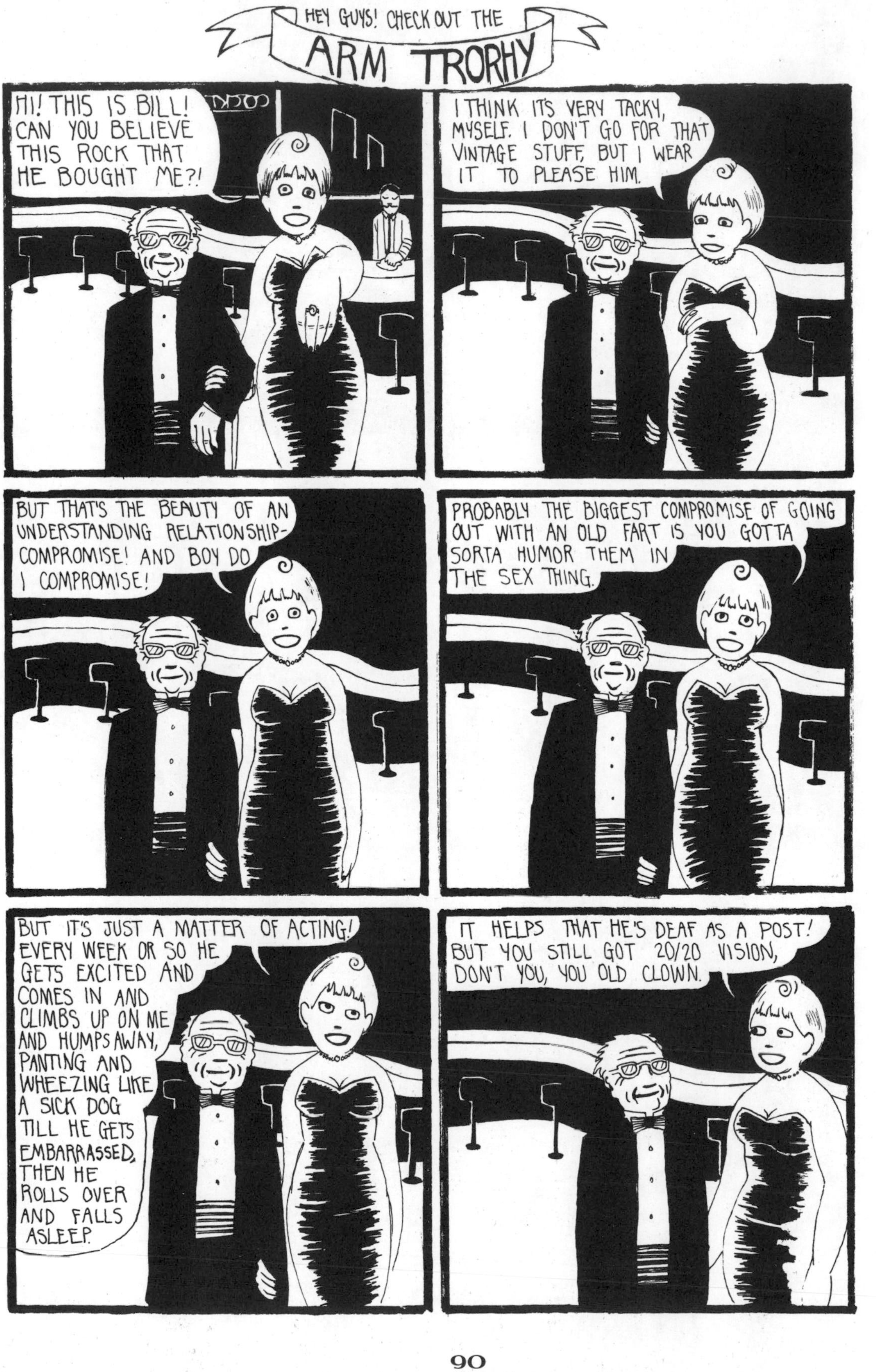
HEY GUYS! CHECK OUT THE
ARM TRORHY
HI! THIS IS BILL! CAN YOU BELIEVE THIS ROCK THAT HE BOUGHT ME?!
I THINK IT'S VERY TACKY, MYSELF. I DON'T GO FOR THAT VINTAGE STUFF, BUT I WEAR IT TO PLEASE HIM.
BUT THAT'S THE BEAUTY OF AN UNDERSTANDING RELATIONSHIP- COMPROMISE! AND BOY DO I COMPROMISE!
PROBABLY THE BIGGEST COMPROMISE OF GOING OUT WITH AN OLD FART IS YOU GOTTA SORTA HUMOR THEM IN THE SEX THING.
BUT IT'S JUST A MATTER OF ACTING! EVERY WEEK OR SO HE GETS EXCITED AND COMES IN AND CLIMBS UP ON ME AND HUMPS AWAY, PANTING AND WHEEZING LIKE A SICK DOG TILL HE GETS EMBARRASSED, THEN HE ROLLS OVER AND FALLS ASLEEP.
IT HELPS THAT HE'S DEAF AS A POST! BUT YOU STILL GOT 20/20 VISION, DON'T YOU, YOU OLD CLOWN.

GABRIELLA
PICKER-
PACKER
IN
THE
GARDEN

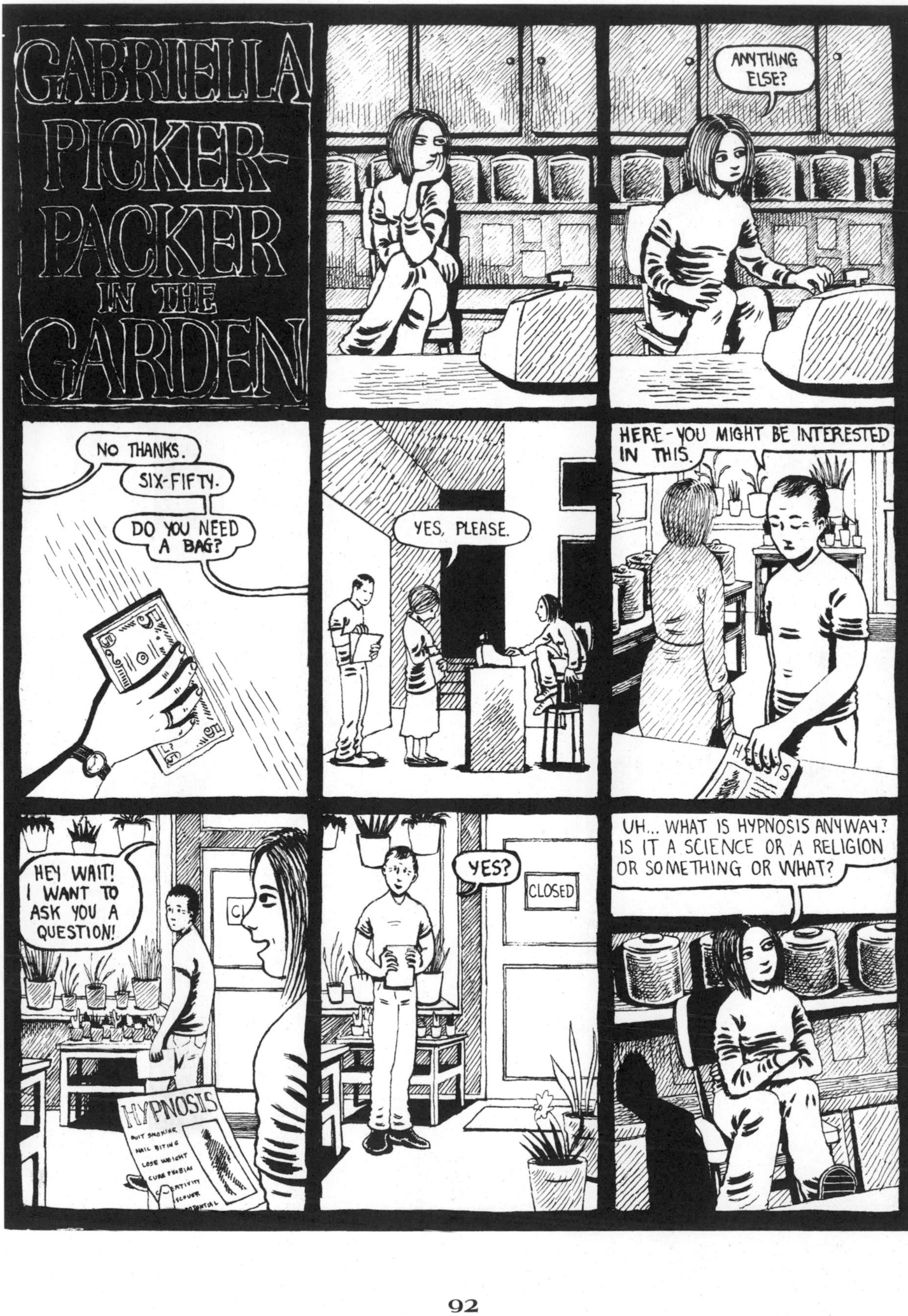
GABRIELLA PICKER-PACKER IN THE GARDEN
ANYTHING ELSE?
NO THANKS.
SIX-FIFTY.
DO YOU NEED A BAG?
YES, PLEASE.
HERE-YOU MIGHT BE INTERESTED IN THIS.
HEY WAIT! I WANT TO ASK YOU A QUESTION!
HYPNOSIS
QUIT SMOKING
NAIL BITING
LOSE WEIGHT
CURE PHOBIAS
YES?
CLOSED
UH... WHAT IS HYPNOSIS ANYWAY? IS IT A SCIENCE OR A RELIGION OR SOMETHING OR WHAT?

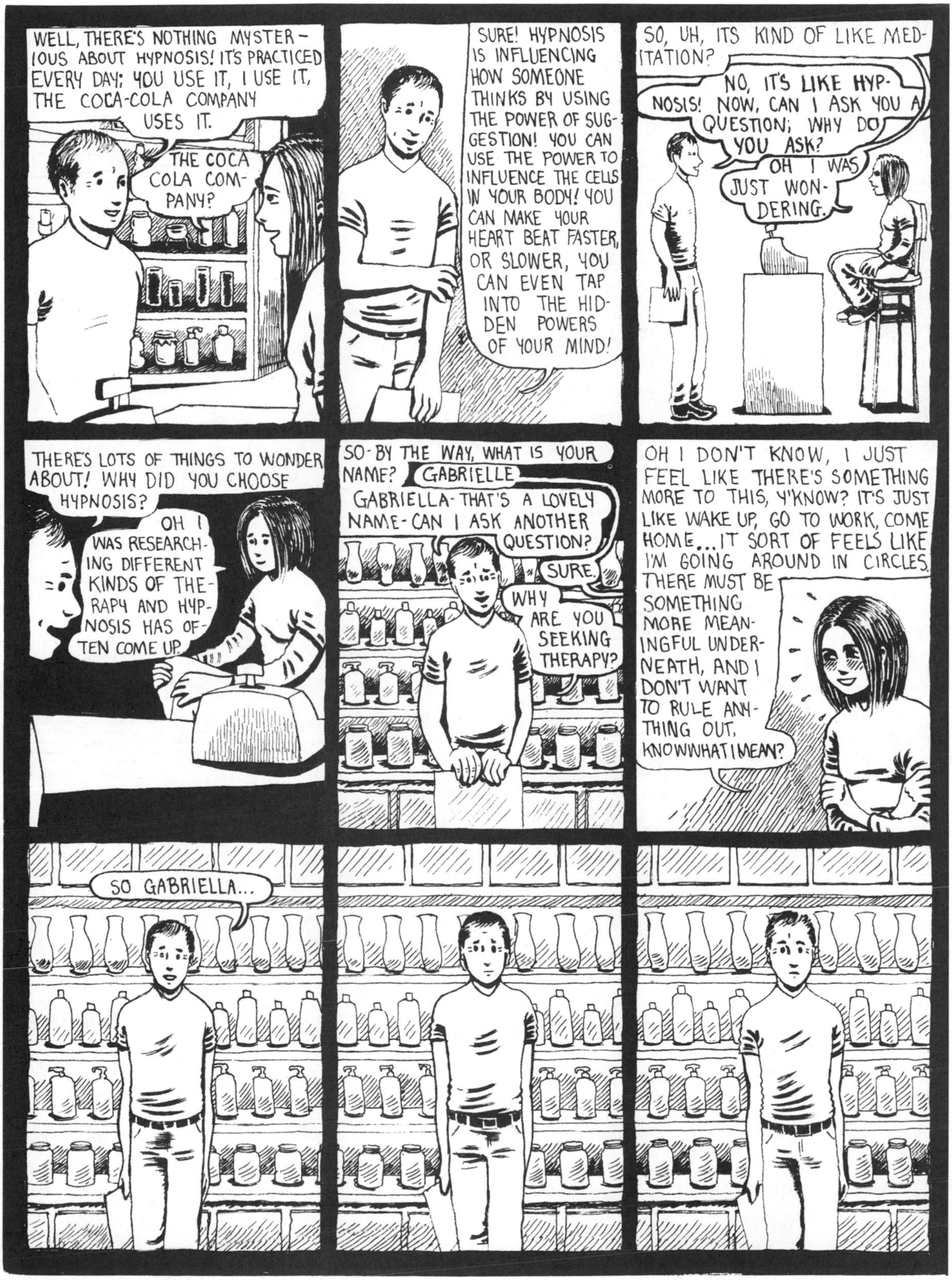
WELL, THERE'S NOTHING MYSTERIOUS ABOUT HYPNOSIS! IT'S PRACTICED EVERY DAY; YOU USE IT, I USE IT, THE COCA-COLA COMPANY USES IT.
THE COCA COLA COMPANY?
SURE! HYPNOSIS IS INFLUENCING HOW SOMEONE THINKS BY USING THE POWER OF SUGGESTION! YOU CAN USE THE POWER TO INFLUENCE THE CELLS IN YOUR BODY! YOU CAN MAKE YOUR HEART BEAT FASTER, OR SLOWER, YOU CAN EVEN TAP INTO THE HIDDEN POWERS OF YOUR MIND!
SO, UH, ITS KIND OF LIKE MEDITATION?
NO, IT'S LIKE HYPNOSIS! NOW, CAN I ASK YOU A QUESTION; WHY DO YOU ASK?
OH I WAS JUST WONDERING.
THERE'S LOTS OF THINGS TO WONDER ABOUT! WHY DID YOU CHOOSE HYPNOSIS?
OH I WAS RESEARCHING DIFFERENT KINDS OF THERAPY AND HYPNOSIS HAS OFTEN COME UP.
SO-BY THE WAY, WHAT IS YOUR NAME?
GABRIELLE
GABRIELLA-THAT'S A LOVELY NAME-CAN I ASK ANOTHER QUESTION?
SURE.
WHY ARE YOU SEEKING THERAPY?
OH I DON'T KNOW, I JUST FEEL LIKE THERE'S SOMETHING MORE TO THIS, Y'KNOW? IT'S JUST LIKE WAKE UP, GO TO WORK, COME HOME... IT SORT OF FEELS LIKE I'M GOING AROUND IN CIRCLES.
THERE MUST BE SOMETHING MORE MEANINGFUL UNDERNEATH, AND I DON'T WANT TO RULE ANYTHING OUT. KNOWWHATIMEAN?
SO GABRIELLA...

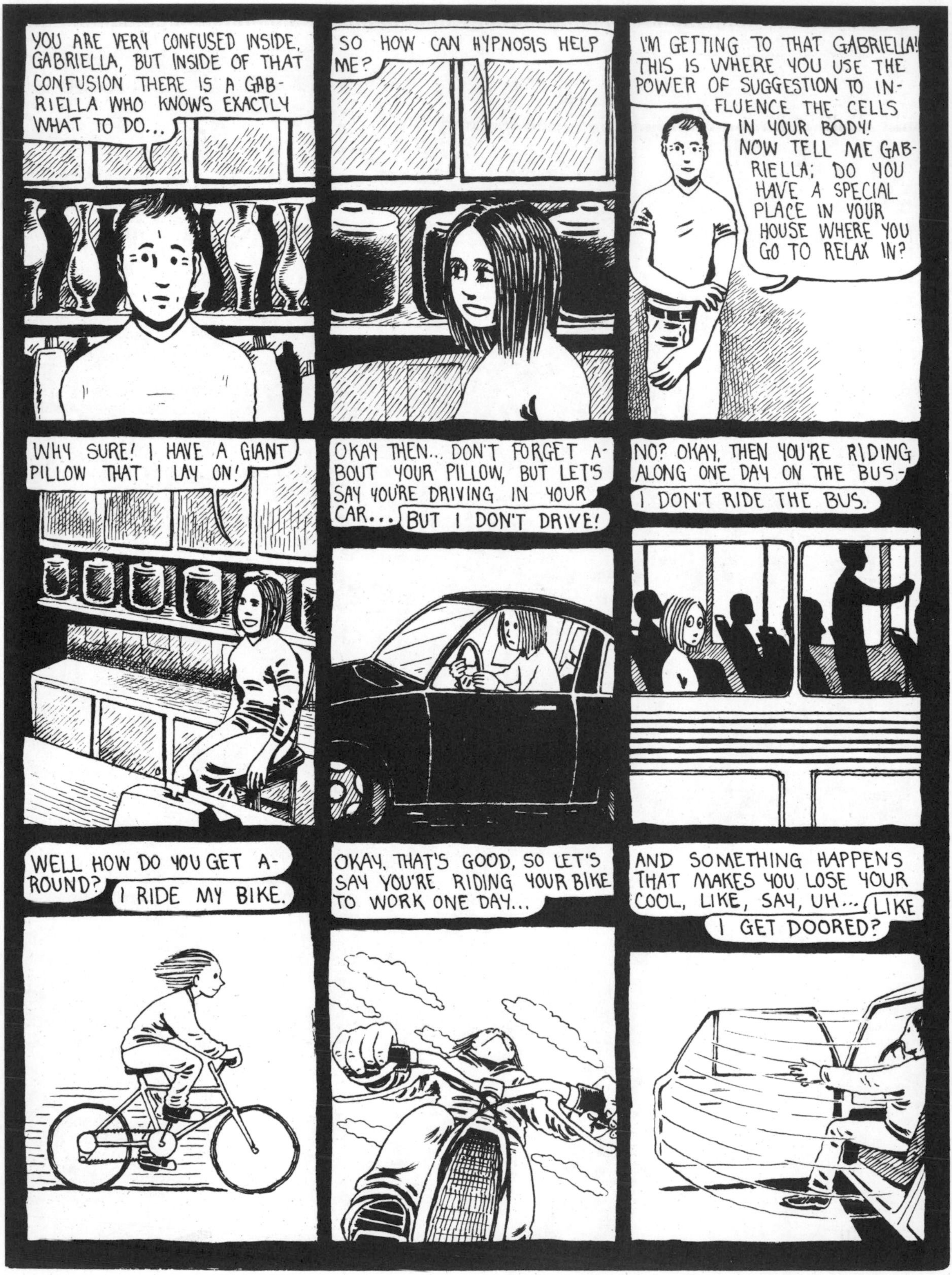
YOU ARE VERY CONFUSED INSIDE, GABRIELLA, BUT INSIDE OF THAT CONFUSION THERE IS A GABRIELLA WHO KNOWS EXACTLY WHAT TO DO...
SO HOW CAN HYPNOSIS HELP ME?
I'M GETTING TO THAT GABRIELLA! THIS IS WHERE YOU USE THE POWER OF SUGGESTION TO INFLUENCE THE CELLS IN YOUR BODY! NOW TELL ME GABRIELLA; DO YOU HAVE A SPECIAL PLACE IN YOUR HOUSE WHERE YOU GO TO RELAX IN?
WHY SURE! I HAVE A GIANT PILLOW THAT I LAY ON!
OKAY THEN... DON'T FORGET ABOUT YOUR PILLOW, BUT LET'S SAY YOU'RE DRIVING IN YOUR CAR...
BUT I DON'T DRIVE!
NO? OKAY, THEN YOU'RE RIDING ALONG ONE DAY ON THE BUS-
I DON'T RIDE THE BUS.
WELL HOW DO YOU GET AROUND?
I RIDE MY BIKE.
OKAY, THAT'S GOOD, SO LET'S SAY YOU'RE RIDING YOUR BIKE TO WORK ONE DAY...
AND SOMETHING HAPPENS THAT MAKES YOU LOSE YOUR COOL, LIKE, SAY, UH...
LIKE I GET DOORED?

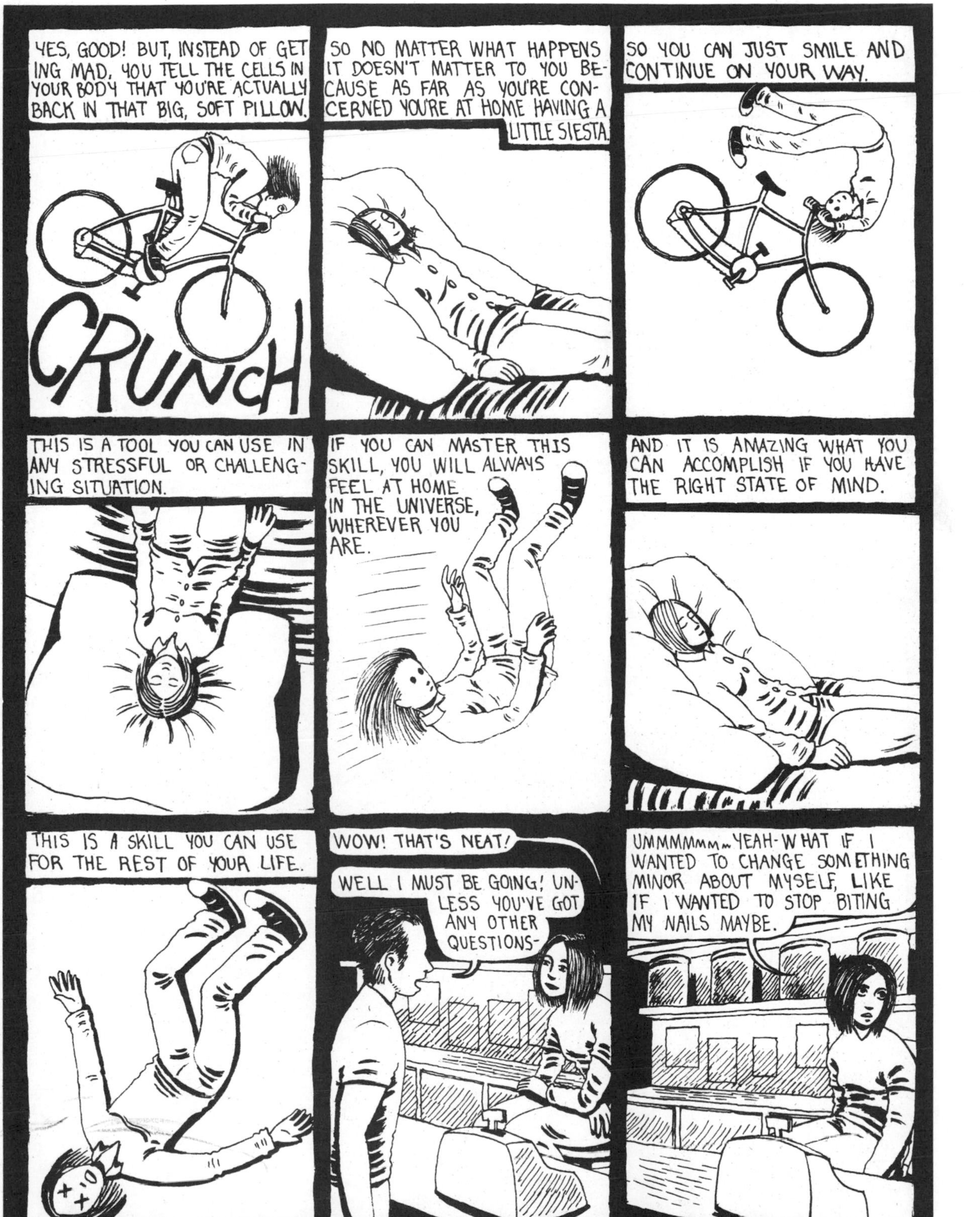
YES, GOOD! BUT, INSTEAD OF GETTING MAD, YOU TELL THE CELLS IN YOUR BODY THAT YOU'RE ACTUALLY BACK IN THAT BIG, SOFT PILLOW.
CRUNCH
SO NO MATTER WHAT HAPPENS IT DOESN'T MATTER TO YOU BECAUSE AS FAR AS YOU'RE CONCERNED YOU'RE AT HOME HAVING A LITTLE SIESTA.
SO YOU CAN JUST SMILE AND CONTINUE ON YOUR WAY.
THIS IS A TOOL YOU CAN USE IN ANY STRESSFUL OR CHALLENGING SITUATION.
IF YOU CAN MASTER THIS SKILL, YOU WILL ALWAYS FEEL AT HOME IN THE UNIVERSE, WHEREVER YOU ARE.
AND IT IS AMAZING WHAT YOU CAN ACCOMPLISH IF YOU HAVE THE RIGHT STATE OF MIND.
THIS IS A SKILL YOU CAN USE FOR THE REST OF YOUR LIFE.
WOW! THAT'S NEAT!
WELL I MUST BE GOING! UNLESS YOU'VE GOT ANY OTHER QUESTIONS-
UMMMMMM... YEAH- WHAT IF I WANTED TO CHANGE SOMETHING MINOR ABOUT MYSELF, LIKE IF I WANTED TO STOP BITING MY NAILS MAYBE.

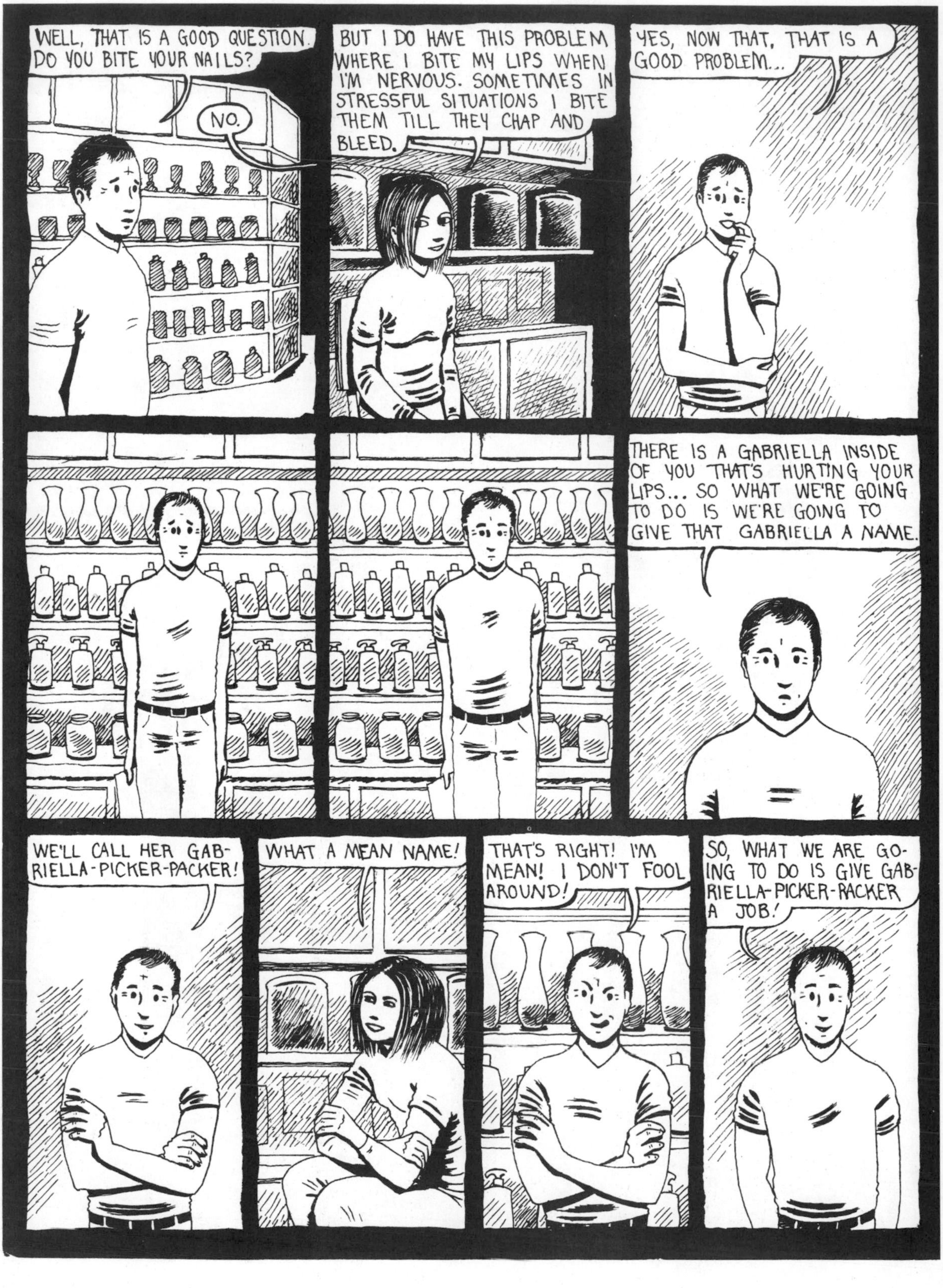
WELL, THAT IS A GOOD QUESTION. DO YOU BITE YOUR NAILS?
NO.
BUT I DO HAVE THIS PROBLEM WHERE I BITE MY LIPS WHEN I'M NERVOUS. SOMETIMES IN STRESSFUL SITUATIONS I BITE THEM TILL THEY CHAP AND BLEED.
YES, NOW THAT. THAT IS A GOOD PROBLEM...
THERE IS A GABRIELLA INSIDE OF YOU THAT'S HURTING YOUR LIPS... SO WHAT WE'RE GOING TO DO IS WE'RE GOING TO GIVE THAT GABRIELLA A NAME.
WE'LL CALL HER GAB-RIELLA-PICKER-PACKER!
WHAT A MEAN NAME!
THAT'S RIGHT! I'M MEAN! I DON'T FOOL AROUND!
SO, WHAT WE ARE GO-ING TO DO IS GIVE GAB-RIELLA-PICKER-RACKER A JOB!

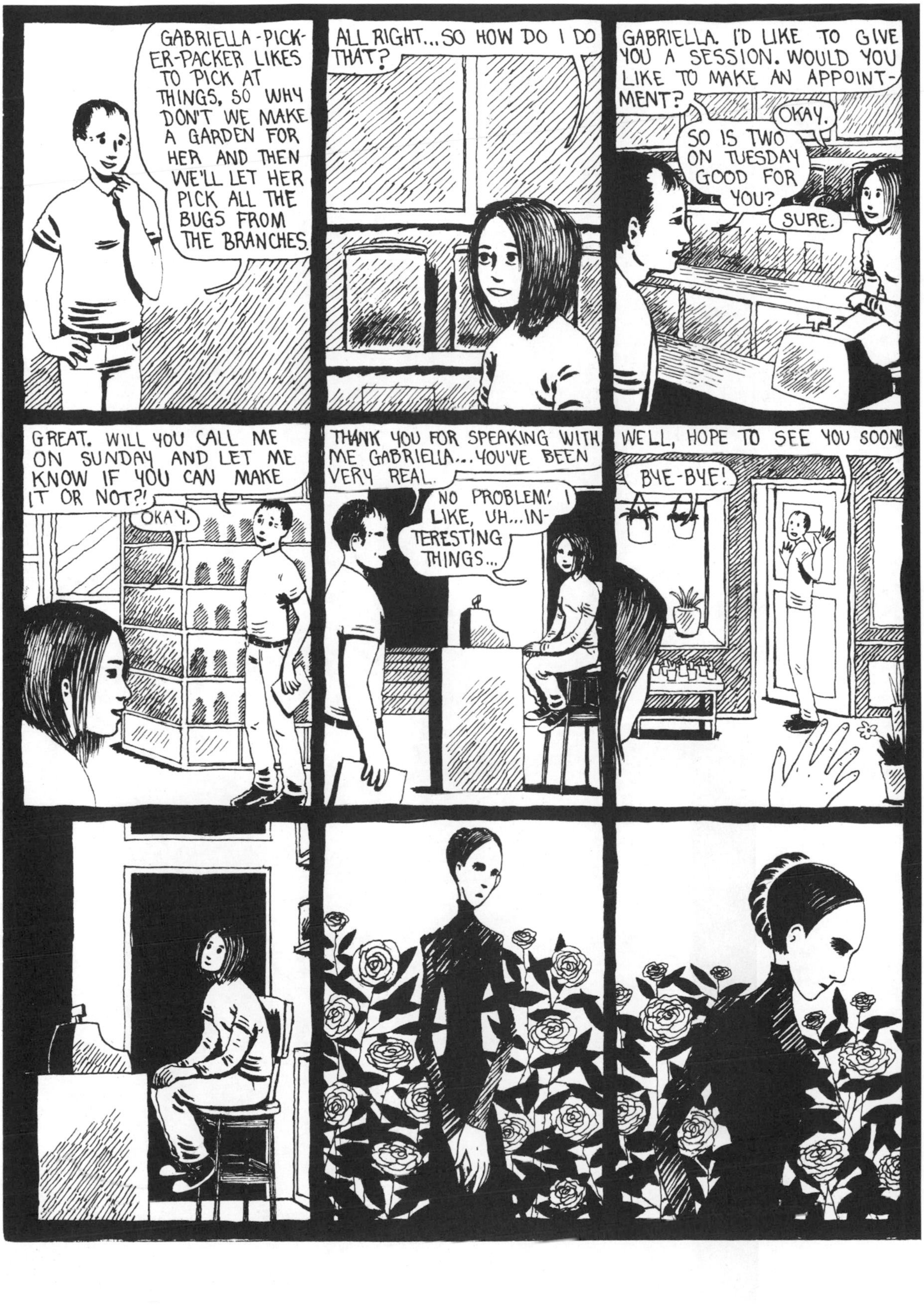
GABRIELLA-PICKER-PACKER LIKES TO PICK AT THINGS, SO WHY DON'T WE MAKE A GARDEN FOR HER AND THEN WE'LL LET HER PICK ALL THE BUGS FROM THE BRANCHES.
ALL RIGHT... SO HOW DO I DO THAT?
GABRIELLA. I'D LIKE TO GIVE YOU A SESSION. WOULD YOU LIKE TO MAKE AN APPOINTMENT?
OKAY.
SO IS TWO ON TUESDAY GOOD FOR YOU?
SURE.
GREAT. WILL YOU CALL ME ON SUNDAY AND LET ME KNOW IF YOU CAN MAKE IT OR NOT?!
OKAY.
THANK YOU FOR SPEAKING WITH ME GABRIELLA... YOU'VE BEEN VERY REAL.
NO PROBLEM! I LIKE, UH... INTERESTING THINGS...
WELL, HOPE TO SEE YOU SOON!
BYE-BYE!

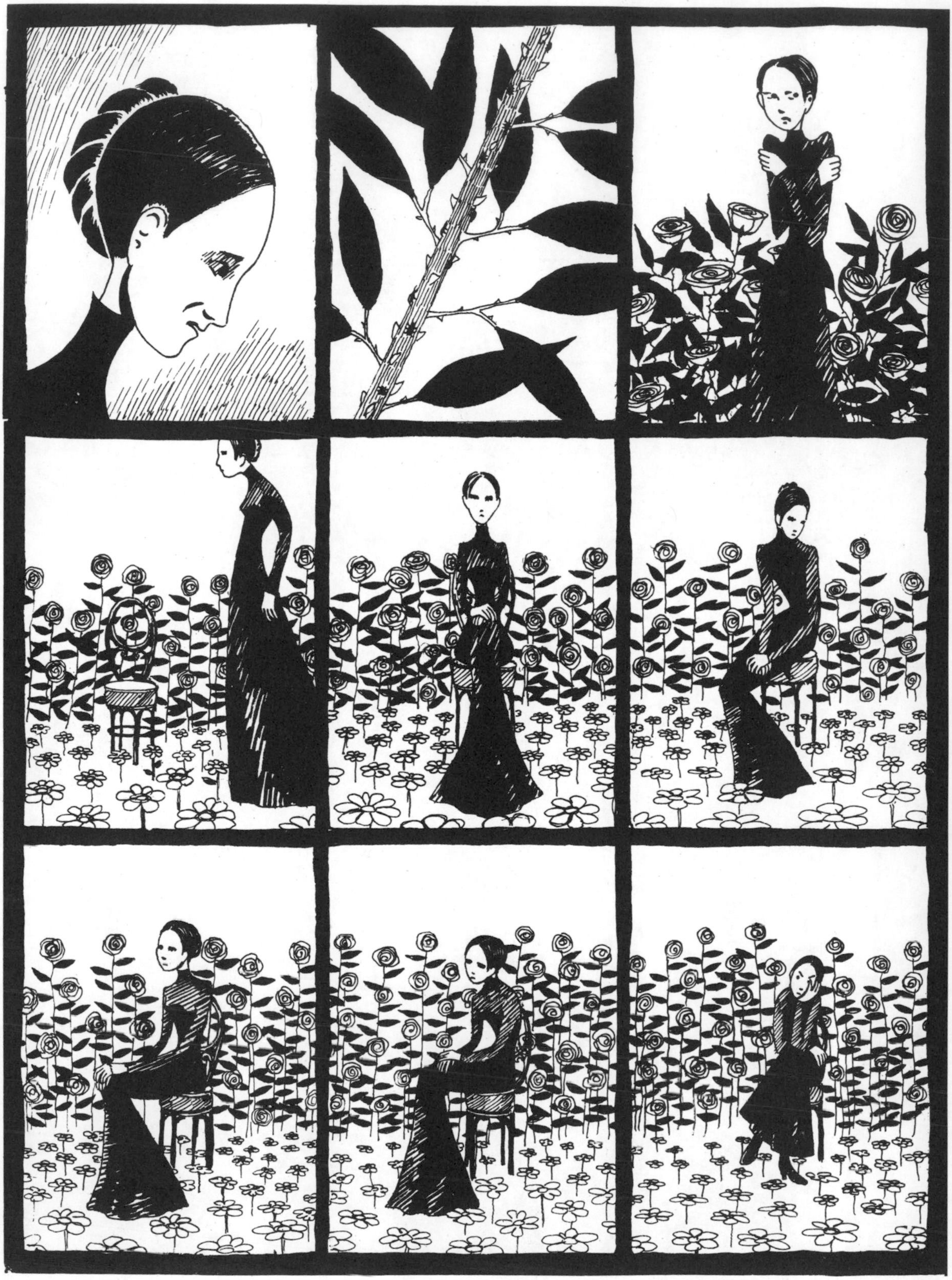

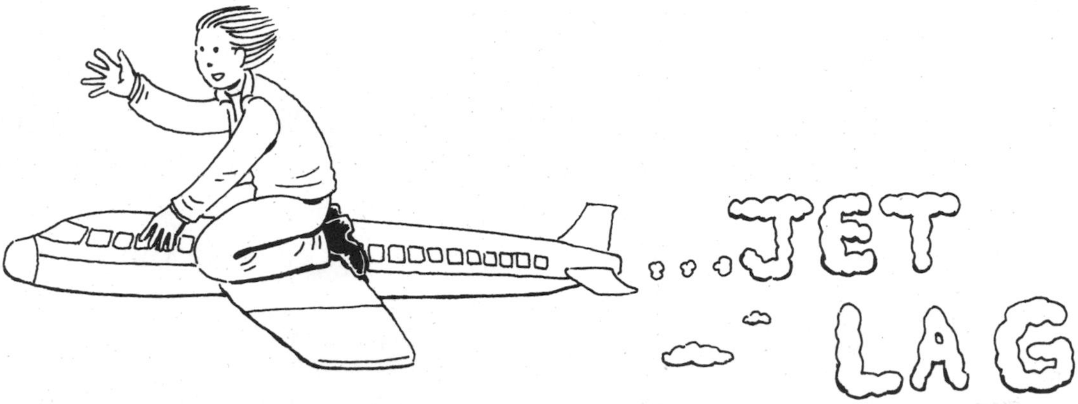
...JET
LAG

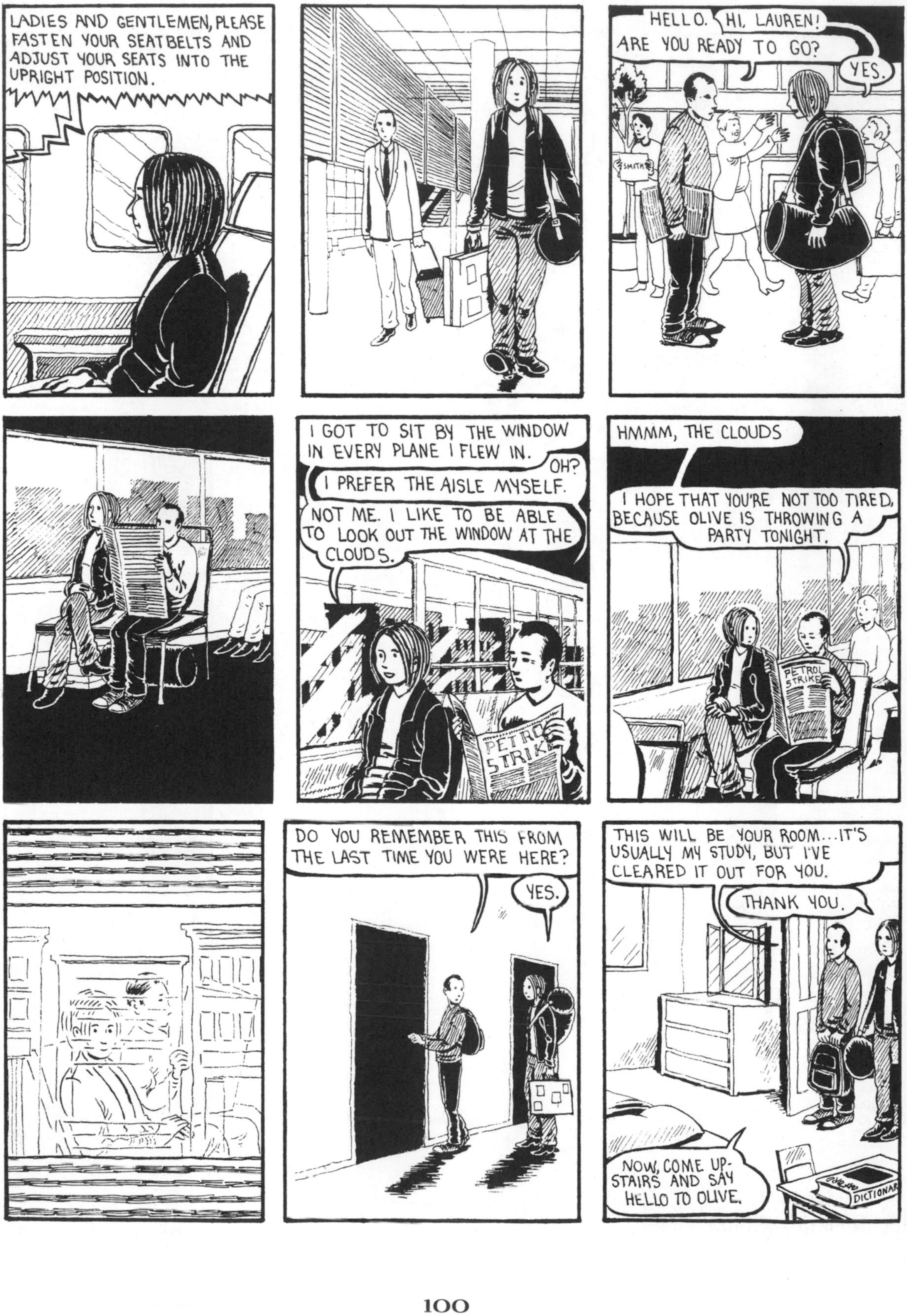

LADIES AND GENTLEMEN, PLEASE FASTEN YOUR SEATBELTS AND ADJUST YOUR SEATS INTO THE UPRIGHT POSITION.
HELLO.
HI, LAUREN!
ARE YOU READY TO GO?
YES.
SMITH
I GOT TO SIT BY THE WINDOW IN EVERY PLANE I FLEW IN.
OH?
I PREFER THE AISLE MYSELF.
NOT ME. I LIKE TO BE ABLE TO LOOK OUT THE WINDOW AT THE CLOUDS.
PETROL STRIKE
HMMM, THE CLOUDS
I HOPE THAT YOU'RE NOT TOO TIRED, BECAUSE OLIVE IS THROWING A PARTY TONIGHT.
PETROL STRIKE
DO YOU REMEMBER THIS FROM THE LAST TIME YOU WERE HERE?
YES.
THIS WILL BE YOUR ROOM... IT'S USUALLY MY STUDY, BUT I'VE CLEARED IT OUT FOR YOU.
THANK YOU.
NOW, COME UPSTAIRS AND SAY HELLO TO OLIVE.
DICTIONAR

HELLO, DEAR! YOU LOOK LOVELY!

HI GRANDMA

I HOPE YOU DON'T MIND, I'M HAVING A LITTLE PARTY TONIGHT. I INVITED ALL THESE PEOPLE OVER AND COMPLETELY FORGOT YOU WERE COMING!

NO, THAT SOUNDS FUN! HERE'S YOUR GIN!

OH! ME DUTY-FREE! YOU RE-MEMBERED!

AND HOW IS YOUR BROTHER?

HE'S DOING WELL! HE'S GOING TO COLLEGE AND WORKING IN... UM... COMPUTER STUFF!

OH THAT'S WONDER-FUL! I HOPE HE COMES TO VISIT SOON.

AND I HEAR YOU'RE DOING WELL YOURSELF.

IS THERE ANYTHING SPECIAL YOU'D LIKE TO DO IN LON-DON?

WELL, I WAS THINK-ING I'D LIKE TO BUY A BICYCLE... DO YOU KNOW WHERE I COULD GET ONE?

OH, NO, DEAR, YOU CAWN'T RIDE A BICYCLE IN LONDON. THE TRAFFIC IS TOO DANGEROUS!

WELL, JUST FOR AROUND HERE, LIKE UP AND DOWN PORTOBELLO ROAD...

NOW LAUREN SHOULD KNOW BETTER THAN I. LET ME JUST ASK HIM.

OH, LAUREN!

YES?

DO YOU KNOW WHERE GAB-RIELLE CAN BUY A BICYCLE?

YOU CAN'T RIDE A BICYCLE A-ROUND HERE! IT'S TOO DANGEROUS!

IT DOESN'T MATTER! I THINK I'M GOING TO LAY DOWN FOR AWHILE. I HAVEN'T SLEPT MUCH FOR THE PAST TWENTY-FOUR HOURS!

ALL RIGHT, DEAR! JUST COME UP FOR THE PARTY AROUND FIVE!

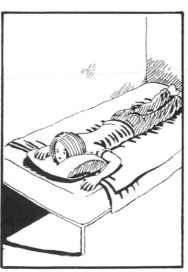

OH, THERE SHE IS! HELLO GABRIELLE! DO YOU REMEMBER GRETA?

HI DARLING! DID YOU MANAGE TO GET SOME SLEEP?

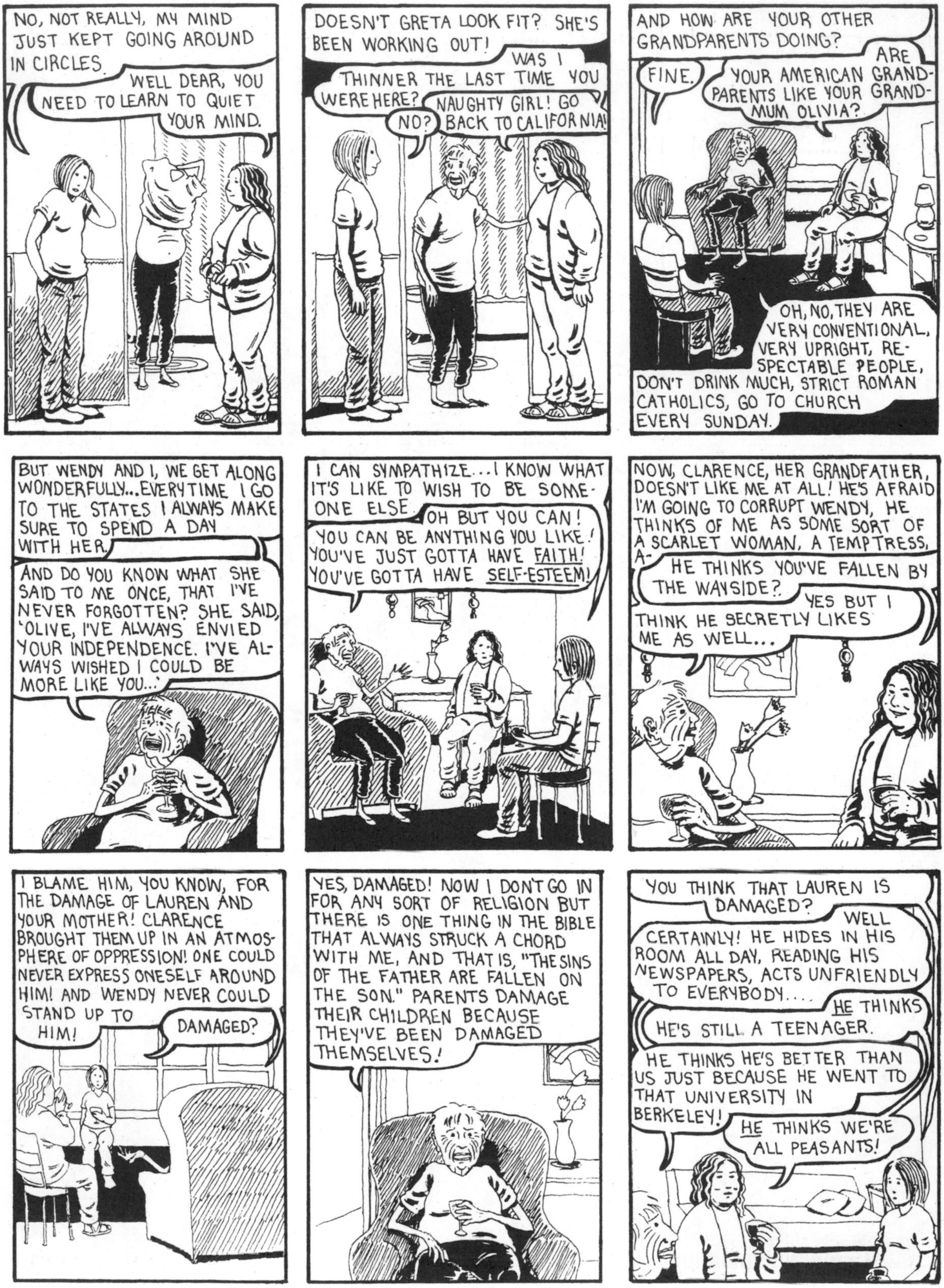

NO, NOT REALLY, MY MIND JUST KEPT GOING AROUND IN CIRCLES.
WELL DEAR, YOU NEED TO LEARN TO QUIET YOUR MIND.
DOESN'T GRETA LOOK FIT? SHE'S BEEN WORKING OUT!
WAS I THINNER THE LAST TIME YOU WERE HERE?
NO?
NAUGHTY GIRL! GO BACK TO CALIFORNIA!
AND HOW ARE YOUR OTHER GRANDPARENTS DOING?
FINE.
ARE YOUR AMERICAN GRANDPARENTS LIKE YOUR GRANDMUM OLIVIA?
OH, NO, THEY ARE VERY CONVENTIONAL, VERY UPRIGHT, RESPECTABLE PEOPLE, DON'T DRINK MUCH, STRICT ROMAN CATHOLICS, GO TO CHURCH EVERY SUNDAY.
BUT WENDY AND I, WE GET ALONG WONDERFULLY... EVERYTIME I GO TO THE STATES I ALWAYS MAKE SURE TO SPEND A DAY WITH HER.
AND DO YOU KNOW WHAT SHE SAID TO ME ONCE, THAT I'VE NEVER FORGOTTEN? SHE SAID, 'OLIVE, I'VE ALWAYS ENVIED YOUR INDEPENDENCE. I'VE ALWAYS WISHED I COULD BE MORE LIKE YOU...'
I CAN SYMPATHIZE... I KNOW WHAT IT'S LIKE TO WISH TO BE SOMEONE ELSE.
OH BUT YOU CAN! YOU CAN BE ANYTHING YOU LIKE! YOU'VE JUST GOTTA HAVE FAITH! YOU'VE GOTTA HAVE SELF-ESTEEM!
NOW, CLARENCE, HER GRANDFATHER, DOESN'T LIKE ME AT ALL! HE'S AFRAID I'M GOING TO CORRUPT WENDY, HE THINKS OF ME AS SOME SORT OF A SCARLET WOMAN, A TEMPTRESS, A-
HE THINKS YOU'VE FALLEN BY THE WAYSIDE?
YES BUT I THINK HE SECRETLY LIKES ME AS WELL...
I BLAME HIM, YOU KNOW, FOR THE DAMAGE OF LAUREN AND YOUR MOTHER! CLARENCE BROUGHT THEM UP IN AN ATMOSPHERE OF OPPRESSION! ONE COULD NEVER EXPRESS ONESELF AROUND HIM! AND WENDY NEVER COULD STAND UP TO HIM!
DAMAGED?
YES, DAMAGED! NOW I DON'T GO IN FOR ANY SORT OF RELIGION BUT THERE IS ONE THING IN THE BIBLE THAT ALWAYS STRUCK A CHORD WITH ME, AND THAT IS, "THE SINS OF THE FATHER ARE FALLEN ON THE SON." PARENTS DAMAGE THEIR CHILDREN BECAUSE THEY'VE BEEN DAMAGED THEMSELVES!
YOU THINK THAT LAUREN IS DAMAGED?
WELL CERTAINLY! HE HIDES IN HIS ROOM ALL DAY, READING HIS NEWSPAPERS, ACTS UNFRIENDLY TO EVERYBODY....
HE THINKS HE'S STILL A TEENAGER.
HE THINKS HE'S BETTER THAN US JUST BECAUSE HE WENT TO THAT UNIVERSITY IN BERKELEY!
HE THINKS WE'RE ALL PEASANTS!

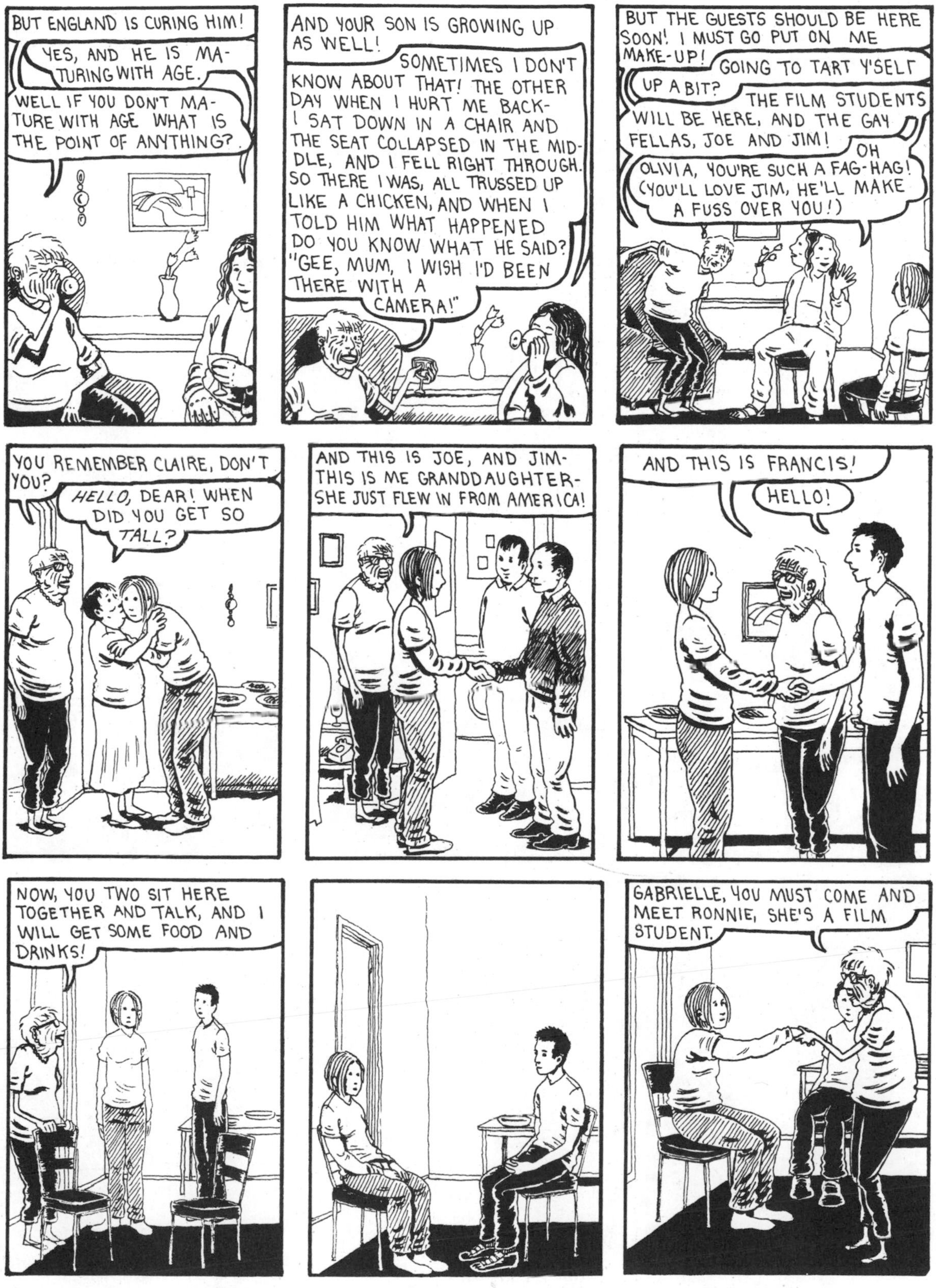
BUT ENGLAND IS CURING HIM!
YES, AND HE IS MATURING WITH AGE.
WELL IF YOU DON'T MATURE WITH AGE WHAT IS THE POINT OF ANYTHING?
AND YOUR SON IS GROWING UP AS WELL!
SOMETIMES I DON'T KNOW ABOUT THAT! THE OTHER DAY WHEN I HURT ME BACK- I SAT DOWN IN A CHAIR AND THE SEAT COLLAPSED IN THE MIDDLE, AND I FELL RIGHT THROUGH. SO THERE I WAS, ALL TRUSSED UP LIKE A CHICKEN, AND WHEN I TOLD HIM WHAT HAPPENED DO YOU KNOW WHAT HE SAID? "GEE, MUM, I WISH I'D BEEN THERE WITH A CAMERA!"
BUT THE GUESTS SHOULD BE HERE SOON! I MUST GO PUT ON ME MAKE-UP!
GOING TO TART Y'SELF UP A BIT?
THE FILM STUDENTS WILL BE HERE, AND THE GAY FELLAS, JOE AND JIM!
OH OLIVIA, YOU'RE SUCH A FAG-HAG! (YOU'LL LOVE JIM, HE'LL MAKE A FUSS OVER YOU!)
YOU REMEMBER CLAIRE, DON'T YOU?
HELLO, DEAR! WHEN DID YOU GET SO *TALL?*
AND THIS IS JOE, AND JIM- THIS IS ME GRANDDAUGHTER- SHE JUST FLEW IN FROM AMERICA!
AND THIS IS FRANCIS!
HELLO!
NOW, YOU TWO SIT HERE TOGETHER AND TALK, AND I WILL GET SOME FOOD AND DRINKS!
GABRIELLE, YOU MUST COME AND MEET RONNIE, SHE'S A FILM STUDENT.

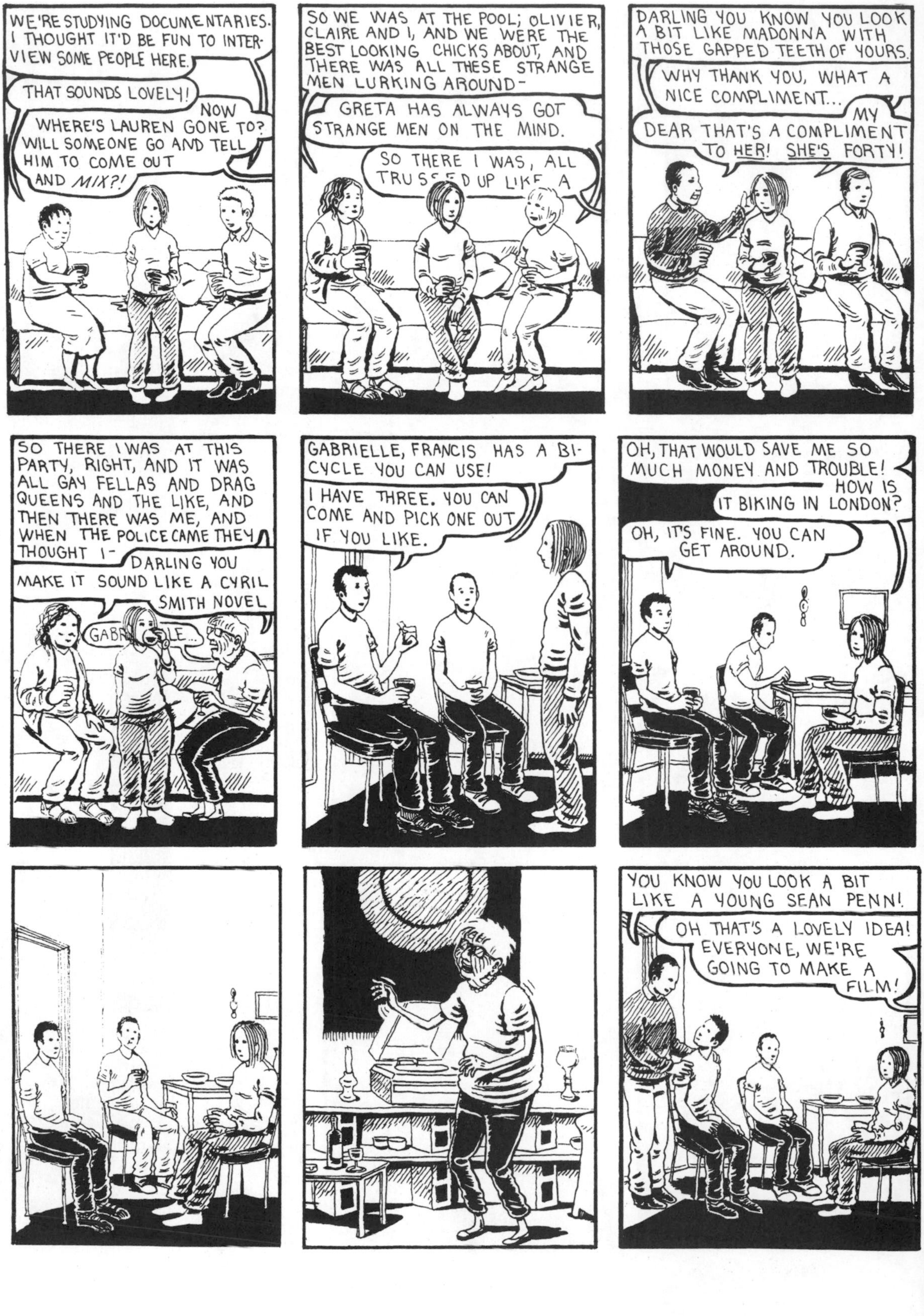
WE'RE STUDYING DOCUMENTARIES. I THOUGHT IT'D BE FUN TO INTERVIEW SOME PEOPLE HERE.
THAT SOUNDS LOVELY!
NOW WHERE'S LAUREN GONE TO? WILL SOMEONE GO AND TELL HIM TO COME OUT AND *MIX?!*
SO WE WAS AT THE POOL; OLIVIER, CLAIRE AND I, AND WE WERE THE BEST LOOKING CHICKS ABOUT, AND THERE WAS ALL THESE STRANGE MEN LURKING AROUND-
GRETA HAS ALWAYS GOT STRANGE MEN ON THE MIND.
SO THERE I WAS, ALL TRUS ED UP LIKE A
DARLING YOU KNOW YOU LOOK A BIT LIKE MADONNA WITH THOSE GAPPED TEETH OF YOURS.
WHY THANK YOU, WHAT A NICE COMPLIMENT...
MY DEAR THAT'S A COMPLIMENT TO HER! SHE'S FORTY!
SO THERE I WAS AT THIS PARTY, RIGHT, AND IT WAS ALL GAY FELLAS AND DRAG QUEENS AND THE LIKE, AND THEN THERE WAS ME, AND WHEN THE POLICE CAME THEY THOUGHT I-
DARLING YOU MAKE IT SOUND LIKE A CYRIL SMITH NOVEL
GABR LE...
GABRIELLE, FRANCIS HAS A BICYCLE YOU CAN USE!
I HAVE THREE. YOU CAN COME AND PICK ONE OUT IF YOU LIKE.
OH, THAT WOULD SAVE ME SO MUCH MONEY AND TROUBLE!
HOW IS IT BIKING IN LONDON?
OH, IT'S FINE. YOU CAN GET AROUND.
YOU KNOW YOU LOOK A BIT LIKE A YOUNG SEAN PENN!
OH THAT'S A LOVELY IDEA! EVERYONE, WE'RE GOING TO MAKE A FILM!

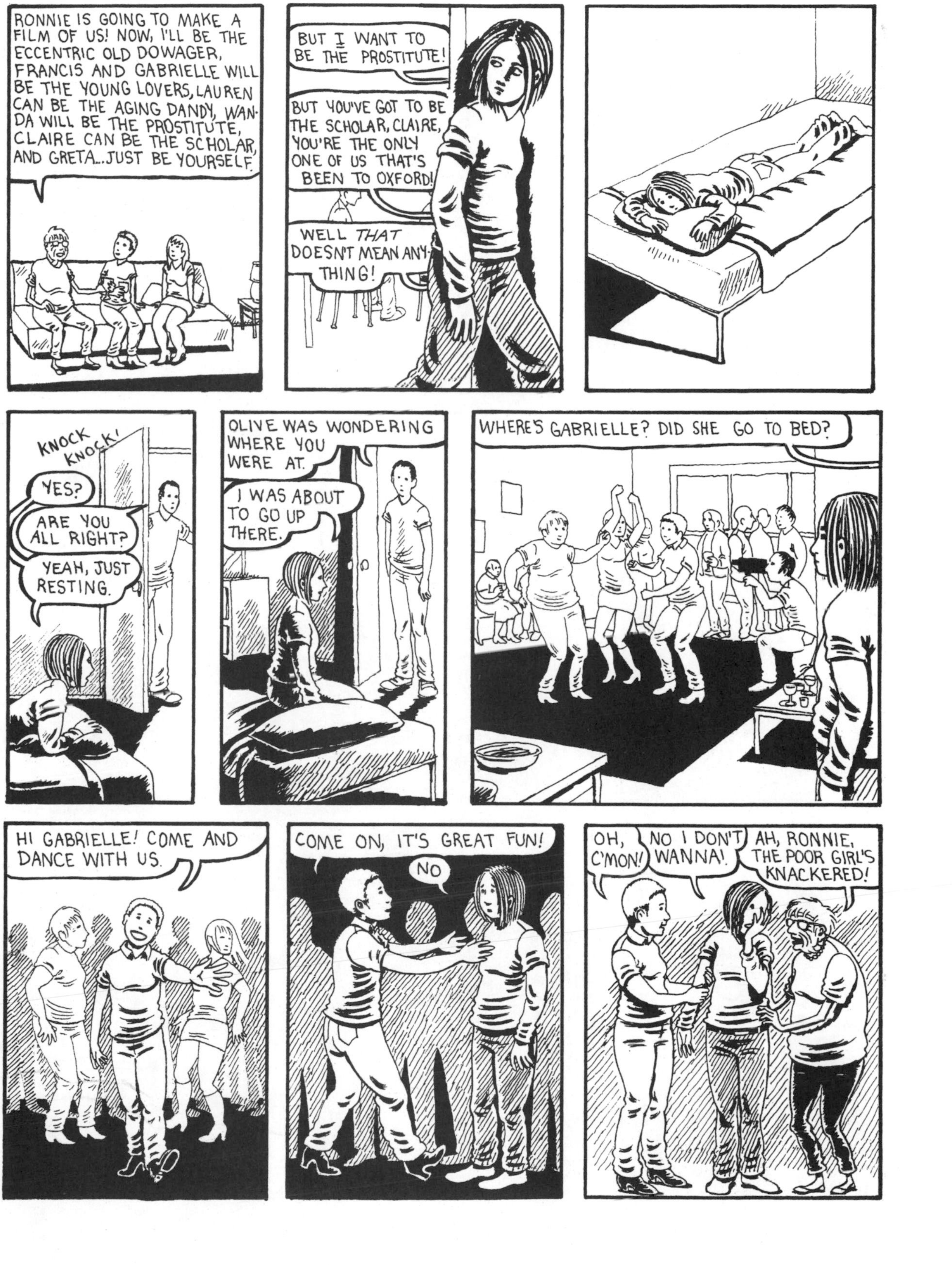
RONNIE IS GOING TO MAKE A FILM OF US! NOW, I'LL BE THE ECCENTRIC OLD DOWAGER, FRANCIS AND GABRIELLE WILL BE THE YOUNG LOVERS, LAUREN CAN BE THE AGING DANDY, WANDA WILL BE THE PROSTITUTE, CLAIRE CAN BE THE SCHOLAR, AND GRETA...JUST BE YOURSELF.
BUT I WANT TO BE THE PROSTITUTE!
BUT YOU'VE GOT TO BE THE SCHOLAR, CLAIRE, YOU'RE THE ONLY ONE OF US THAT'S BEEN TO OXFORD!
WELL *THAT* DOESN'T MEAN ANYTHING!
KNOCK KNOCK!
YES?
ARE YOU ALL RIGHT?
YEAH, JUST RESTING.
OLIVE WAS WONDERING WHERE YOU WERE AT.
I WAS ABOUT TO GO UP THERE.
WHERE'S GABRIELLE? DID SHE GO TO BED?
HI GABRIELLE! COME AND DANCE WITH US.
COME ON, IT'S GREAT FUN!
NO
OH, C'MON!
NO I DON'T WANNA!
AH, RONNIE, THE POOR GIRL'S KNACKERED!

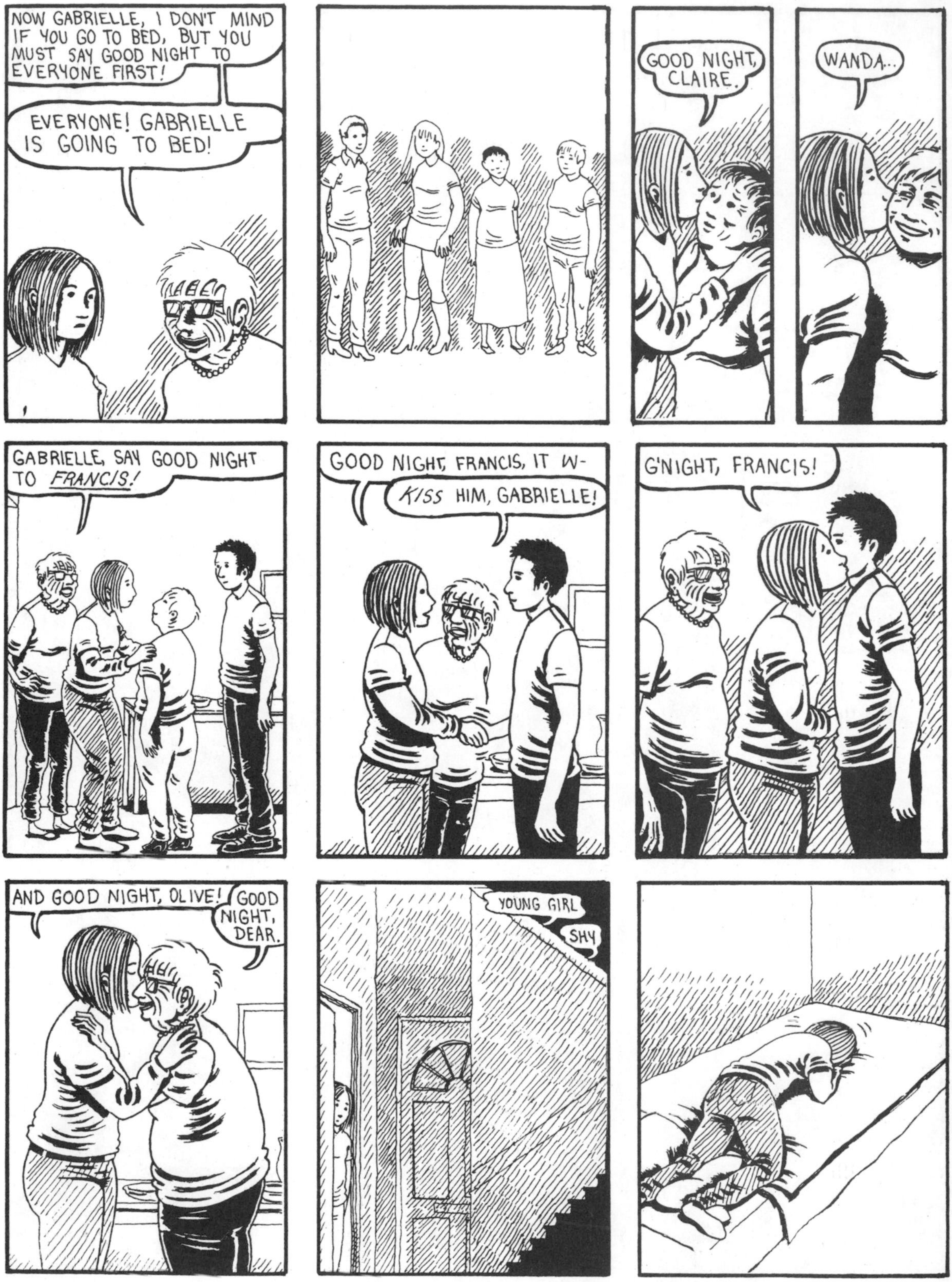
NOW GABRIELLE, I DON'T MIND IF YOU GO TO BED, BUT YOU MUST SAY GOOD NIGHT TO EVERYONE FIRST!
EVERYONE! GABRIELLE IS GOING TO BED!
GOOD NIGHT, CLAIRE.
WANDA...
GABRIELLE, SAY GOOD NIGHT TO FRANCIS!
GOOD NIGHT, FRANCIS, IT W-
KISS HIM, GABRIELLE!
G'NIGHT, FRANCIS!
AND GOOD NIGHT, OLIVE!
GOOD NIGHT, DEAR.
YOUNG GIRL
SHY

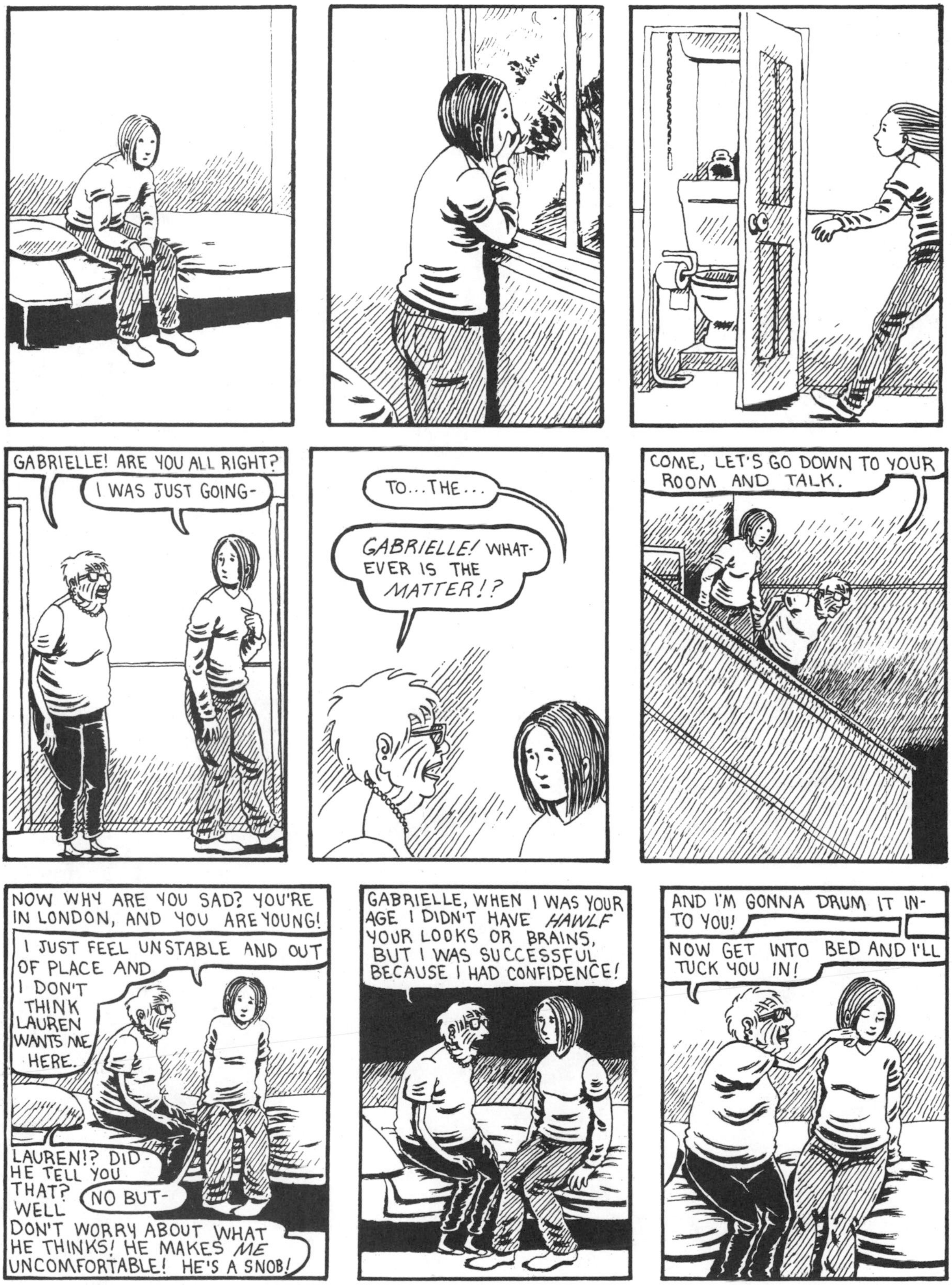
GABRIELLE! ARE YOU ALL RIGHT?
I WAS JUST GOING-
TO...THE...
GABRIELLE! WHATEVER IS THE MATTER!?
COME, LET'S GO DOWN TO YOUR ROOM AND TALK.
NOW WHY ARE YOU SAD? YOU'RE IN LONDON, AND YOU ARE YOUNG!
I JUST FEEL UNSTABLE AND OUT OF PLACE AND I DON'T THINK LAUREN WANTS ME HERE.
LAUREN!? DID HE TELL YOU THAT?
NO BUT-
WELL DON'T WORRY ABOUT WHAT HE THINKS! HE MAKES ME UNCOMFORTABLE! HE'S A SNOB!
GABRIELLE, WHEN I WAS YOUR AGE I DIDN'T HAVE HAWLF YOUR LOOKS OR BRAINS, BUT I WAS SUCCESSFUL BECAUSE I HAD CONFIDENCE!
AND I'M GONNA DRUM IT INTO YOU!
NOW GET INTO BED AND I'LL TUCK YOU IN!

RIGHT...YOU DON'T SLEEP IN YOUR TROUSERS, DO YOU?

DO YOU KNOW I USED TO TUCK YOU AND YOUR BROTHER INTO THIS VERY BED WHEN YOU WERE BABIES.

YOU KNOW YOU REMIND ME SO MUCH OF MYSELF WHEN I WAS YOUR AGE.

NOW WHY ARE YOU CRYING AGAIN?

OH, YOU'RE DAMAGED! I NEGLECTED YOUR FATHER SO HE NEGLECTED YOU AND NOW YOUR RUINED BECAUSE OF ME!

AND I'M *NOT* GOING TO SAY I DIDN'T KNOW ANY BETTER.

BUT THEN, I TRIED HARD TO GET YOUR MOTHER TO STAY HERE IN LONDON WITH ME...BUT THERE WAS NO CONVINCING HER.

OH, WHAT'S THE USE OF BLAMING ANYONE? THE POINT IS THAT YOU'RE DAMAGED AND IT'S ALL MY FAULT!

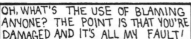

NO GRANDMA! I'M ALL RIGHT! REALLY! I JUST GOT A LITTLE UPSET IS ALL! I'LL BE OKAY IN THE MORNING!

SOB!!!

DO YOU...CARE ABOUT ANYONE? I MEAN, DO YOU LOVE ANYBODY...BECAUSE I THINK IT'S A SIGN OF HEALING WHEN YOU CAN CARE ABOUT SOMEONE, ANYONE BESIDES YOURSELF. AS FOR ME, I'VE HAD PLENTY OF FRIENDS, LOVERS AND HUSBANDS, AND THEY'VE GIVEN ME A LOT OF LOVE, BUT I NEVER CARED WHETHER THEY CAME OR WENT!

I, UH... I GUESS IT'S BECAUSE ME OWN PARENTS FARMED ME OFF TO MY GRANDPARENTS. I WAS ALWAYS FOND OF ME GRANDMUM AND GRANDDAD, BUT I COULD NEVER LOVE THEM, NOR COULD I LOVE MY REAL PARENTS, THOUGH I DO HAVE FOND MEMORIES OF THEM.

I REMEMBER GOING TO VISIT ME MOTHER ONCE, AND SHE WANTED TO MAKE ME A DRESS, SO SHE GOT OUT THE MATERIAL, MEASURED IT OUT, AND THEN PUT IT AWAY FOR LATER, BUT I SAID, 'NO, MUM, I WANT YOU TO MAKE IT NOW!'

AND SO SHE TOOK IT OUT, AND MADE IT FOR ME RIGHT THEN.

I WAS ALWAYS GRATEFUL TO HER FOR THAT, BUT I COULD NEVER LOVE HER.

I'M ONLY JUST BEGINNING TO LEARN HOW TO CARE, HOW TO GIVE. CAN YOU IMAGINE? EIGHTY-TWO YEARS OLD AND ONLY BEGINNING TO LEARN TO CARE.

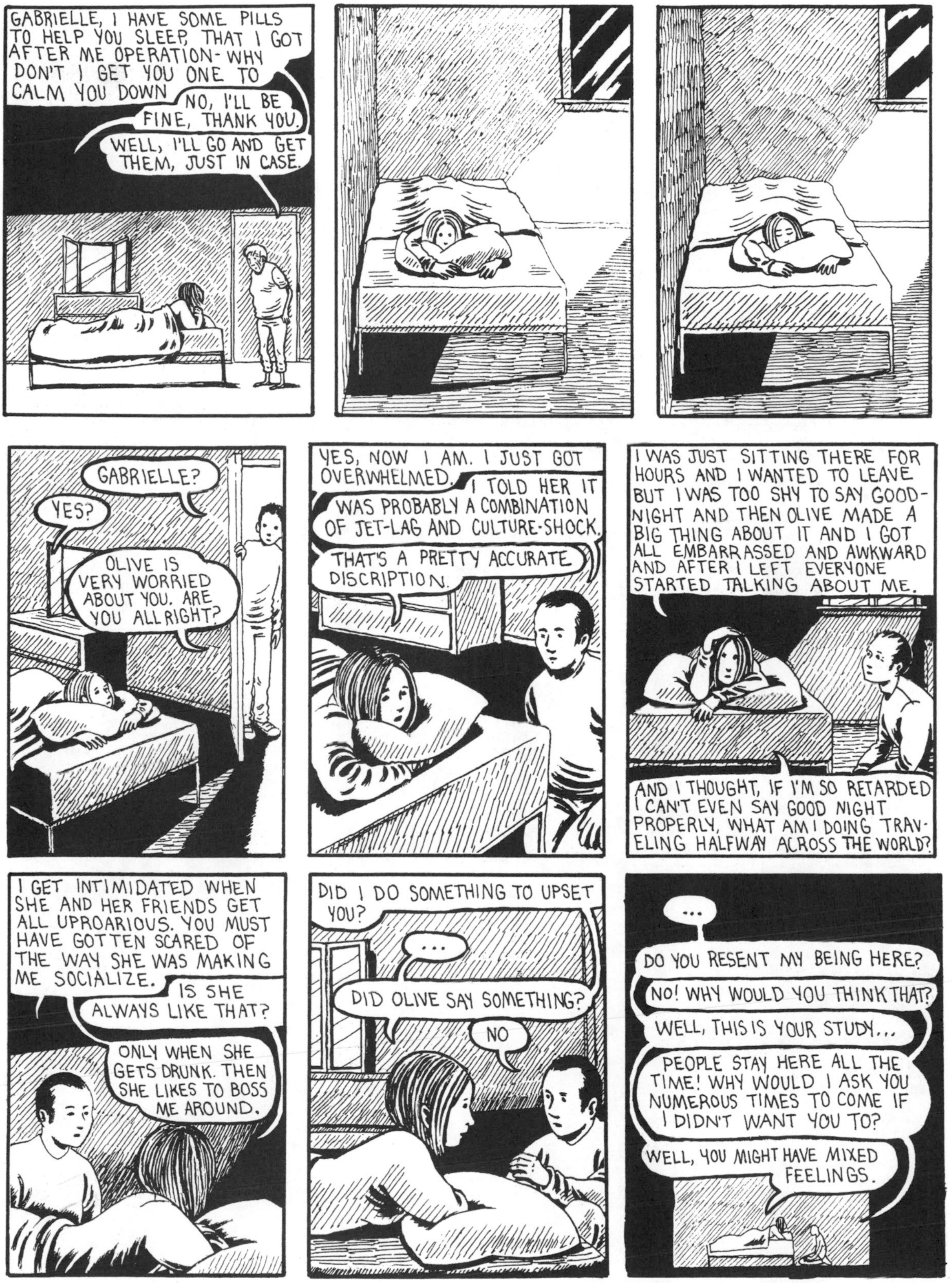
GABRIELLE, I HAVE SOME PILLS TO HELP YOU SLEEP, THAT I GOT AFTER ME OPERATION- WHY DON'T I GET YOU ONE TO CALM YOU DOWN
NO, I'LL BE FINE, THANK YOU.
WELL, I'LL GO AND GET THEM, JUST IN CASE.
GABRIELLE?
YES?
OLIVE IS VERY WORRIED ABOUT YOU. ARE YOU ALL RIGHT?
YES, NOW I AM. I JUST GOT OVERWHELMED.
I TOLD HER IT WAS PROBABLY A COMBINATION OF JET-LAG AND CULTURE-SHOCK.
THAT'S A PRETTY ACCURATE DISCRIPTION.
I WAS JUST SITTING THERE FOR HOURS AND I WANTED TO LEAVE BUT I WAS TOO SHY TO SAY GOOD-NIGHT AND THEN OLIVE MADE A BIG THING ABOUT IT AND I GOT ALL EMBARRASSED AND AWKWARD AND AFTER I LEFT EVERYONE STARTED TALKING ABOUT ME.
AND I THOUGHT, IF I'M SO RETARDED I CAN'T EVEN SAY GOOD NIGHT PROPERLY, WHAT AM I DOING TRAVELING HALFWAY ACROSS THE WORLD?
I GET INTIMIDATED WHEN SHE AND HER FRIENDS GET ALL UPROARIOUS. YOU MUST HAVE GOTTEN SCARED OF THE WAY SHE WAS MAKING ME SOCIALIZE.
IS SHE ALWAYS LIKE THAT?
ONLY WHEN SHE GETS DRUNK. THEN SHE LIKES TO BOSS ME AROUND.
DID I DO SOMETHING TO UPSET YOU?
...
DID OLIVE SAY SOMETHING?
NO
...
DO YOU RESENT MY BEING HERE?
NO! WHY WOULD YOU THINK THAT?
WELL, THIS IS YOUR STUDY...
PEOPLE STAY HERE ALL THE TIME! WHY WOULD I ASK YOU NUMEROUS TIMES TO COME IF I DIDN'T WANT YOU TO?
WELL, YOU MIGHT HAVE MIXED FEELINGS.

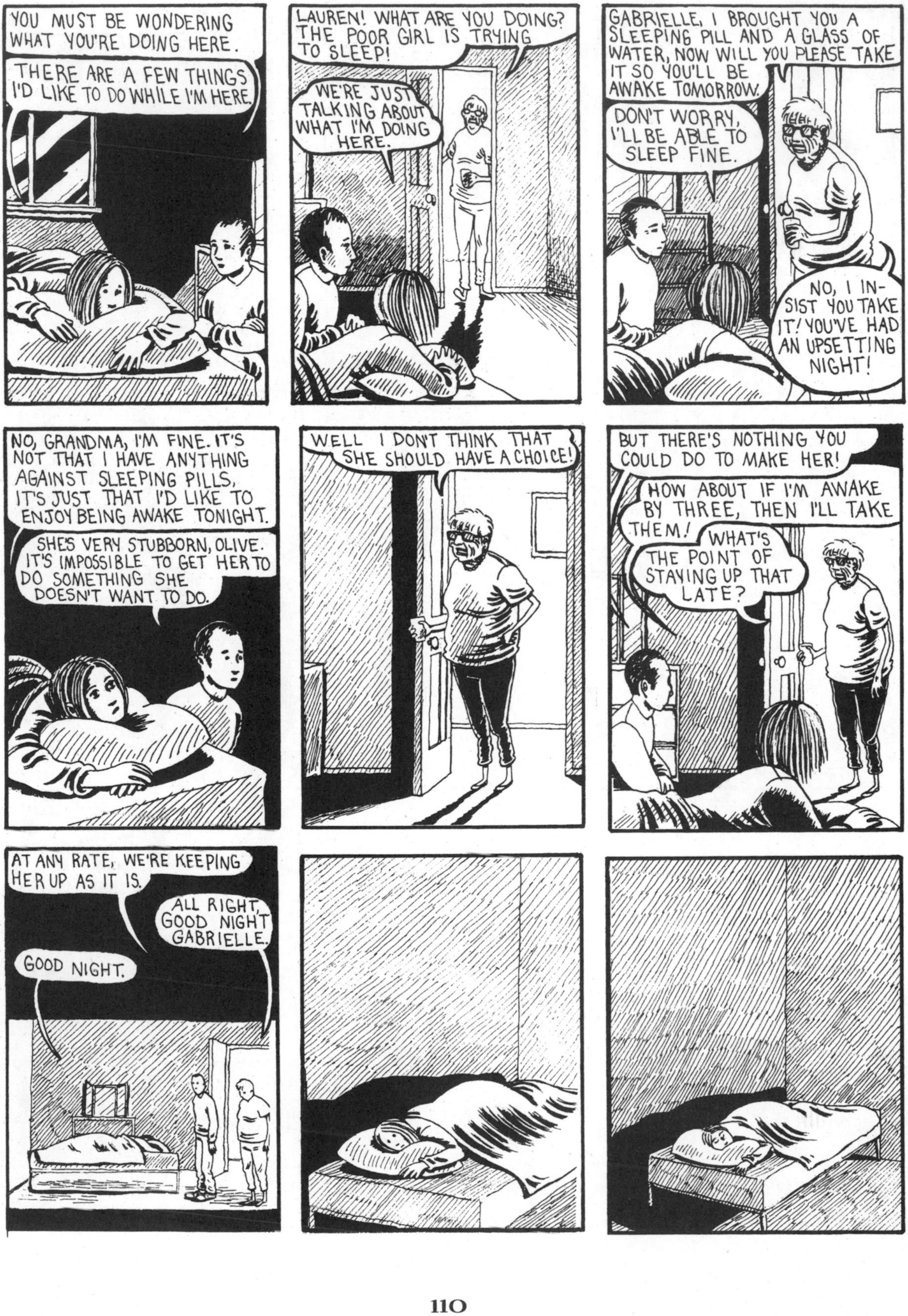
YOU MUST BE WONDERING WHAT YOU'RE DOING HERE.
THERE ARE A FEW THINGS I'D LIKE TO DO WHILE I'M HERE.
LAUREN! WHAT ARE YOU DOING? THE POOR GIRL IS TRYING TO SLEEP!
WE'RE JUST TALKING ABOUT WHAT I'M DOING HERE.
GABRIELLE, I BROUGHT YOU A SLEEPING PILL AND A GLASS OF WATER, NOW WILL YOU PLEASE TAKE IT SO YOU'LL BE AWAKE TOMORROW.
DON'T WORRY, I'LL BE ABLE TO SLEEP FINE.
NO, I INSIST YOU TAKE IT! YOU'VE HAD AN UPSETTING NIGHT!
NO, GRANDMA, I'M FINE. IT'S NOT THAT I HAVE ANYTHING AGAINST SLEEPING PILLS, IT'S JUST THAT I'D LIKE TO ENJOY BEING AWAKE TONIGHT.
SHE'S VERY STUBBORN, OLIVE. IT'S IMPOSSIBLE TO GET HER TO DO SOMETHING SHE DOESN'T WANT TO DO.
WELL I DON'T THINK THAT SHE SHOULD HAVE A CHOICE!
BUT THERE'S NOTHING YOU COULD DO TO MAKE HER!
HOW ABOUT IF I'M AWAKE BY THREE, THEN I'LL TAKE THEM!
WHAT'S THE POINT OF STAYING UP THAT LATE?
AT ANY RATE, WE'RE KEEPING HER UP AS IT IS.
ALL RIGHT, GOOD NIGHT GABRIELLE.
GOOD NIGHT.

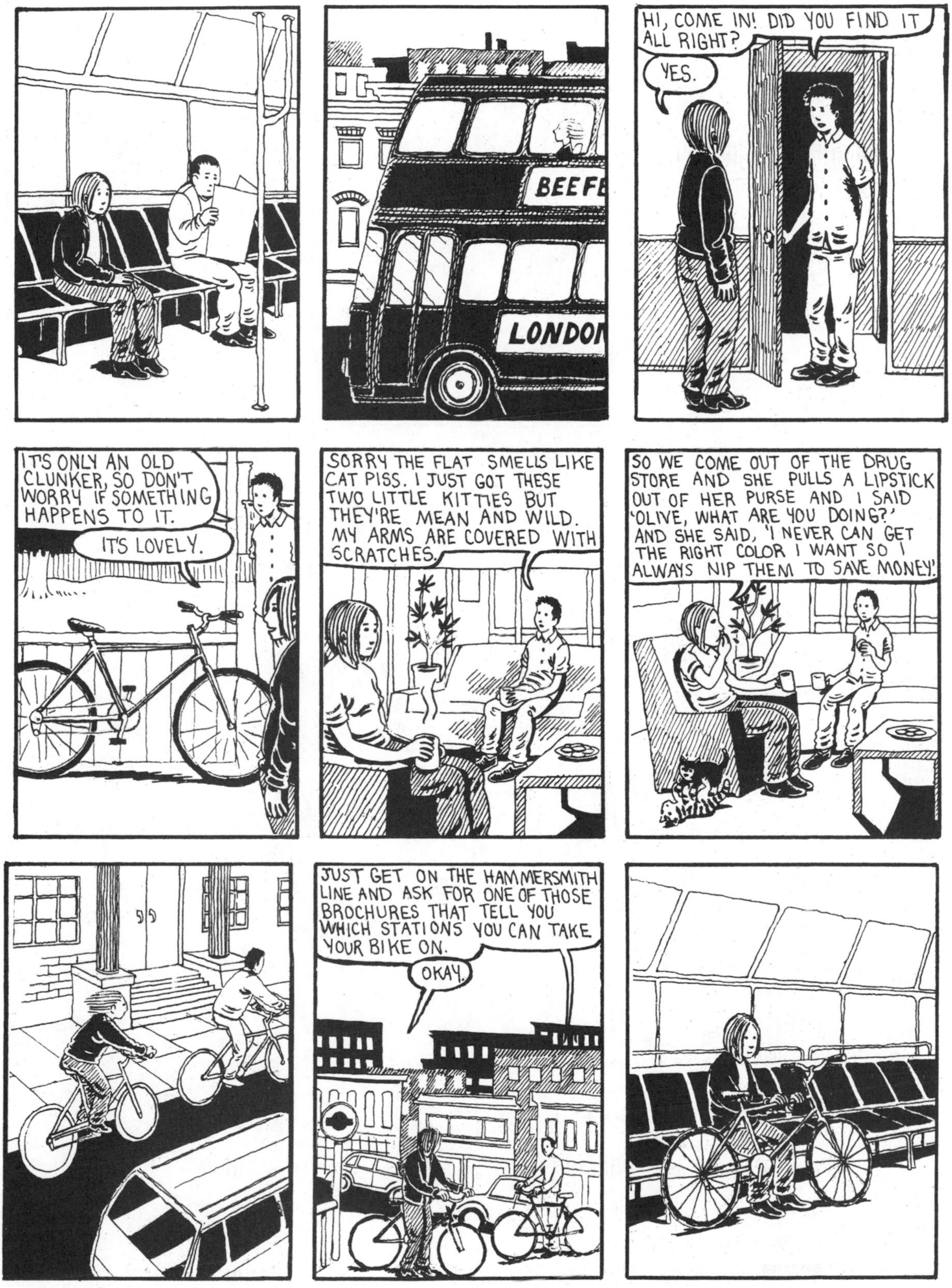
BEEFE
LONDON
HI, COME IN! DID YOU FIND IT ALL RIGHT?
YES.
IT'S ONLY AN OLD CLUNKER, SO DON'T WORRY IF SOMETHING HAPPENS TO IT.
IT'S LOVELY.
SORRY THE FLAT SMELLS LIKE CAT PISS. I JUST GOT THESE TWO LITTLE KITTIES BUT THEY'RE MEAN AND WILD. MY ARMS ARE COVERED WITH SCRATCHES.
SO WE COME OUT OF THE DRUG STORE AND SHE PULLS A LIPSTICK OUT OF HER PURSE AND I SAID 'OLIVE, WHAT ARE YOU DOING?' AND SHE SAID, 'I NEVER CAN GET THE RIGHT COLOR I WANT SO I ALWAYS NIP THEM TO SAVE MONEY.'
JUST GET ON THE HAMMERSMITH LINE AND ASK FOR ONE OF THOSE BROCHURES THAT TELL YOU WHICH STATIONS YOU CAN TAKE YOUR BIKE ON.
OKAY.

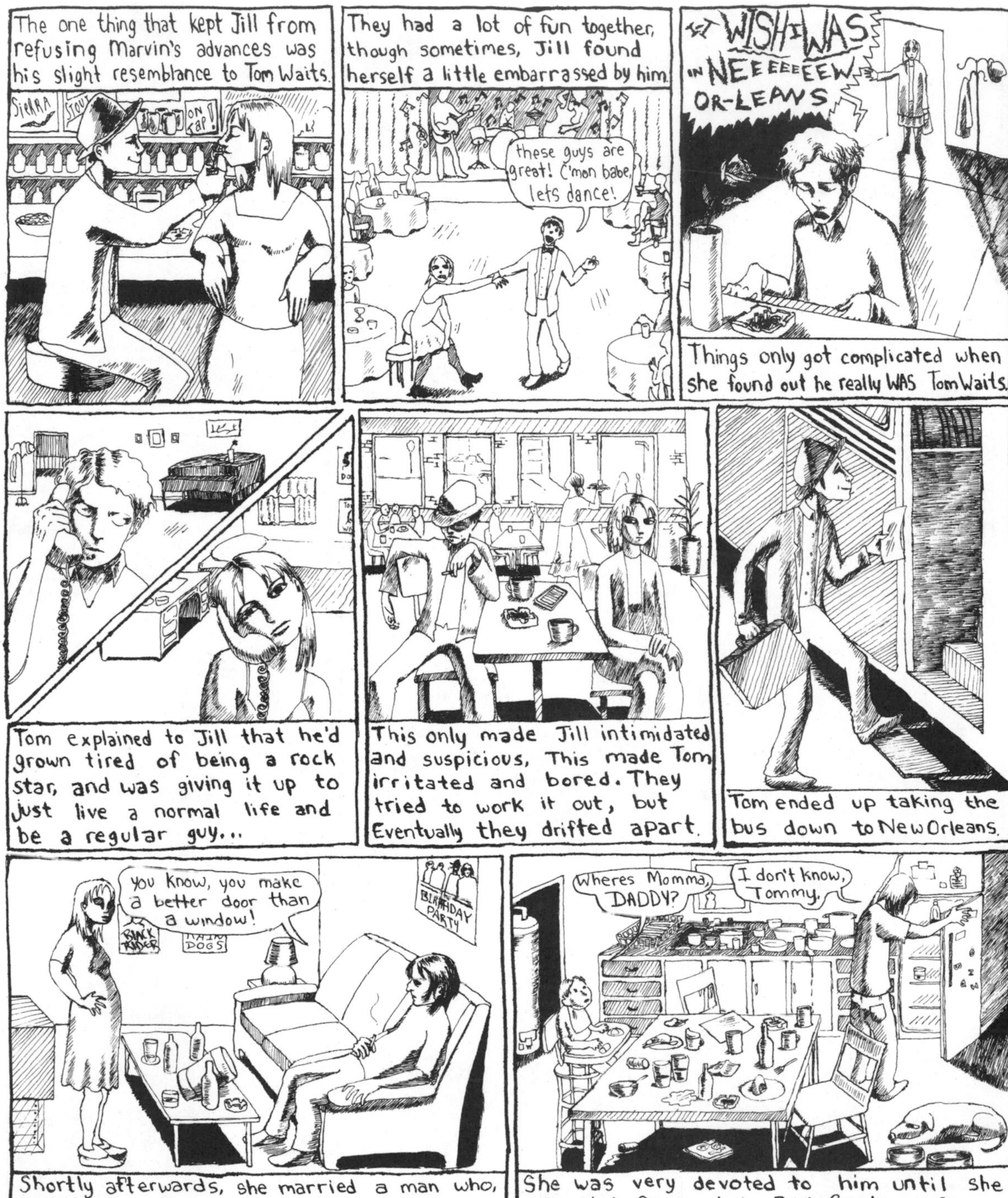
The one thing that kept Jill from refusing Marvin's advances was his slight resemblance to Tom Waits.
SIERRA
STOUT
ON TAP!
They had a lot of fun together, though sometimes, Jill found herself a little embarrassed by him.
these guys are great! C'mon babe, lets dance!
I WISH I WAS IN NEEEEEEEW OR-LEANS
Things only got complicated when she found out he really WAS Tom Waits.
Tom explained to Jill that he'd grown tired of being a rock star, and was giving it up to just live a normal life and be a regular guy...
This only made Jill intimidated and suspicious, This made Tom irritated and bored. They tried to work it out, but Eventually they drifted apart.
Tom ended up taking the bus down to New Orleans.
you know, you make a better door than a window!
BLACK RIDER
RAIN DOGS
BIRTHDAY PARTY
Shortly afterwards, she married a man who, except for his paunch, the resigned wrinkles and the Iroquois nose, bore an uncanny likeness to Nick Cave.
Wheres Momma, DADDY?
I don't know, Tommy.
She was very devoted to him until she saw Nick Cave and the Bad Seeds perform at Lollapalooza, after which she grew disgusted with her husband, and left him.

ANATOMY OF THE HEART

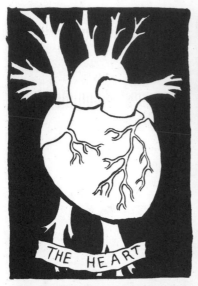

THE HEART

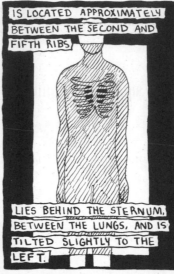

IS LOCATED APPROXIMATELY BETWEEN THE SECOND AND FIFTH RIBS.

LIES BEHIND THE STERNUM, BETWEEN THE LUNGS, AND IS TILTED SLIGHTLY TO THE LEFT.

THE HEART RECEIVES DIOXY-GENATED BLOOD FROM THE BODY THROUGH THE SUPERIOR AND IN-FERIOR VENA CAVA, LOCATED AT THE TOP AND BOTTEM OF THE HEART, RESPECTIVELY.

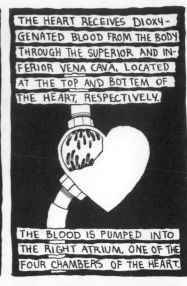

THE BLOOD IS PUMPED INTO THE RIGHT ATRIUM, ONE OF THE FOUR CHAMBERS OF THE HEART.

THE ATRIUM FILLS WITH BLOOD, EXERTING PRESSURE ON THE ATRIOVENTRICULAR VALVES, WHICH SQUEEZES THE BLOOD INTO THE RIGHT VENTRICLE. ANOTHER OF THE FOUR CHAMBERS OF THE HEART.

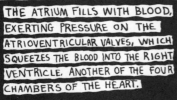

THE AV VALVES SHUT TIGHT BE-HIND IT, EMITTING A SOUND THAT IS OFTEN DESCRIBED AS A "LUB".

THE RIGHT VENTRICLE FILLS WITH BLOOD, OPENING THE SEMILUNAR VALVES, AND FORCES IT INTO THE PULMONARY ARTERIES, LOCATED BETWEEN THE RIGHT AND LEFT ATRIUM.

THE SEMILUNAR VALVES SLAM BEHIND IT, MAKING A NOISE WHICH HAS BEEN SAID TO SOUND LIKE A "DUB".

THE BLOOD SQUIRTS FROM THE PULMONARY ARTERIES TO THE LUNGS.

IN THE LUNGS, CARBON-DIOXIDE IS EXCHANGED FOR OXYGEN.

MEANWHILE, BLOOD POURS FROM THE LUNG INTO THE LEFT ATRIUM, VIA THE PULMONARY VEINS, JUST TO THE LEFT OF THE LEFT ATRIUM.

THE LEFT ATRIUM FILLS, SENDS THE BLOOD THROUGH THE AV VALVES, (MAKING THAT "LUB" SOUND) AND INTO THE LEFT VENTRICLE.

FROM THE LEFT VENTRICLE, THE BLOOD SPURTS THROUGH THE AORTAL SEMILUNAR VALVE, (MAK-THE "DUB" SOUND) AND INTO THE AORTA.

THE AORTA IS A BIG, FAT ART-ERY AT THE TOP OF THE HEART.

FROM THE AORTA, BLOOD IS DISTRIBUTED TO OTHER ART-ERIES.

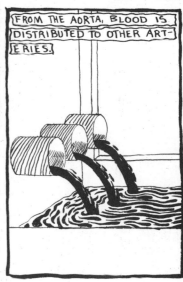

THE ARTERIES DIVIDE INTO SMALLER VESSELS CALLED ARTERIOLES, WHICH THEN ENTER THE ORGANS AND TISSUES WHERE THEY FURTHER DIVIDE INTO CAPILLARIES.

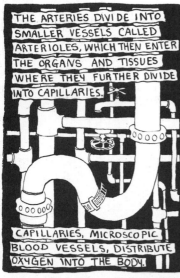

CAPILLARIES, MICROSCOPIC BLOOD VESSELS, DISTRIBUTE OXYGEN INTO THE BODY.

THE CAPILLARIES GATHER TO FORM VENULES (ALSO VESSELS) WHICH MERGE TO FORM VEINS.

THE VEINS ARE WHAT CARRY BLOOD BACK TO THE HEART.

THE BLOOD ENTERS THE RIGHT ATRIUM, THROUGH THE VENA-CAVA, AND THE WHOLE PROCESS BEGINS AGAIN.

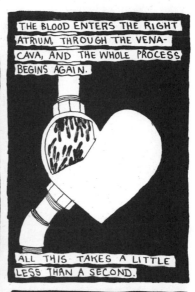

ALL THIS TAKES A LITTLE LESS THAN A SECOND.

I KNOW WHAT YOU'RE THINKING; ENDLESSLY FASCINATING, BUT STILL IT LEAVES SOME HOLES IN OUR UNDERSTANDING OF THE HUMAN HEART.

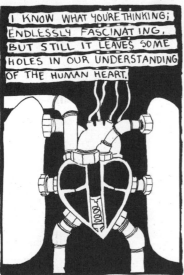

LIKE, FOR EXAMPLE, HOW DOES IT SWELL WITH JOY, OR ACHE WITH SADNESS, AND WHAT IS THE CURE FOR A BROKEN HEART?

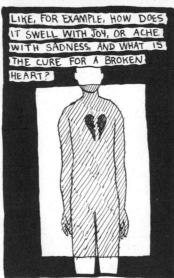

I DON'T KNOW EITHER. LET'S TRY AND FIND SOMEBODY WHO DOES.

HOSPITAL ENTRANCE

SOMEBODY IN HERE MUST KNOW.

MAYBE WE'LL FIND WHAT WE'RE LOOKING FOR IN HERE.

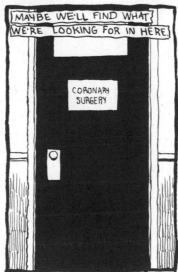

CORONARY SURGERY

EXCUSE ME, DO YOU KNOW ANY-THING ABOUT THE HUMAN HEART? YES, BUT I'M VERY BUSY NOW.

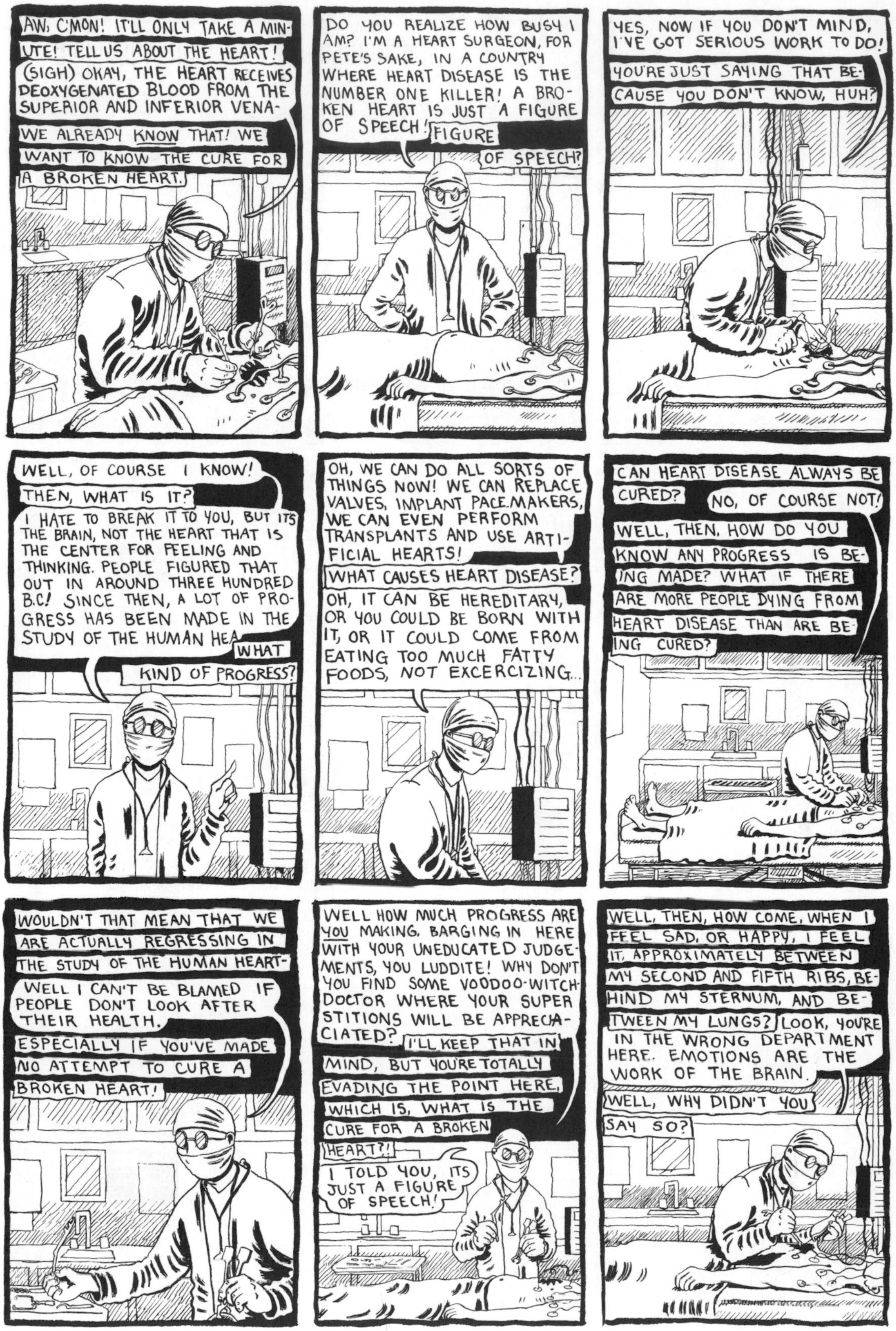
AW, C'MON! IT'LL ONLY TAKE A MINUTE! TELL US ABOUT THE HEART!
(SIGH) OKAY, THE HEART RECEIVES DEOXYGENATED BLOOD FROM THE SUPERIOR AND INFERIOR VENA-
WE ALREADY KNOW THAT! WE WANT TO KNOW THE CURE FOR A BROKEN HEART.
DO YOU REALIZE HOW BUSY I AM? I'M A HEART SURGEON, FOR PETE'S SAKE, IN A COUNTRY WHERE HEART DISEASE IS THE NUMBER ONE KILLER! A BROKEN HEART IS JUST A FIGURE OF SPEECH!
FIGURE OF SPEECH?
YES, NOW IF YOU DON'T MIND, I'VE GOT SERIOUS WORK TO DO!
YOU'RE JUST SAYING THAT BECAUSE YOU DON'T KNOW, HUH?
WELL, OF COURSE I KNOW!
THEN, WHAT IS IT?
I HATE TO BREAK IT TO YOU, BUT ITS THE BRAIN, NOT THE HEART THAT IS THE CENTER FOR FEELING AND THINKING. PEOPLE FIGURED THAT OUT IN AROUND THREE HUNDRED B.C! SINCE THEN, A LOT OF PROGRESS HAS BEEN MADE IN THE STUDY OF THE HUMAN HEA
WHAT KIND OF PROGRESS?
OH, WE CAN DO ALL SORTS OF THINGS NOW! WE CAN REPLACE VALVES, IMPLANT PACEMAKERS, WE CAN EVEN PERFORM TRANSPLANTS AND USE ARTIFICIAL HEARTS!
WHAT CAUSES HEART DISEASE?
OH, IT CAN BE HEREDITARY, OR YOU COULD BE BORN WITH IT, OR IT COULD COME FROM EATING TOO MUCH FATTY FOODS, NOT EXCERCIZING...
CAN HEART DISEASE ALWAYS BE CURED?
NO, OF COURSE NOT!
WELL, THEN, HOW DO YOU KNOW ANY PROGRESS IS BEING MADE? WHAT IF THERE ARE MORE PEOPLE DYING FROM HEART DISEASE THAN ARE BEING CURED?
WOULDN'T THAT MEAN THAT WE ARE ACTUALLY REGRESSING IN THE STUDY OF THE HUMAN HEART-
WELL I CAN'T BE BLAMED IF PEOPLE DON'T LOOK AFTER THEIR HEALTH.
ESPECIALLY IF YOU'VE MADE NO ATTEMPT TO CURE A BROKEN HEART!
WELL HOW MUCH PROGRESS ARE YOU MAKING, BARGING IN HERE WITH YOUR UNEDUCATED JUDGEMENTS, YOU LUDDITE! WHY DON'T YOU FIND SOME VOODOO-WITCH-DOCTOR WHERE YOUR SUPERSTITIONS WILL BE APPRECACIATED?
I'LL KEEP THAT IN MIND, BUT YOU'RE TOTALLY EVADING THE POINT HERE, WHICH IS, WHAT IS THE CURE FOR A BROKEN HEART?!
I TOLD YOU, ITS JUST A FIGURE OF SPEECH!
WELL, THEN, HOW COME, WHEN I FEEL SAD, OR HAPPY, I FEEL IT, APPROXIMATELY BETWEEN MY SECOND AND FIFTH RIBS, BEHIND MY STERNUM, AND BETWEEN MY LUNGS?
LOOK, YOU'RE IN THE WRONG DEPARTMENT HERE. EMOTIONS ARE THE WORK OF THE BRAIN.
WELL, WHY DIDN'T YOU SAY SO?

WHAT A GRUMP.

NOW LET'S SEE, THE BRAIN...

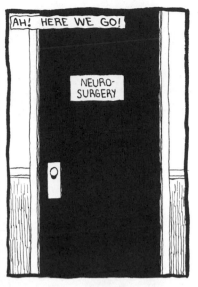

AH! HERE WE GO!

NEURO-SURGERY

UM, EXCUSE ME?

OH HELLO! HOW ARE YOU? DON'T BE SHY, COME ON IN! WHAT CAN I DO FOR YOU?

ER, THANK YOU. WE WERE JUST TALKING TO THE HEART GUY DOWNSTAIRS.

HE'S A CRANKY ONE, ISN'T HE?

UH, YES. WHAT WE WANTED TO ASK YOU WAS—

GOSHDARNIT! HEY, YOU WOULDN'T HAVE A SCALPEL ON YOU, WOULD YOU?

NO

WELL, NO MATTER, THIS THINGY WILL DO...SO YOU WERE JUST TALKING TO. DR. STONEHART?

YES, HE SAID YOU MIGHT KNOW SOMETHING ABOUT THE CURE FOR A BROKEN HEART?

DO YOU THINK I'D BE IN HERE PERFORMING BRAIN SURGERY ON LOW INCOME SENIOR CITIZENS IF I KNEW THAT? HECK NO! I'D BE TOO BUSY TRAVELLING THE WORLD, GIVING LECTURES, WRITING BOOKS, ACCEPTING AWARDS..

SIGH.

AH WELL, WE'VE ALL GOTTA PAY OUR DUES.

BUT SURELY YOU MUST KNOW WHAT MAKES THE HEART FEEL EMOTIONS, DON'T YOU? WHY, SURE I DO! HEY WATCH THIS. GEORGE, COUNT TO TEN!

ONE, TWO, THREE, FOURO, BLEH, NOI, BRU, FRRRR

HA-HA! YOU SEE, I WAS MANIPULATING THE BROCA'S AREA, IN HIS FRONTAL LOBE, WHICH CONTROLS HIS SPEECH...NOW THATS WHAT I CALL MESSING WITH HIS MIND!

SO WHAT IS IT?

WHAT IS WHAT?

WHAT MAKES THE HEART FEEL E-MOTIONS?

HOW DO I KNOW? DO I LOOK LIKE A HEART SURGEON?

BUT YOU SAID YOU DID!

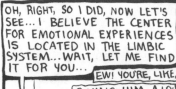

OH, RIGHT, SO I DID, NOW LET'S SEE... I BELIEVE THE CENTER FOR EMOTIONAL EXPERIENCES IS LOCATED IN THE LIMBIC SYSTEM... WAIT, LET ME FIND IT FOR YOU...

EW! YOU'RE, LIKE, GIVING HIM A LO-BOTOMY!

OH, THIS? DON'T WORRY! IT'S ALL PART OF THE NINETY PER-CENT HE DOES-N'T USE!

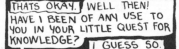

DON'T YOU THINK IT BOTHERS HIM, WHAT YOU'RE DOING TO HIS BRAIN?

HE DOESN'T KNOW! I'VE JUST DISLOCATED HIS VESTIBULOCHLEAR SYSTEM, SO HE CAN'T HEAR A THING!

NOW, THE LIMBIC SYSTEM...

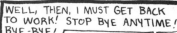

SO, AH, AS I WAS SAYING; THE LIMBIC SYSTEM, IN CONJUNCTION WITH THE HYPOTHALAMUS, COM-MUNICATES WITH THE HEART VIA THE PARASYMPATHETIC NER-VOUS SYSTEM, WHICH SUCRETES NEUROTRANSMITTERS, SUCH AS ACETYLCHOLINE, CAUSING CHANGES IN THE RATE OF THE HEARTBEAT. SO PERHAPS, IN TIMES OF EXTREME EMOTIONAL ACTIVITY, THE HEARTRATE FLUC-TUATES A GREAT DEAL, CAUS-ING A FEELING OF SORENESS IN THE CARDIAC MUSCLE.

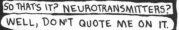

SO THAT'S IT? NEUROTRANSMITTERS?

WELL, DON'T QUOTE ME ON IT.

SO HOW DO WE MAKE IT STOP?

I COULD ALWAYS REMOVE YOUR LIMBIC SYSTEM. OF COURSE, YOU MIGHT HAVE TROUBLE REMEMBERING THINGS, AND YOU PROBABLY WON'T FEEL MUCH OF ANY THING. AND YOU MIGHT MAKE BORING COMPANY.

THATS OKAY.

WELL THEN! HAVE I BEEN OF ANY USE TO YOU IN YOUR LITTLE QUEST FOR KNOWLEDGE?

I GUESS SO.

DO YOU HAVE ANY FURTHER QUESTIONS?

NOT THAT I CAN THINK OF...

WELL, THEN, I MUST GET BACK TO WORK! STOP BYE ANYTIME! BYE-BYE!

BYE-BYE.

SAY BYE-BYE, GEORGE!

gur NRC

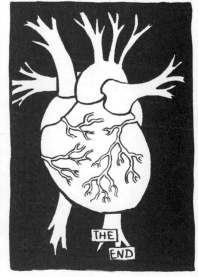

I WONDER WHERE WE COULD FIND A VOO-DOO-WITCH-DOC-TOR'S OFFICE.

THE END

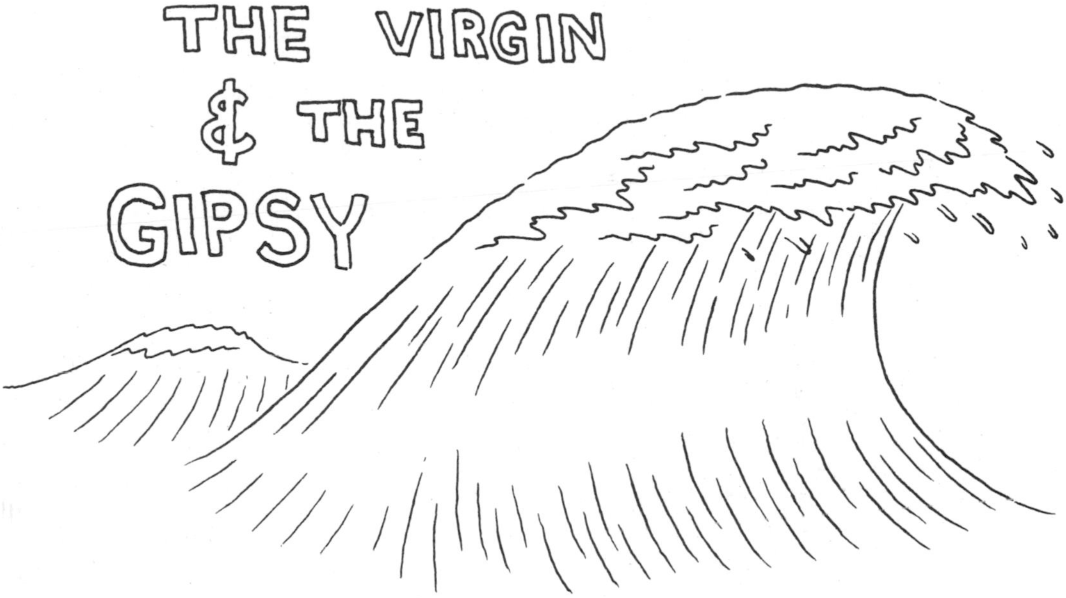
THE VIRGIN
& THE
GIPSY

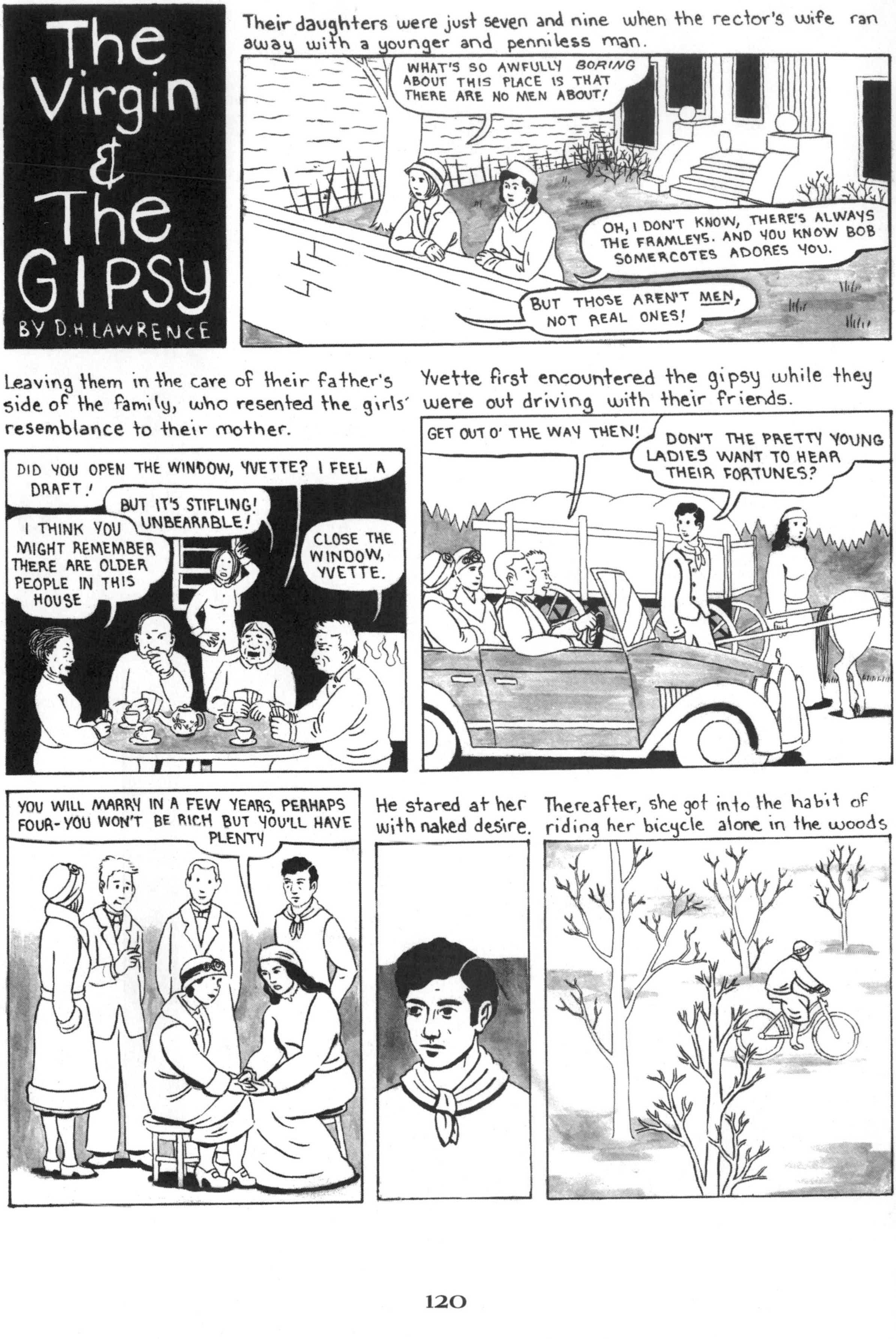
The Virgin & The Gipsy
BY D.H. LAWRENCE
Their daughters were just seven and nine when the rector's wife ran away with a younger and penniless man.
WHAT'S SO AWFULLY BORING ABOUT THIS PLACE IS THAT THERE ARE NO MEN ABOUT!
OH, I DON'T KNOW, THERE'S ALWAYS THE FRAMLEYS. AND YOU KNOW BOB SOMERCOTES ADORES YOU.
BUT THOSE AREN'T MEN, NOT REAL ONES!
Leaving them in the care of their father's side of the family, who resented the girls' resemblance to their mother.
DID YOU OPEN THE WINDOW, YVETTE? I FEEL A DRAFT!
BUT IT'S STIFLING! UNBEARABLE!
I THINK YOU MIGHT REMEMBER THERE ARE OLDER PEOPLE IN THIS HOUSE
CLOSE THE WINDOW, YVETTE.
Yvette first encountered the gipsy while they were out driving with their friends.
GET OUT O' THE WAY THEN!
DON'T THE PRETTY YOUNG LADIES WANT TO HEAR THEIR FORTUNES?
YOU WILL MARRY IN A FEW YEARS, PERHAPS FOUR- YOU WON'T BE RICH BUT YOU'LL HAVE PLENTY
He stared at her with naked desire.
Thereafter, she got into the habit of riding her bicycle alone in the woods

It was a chilly day in February when she came across the gipsy's camp.

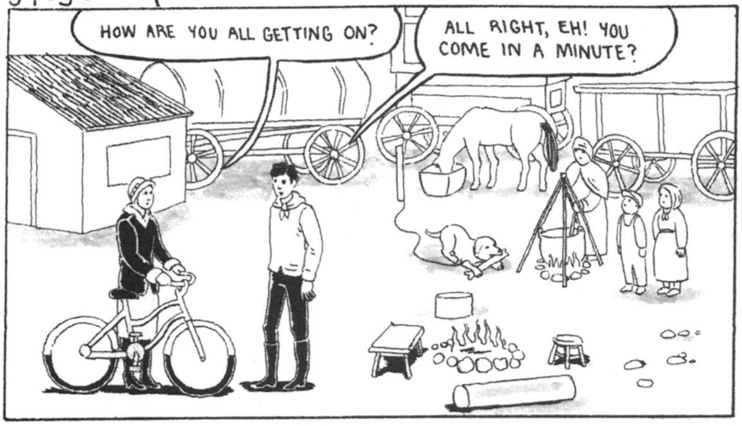
HOW ARE YOU ALL GETTING ON?
ALL RIGHT, EH! YOU COME IN A MINUTE?

They were interrupted by the sound of a motor-car

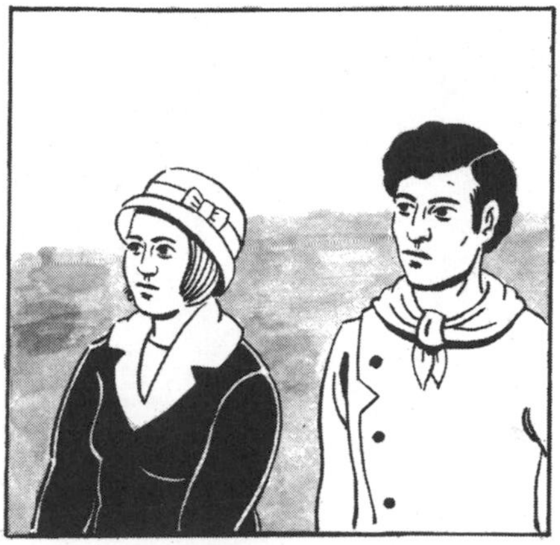

It was a wealthy couple driving in an open car, stopping to warm themselves.

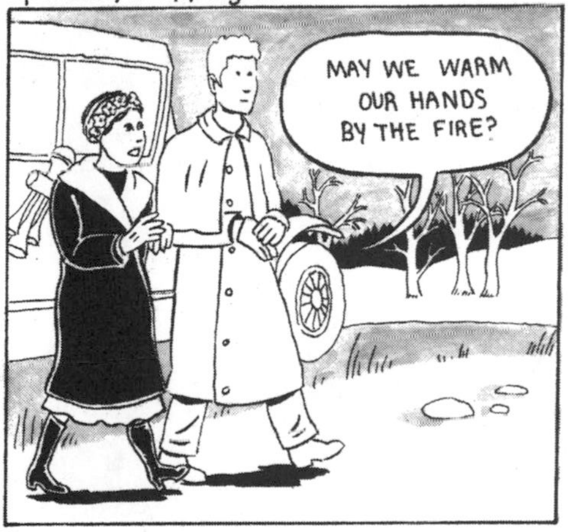
MAY WE WARM OUR HANDS BY THE FIRE?

The woman explained right away that they were on an early honeymoon.

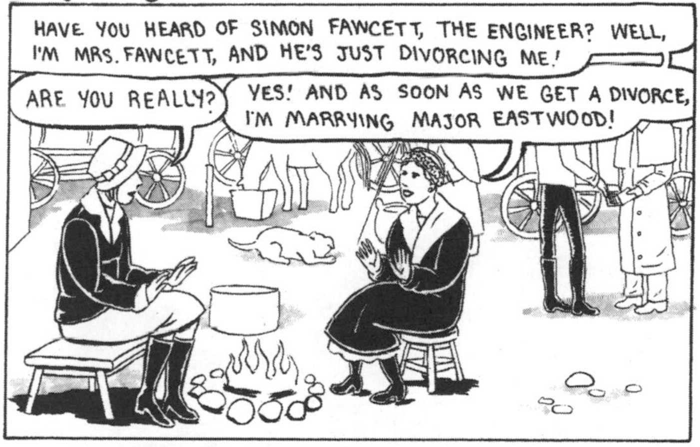
HAVE YOU HEARD OF SIMON FAWCETT, THE ENGINEER? WELL, I'M MRS. FAWCETT, AND HE'S JUST DIVORCING ME!
ARE YOU REALLY?
YES! AND AS SOON AS WE GET A DIVORCE, I'M MARRYING MAJOR EASTWOOD!

They offered Yvette a ride home, and soon they were all good friends.

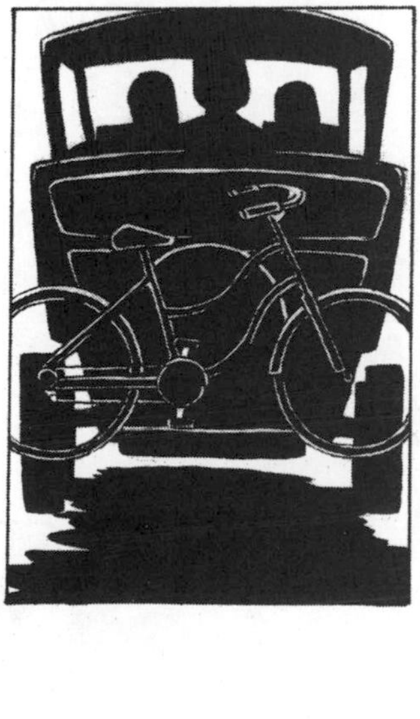

She spent long, pleasant afternoons at the Eastwoods' cottage, talking philosophically.

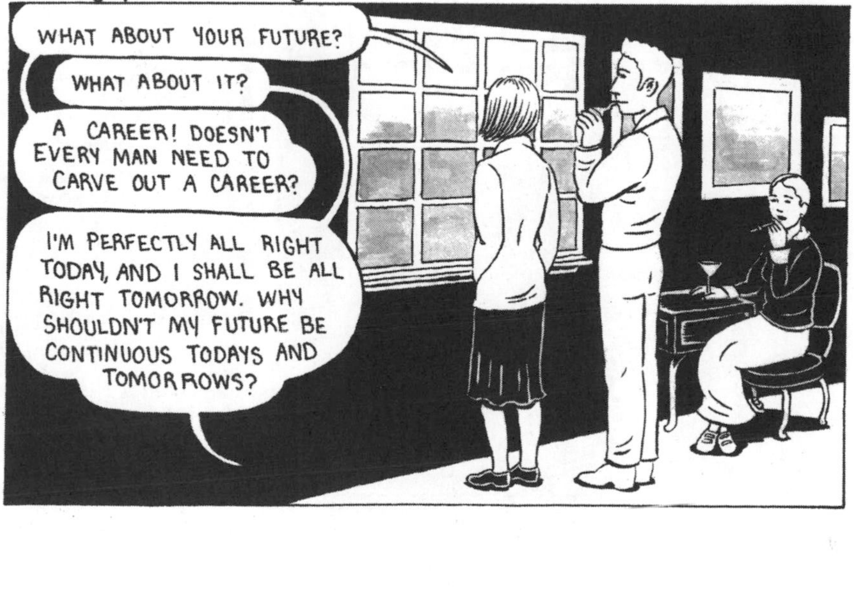
WHAT ABOUT YOUR FUTURE?
WHAT ABOUT IT?
A CAREER! DOESN'T EVERY MAN NEED TO CARVE OUT A CAREER?
I'M PERFECTLY ALL RIGHT TODAY, AND I SHALL BE ALL RIGHT TOMORROW. WHY SHOULDN'T MY FUTURE BE CONTINUOUS TODAYS AND TOMORROWS?

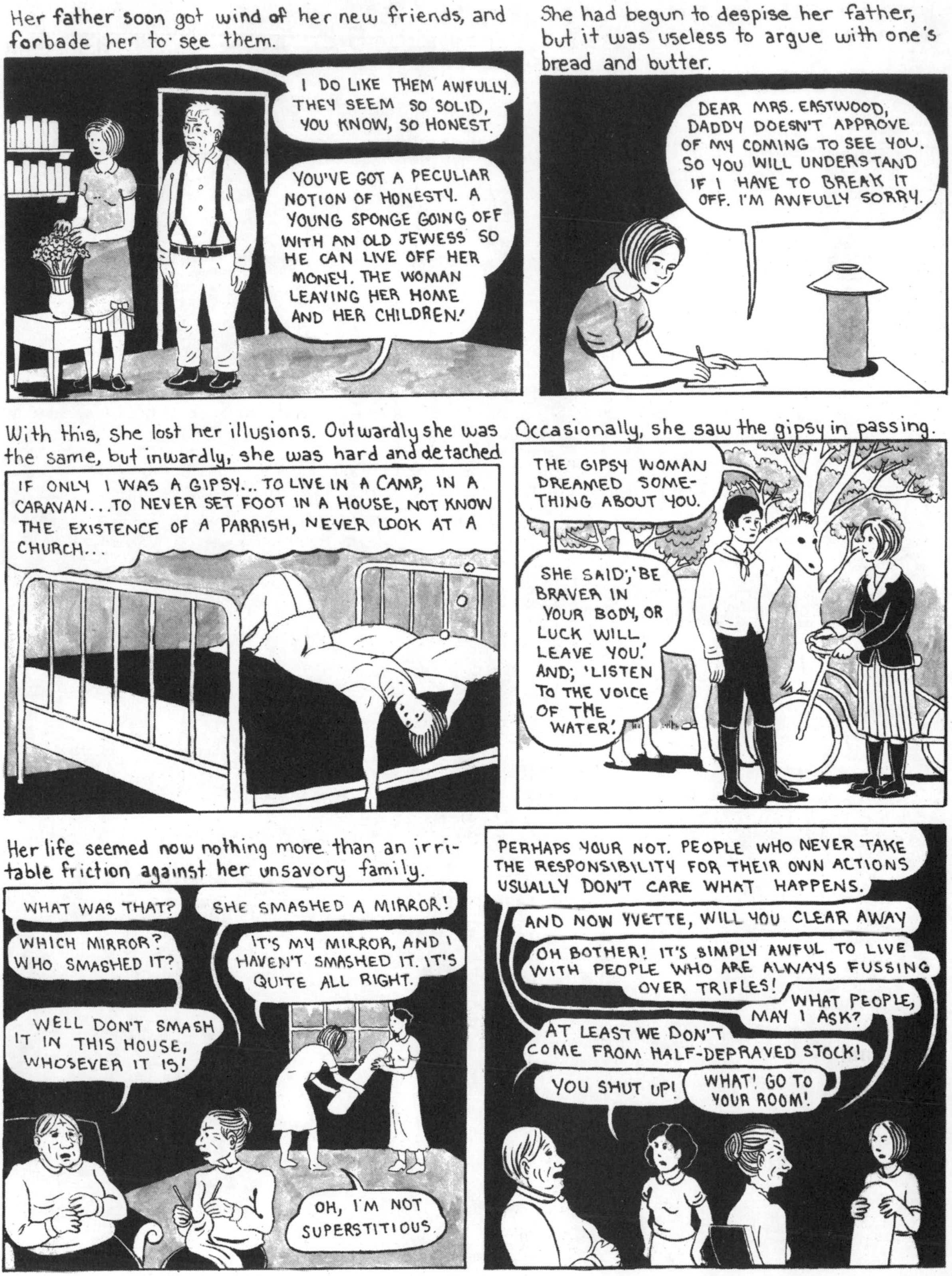

Her father soon got wind of her new friends, and forbade her to see them.
I DO LIKE THEM AWFULLY. THEY SEEM SO SOLID, YOU KNOW, SO HONEST.
YOU'VE GOT A PECULIAR NOTION OF HONESTY. A YOUNG SPONGE GOING OFF WITH AN OLD JEWESS SO HE CAN LIVE OFF HER MONEY. THE WOMAN LEAVING HER HOME AND HER CHILDREN!
She had begun to despise her father, but it was useless to argue with one's bread and butter.
DEAR MRS. EASTWOOD, DADDY DOESN'T APPROVE OF MY COMING TO SEE YOU. SO YOU WILL UNDERSTAND IF I HAVE TO BREAK IT OFF. I'M AWFULLY SORRY.
With this, she lost her illusions. Outwardly she was the same, but inwardly, she was hard and detached.
IF ONLY I WAS A GIPSY... TO LIVE IN A CAMP, IN A CARAVAN... TO NEVER SET FOOT IN A HOUSE, NOT KNOW THE EXISTENCE OF A PARRISH, NEVER LOOK AT A CHURCH...
Occasionally, she saw the gipsy in passing.
THE GIPSY WOMAN DREAMED SOMETHING ABOUT YOU.
SHE SAID; 'BE BRAVER IN YOUR BODY, OR LUCK WILL LEAVE YOU.' AND; 'LISTEN TO THE VOICE OF THE WATER.'
Her life seemed now nothing more than an irritable friction against her unsavory family.
WHAT WAS THAT?
SHE SMASHED A MIRROR!
WHICH MIRROR? WHO SMASHED IT?
IT'S MY MIRROR, AND I HAVEN'T SMASHED IT. IT'S QUITE ALL RIGHT.
WELL DON'T SMASH IT IN THIS HOUSE, WHOSEVER IT IS!
OH, I'M NOT SUPERSTITIOUS.
PERHAPS YOUR NOT. PEOPLE WHO NEVER TAKE THE RESPONSIBILITY FOR THEIR OWN ACTIONS USUALLY DON'T CARE WHAT HAPPENS.
AND NOW YVETTE, WILL YOU CLEAR AWAY
OH BOTHER! IT'S SIMPLY AWFUL TO LIVE WITH PEOPLE WHO ARE ALWAYS FUSSING OVER TRIFLES!
WHAT PEOPLE, MAY I ASK?
AT LEAST WE DON'T COME FROM HALF-DEPRAVED STOCK!
YOU SHUT UP!
WHAT! GO TO YOUR ROOM!

It was a sunny friday in March. Yvette sat outside by the bank of the river, which rolled in an uncanny mass of water.

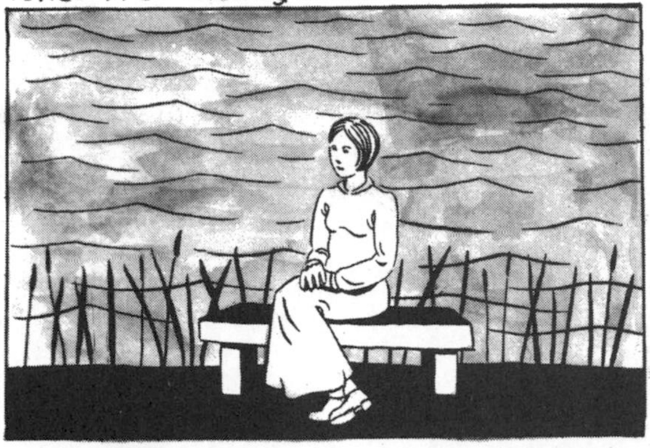

The sound of the river was loud in her ears, and she thought about what the gipsy said.

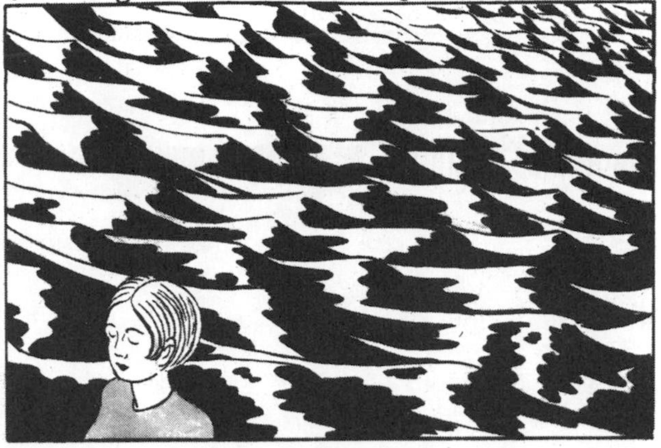

She heard shouting. Down the path the gipsy was bounding, gesticulating wildly. The gardener was also running. She looked around.

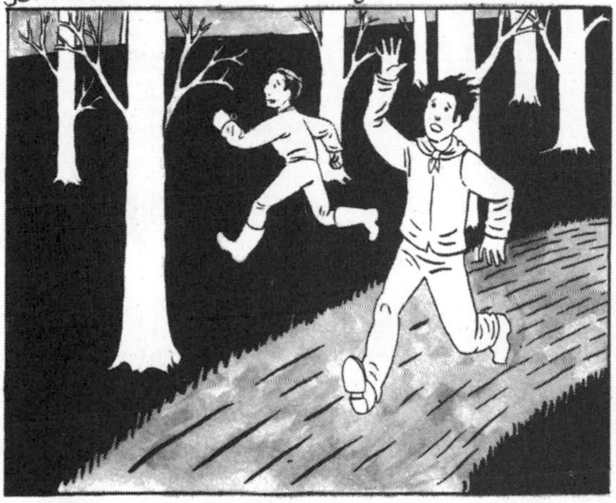

To her horror, round the bend, she saw a wave-front of water, advancing like a wall of lions.

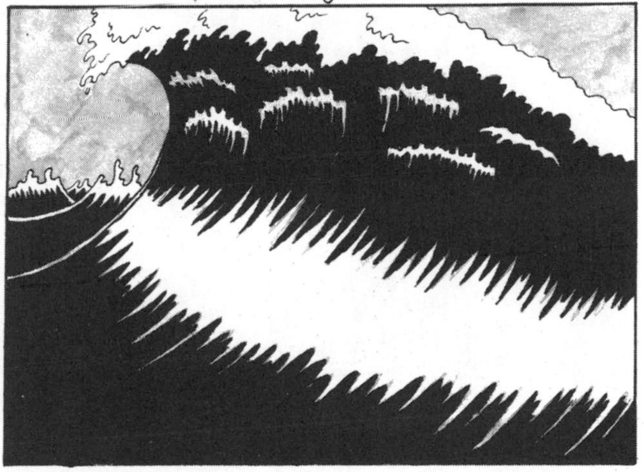

She was powerless, too amazed to move.

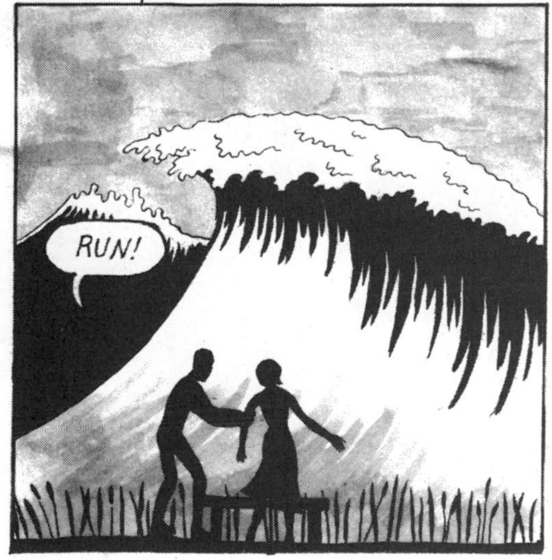
RUN!

In an instant the first wave was washing her feet from under her, swirling in the insane noise, which suddenly seemed to her like stillness. She felt a dull but stunning bruise somewhere.

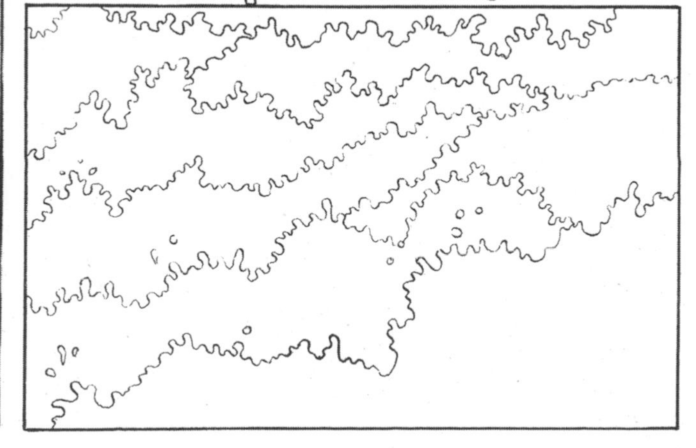

But the gipsy dragged her, heavily, lurching, plunging, towards the house.

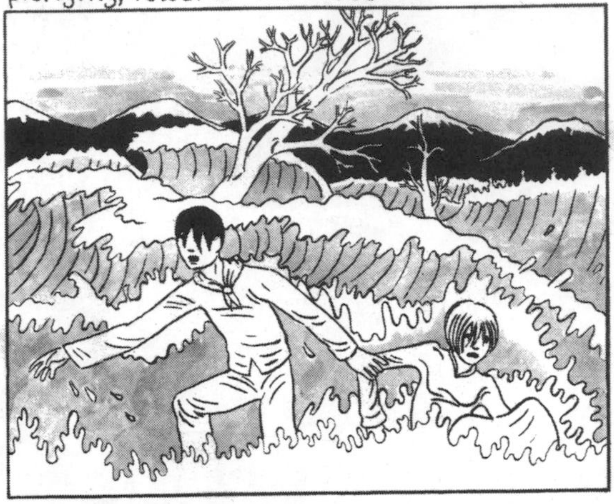

Before they got there a great new surge of water came, mowing them down. He held her arm until it seemed dislocated.

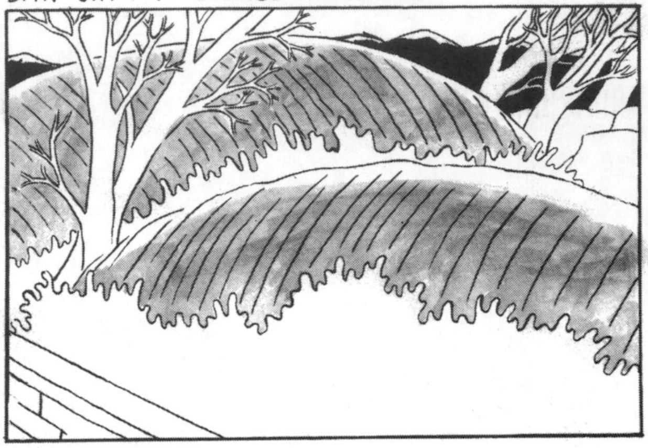

But he pulled her up again, clinging to the wisteria that grew against the wall.

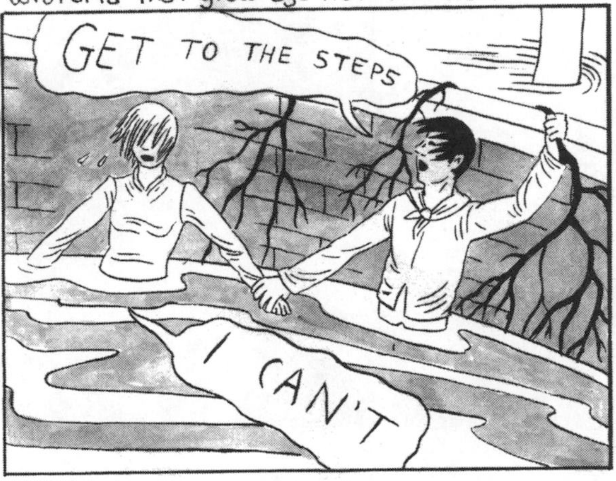
GET TO THE STEPS
I CAN'T

The water abated a little. She staggered, reeled and was pitched up against the porch steps, the man after her.

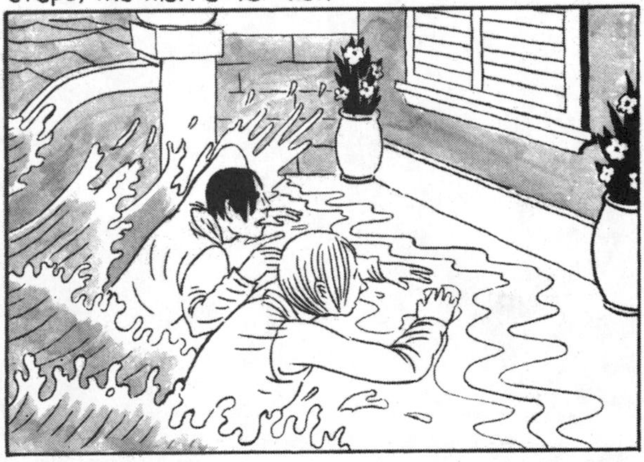

When they got on the steps, another roar was heard amid the roar and the wall shook.

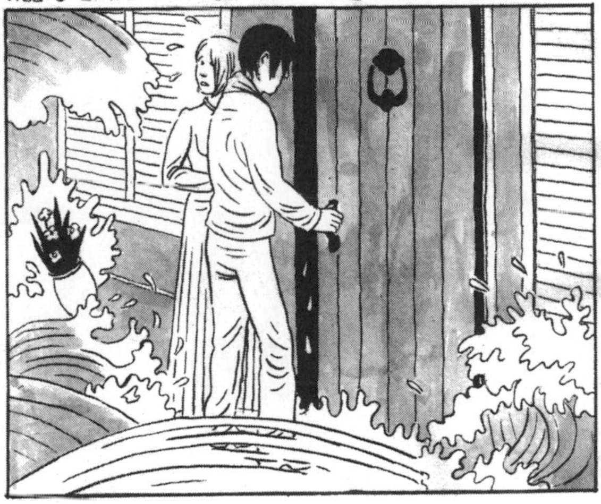

In they poured with the water.

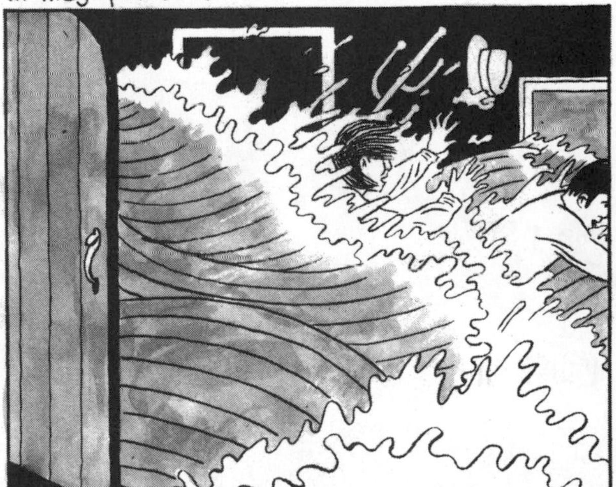

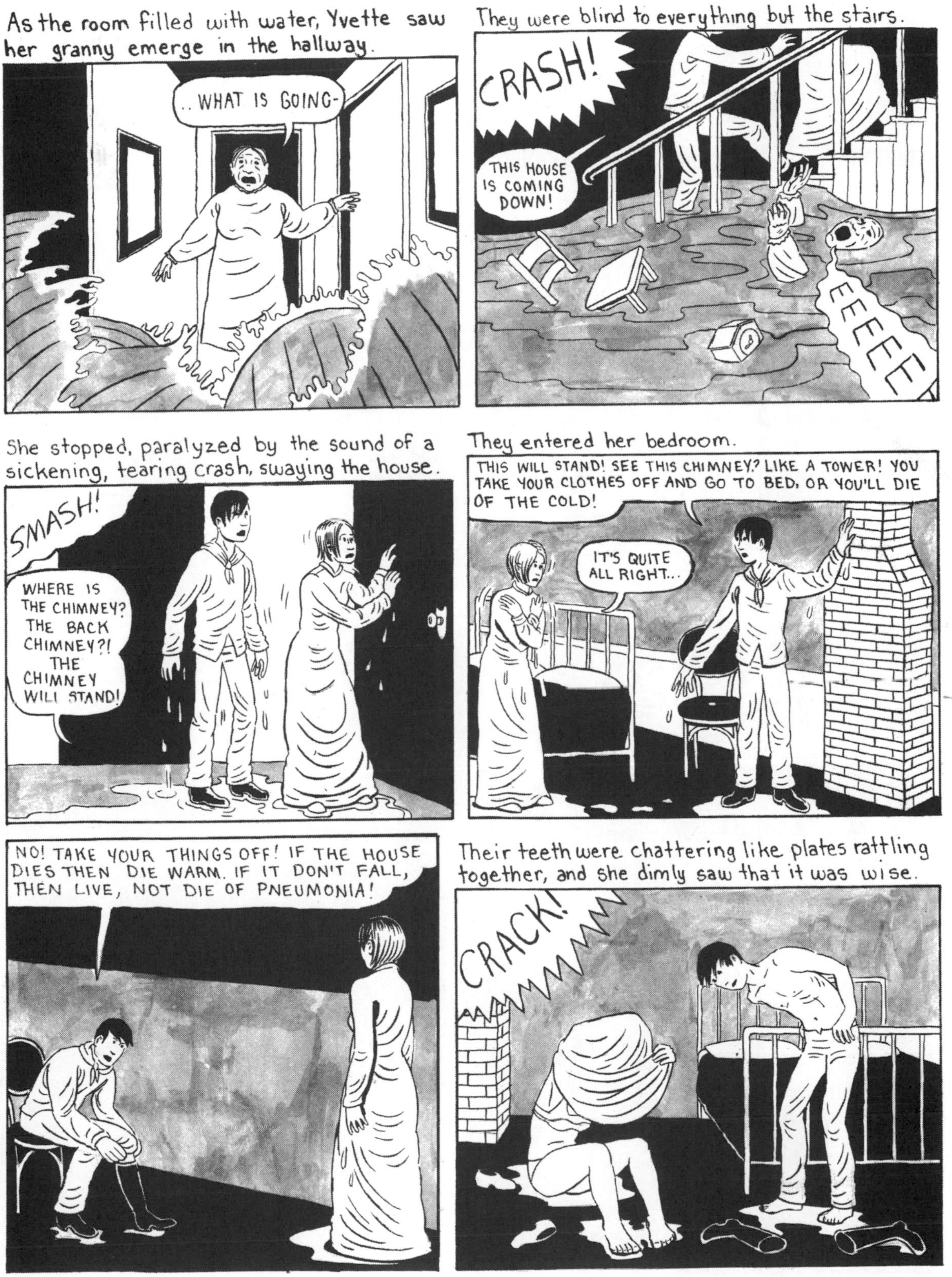
As the room filled with water, Yvette saw her granny emerge in the hallway.
..WHAT IS GOING-
They were blind to everything but the stairs.
CRASH!
THIS HOUSE IS COMING DOWN!
EEEEEE
She stopped, paralyzed by the sound of a sickening, tearing crash, swaying the house.
SMASH!
WHERE IS THE CHIMNEY? THE BACK CHIMNEY?! THE CHIMNEY WILL STAND!
They entered her bedroom.
THIS WILL STAND! SEE THIS CHIMNEY? LIKE A TOWER! YOU TAKE YOUR CLOTHES OFF AND GO TO BED, OR YOU'LL DIE OF THE COLD!
IT'S QUITE ALL RIGHT...
NO! TAKE YOUR THINGS OFF! IF THE HOUSE DIES THEN DIE WARM. IF IT DON'T FALL, THEN LIVE, NOT DIE OF PNEUMONIA!
Their teeth were chattering like plates rattling together, and she dimly saw that it was wise.
CRACK!

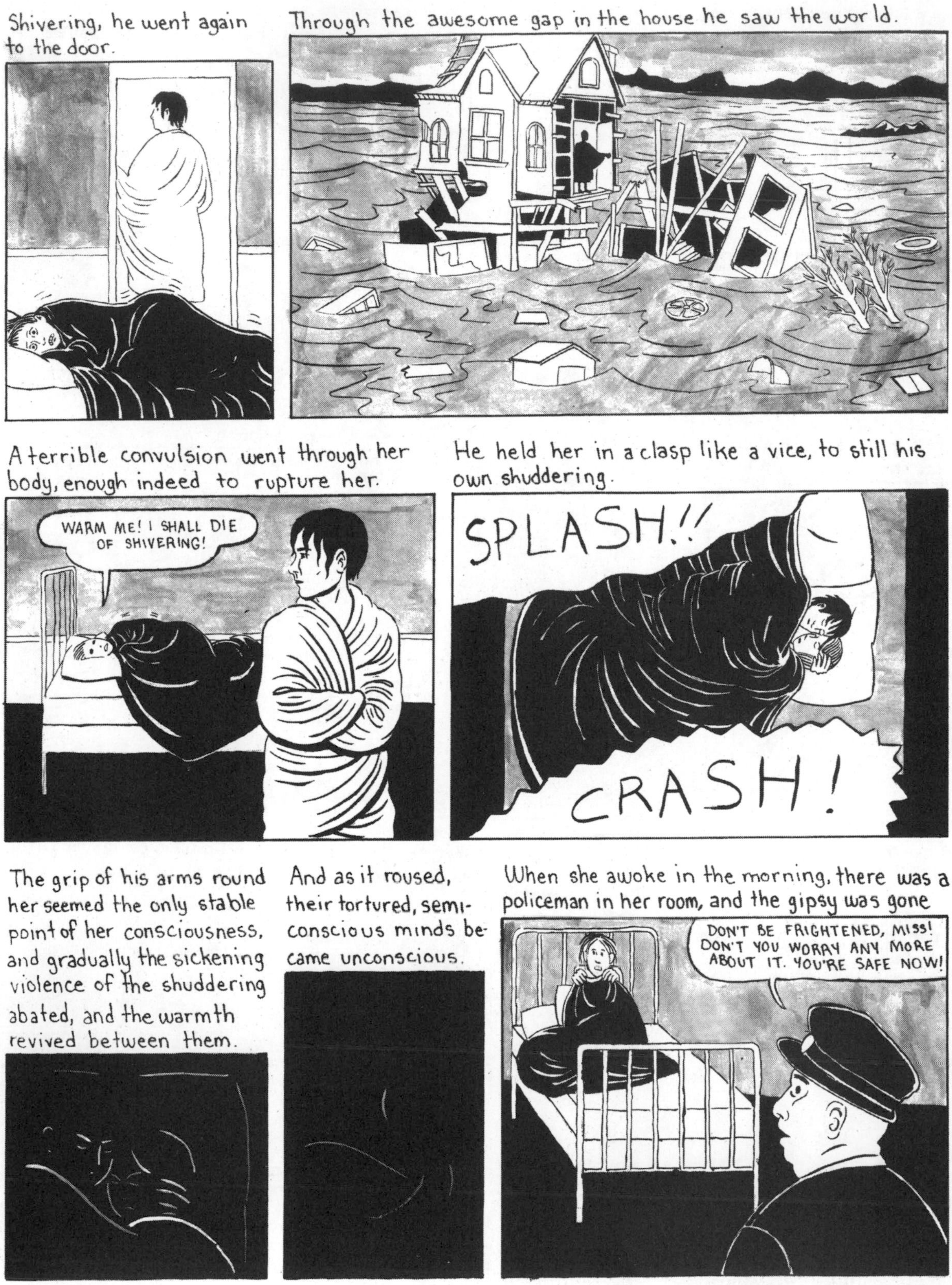
Shivering, he went again to the door.
Through the awesome gap in the house he saw the world.
A terrible convulsion went through her body, enough indeed to rupture her.
WARM ME! I SHALL DIE OF SHIVERING!
He held her in a clasp like a vice, to still his own shuddering.
SPLASH!!
CRASH!
The grip of his arms round her seemed the only stable point of her consciousness, and gradually the sickening violence of the shuddering abated, and the warmth revived between them.
And as it roused, their tortured, semi-conscious minds became unconscious.
When she awoke in the morning, there was a policeman in her room, and the gipsy was gone
DON'T BE FRIGHTENED, MISS! DON'T YOU WORRY ANY MORE ABOUT IT. YOU'RE SAFE NOW!

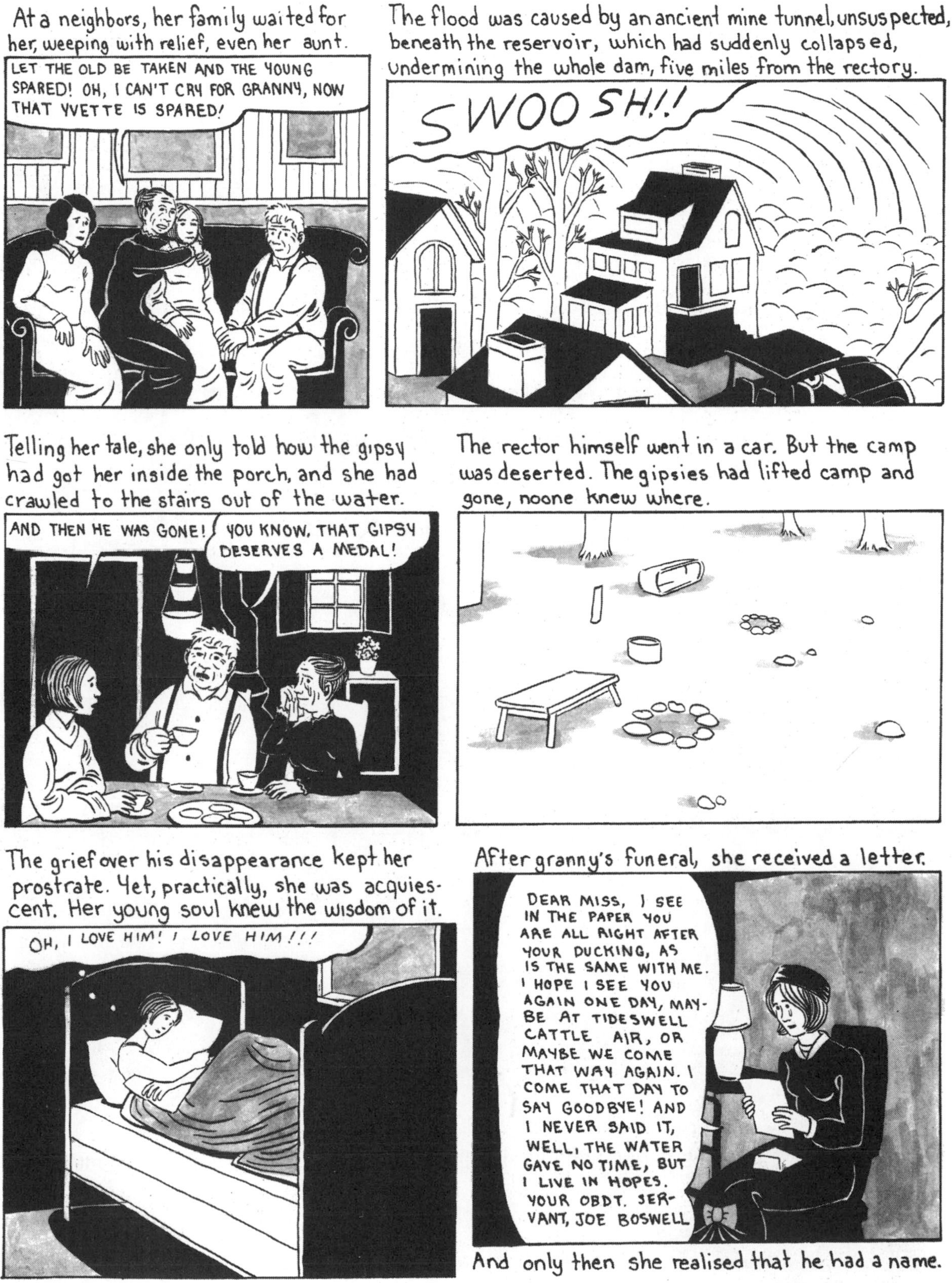
At a neighbors, her family waited for her, weeping with relief, even her aunt.
LET THE OLD BE TAKEN AND THE YOUNG SPARED! OH, I CAN'T CRY FOR GRANNY, NOW THAT YVETTE IS SPARED!
The flood was caused by an ancient mine tunnel, unsuspected, beneath the reservoir, which had suddenly collapsed, undermining the whole dam, five miles from the rectory.
SWOOSH!!
Telling her tale, she only told how the gipsy had got her inside the porch, and she had crawled to the stairs out of the water.
AND THEN HE WAS GONE!
YOU KNOW, THAT GIPSY DESERVES A MEDAL!
The rector himself went in a car. But the camp was deserted. The gipsies had lifted camp and gone, noone knew where.
The grief over his disappearance kept her prostrate. Yet, practically, she was acquiescent. Her young soul knew the wisdom of it.
OH, I LOVE HIM! I LOVE HIM!!!
After granny's funeral, she received a letter.
DEAR MISS, I SEE IN THE PAPER YOU ARE ALL RIGHT AFTER YOUR DUCKING, AS IS THE SAME WITH ME. I HOPE I SEE YOU AGAIN ONE DAY, MAYBE AT TIDESWELL CATTLE AIR, OR MAYBE WE COME THAT WAY AGAIN. I COME THAT DAY TO SAY GOODBYE! AND I NEVER SAID IT, WELL, THE WATER GAVE NO TIME, BUT I LIVE IN HOPES. YOUR OBDT. SERVANT, JOE BOSWELL
And only then she realised that he had a name.

The artist would like to thank;
Jeff Mason, Charles Orr, Tom and Leela, Matt and Jessica, Ron Rege Jr,
Lauren Weinstein, Ben Godfrey, Lawrence Hayes, Olive Bell, Margaret
Hayes and all the good people in the alternative comics community for
indespensible help on the production of this book.

The artist can be contacted at:
gabriellabell@yahoo.com